CORONADIARY

CORONADIARY

100 DAYS THAT CHANGED OUR LIVES AND THREE SKILLS GOVERNMENT HAD BEEN TOLD TO IMPROVE

DAVID FINLAY

ISBN: Paperback: 978-1-80227-079-2
       eBook: 978-1-80227-080-8
       Hardback: 978-1-80227-081-5

CONTENTS

PART 2: AND THREE SKILLS GOVERNMENT HAD BEEN TOLD TO IMPROVE

History is the diary of humankind, to forget it is to try to navigate the future with no memory of the past.

T.L. Riese

INTRODUCTION

On Tuesday 17 March 2020 I took a walk in my local park and observed that life had suddenly changed. On a pleasant sunny day there were not as many people in the park as one would normally expect. Nor the cheerful good humour of friends meeting each other and children from local schools happily running about playing rounders. The world felt strange and subdued. On this first day after we had been told to keep our distance from each other.

As someone who has always kept a diary I recorded what I had seen and the feelings it had evoked. In the days that followed it became clear that we were all exposed to a menace we had not experienced before. A new form of coronavirus, about which little was known, spreading across the UK and bringing with it a life threatening illness. Within a week Prime Minister Boris Johnson informed the nation that we were entering into a full lockdown with the firm instruction to "Stay at home, save lives, protect the NHS."

I realised I was recording in my diary events which might have historical significance. It was also unclear how this story of a dangerous pandemic reaching our shores was going to end. Samuel Pepys, writing in his diary on 30 April 1665, described similar feelings when he became aware of the bubonic illness which would become known as The Great Plague of London: "Great fears of the sickness here in the City, it being said that two or three houses are already shut up. God preserve us all."

Aware that my diary entries in March 2020 might be the first pages of a story which would have lasting importance, I started to type up a daily record interweaving my personal observations, the main news stories and some of the topics we were discussing in my work as a member of the regional NHS Board for Cambridgeshire and Peterborough. My *Coronadiary* had begun.

As the story of the pandemic unfolded I decided to keep my *Coronadiary* for 100 days to see where that took us to in the COVID-19 drama. All of us lived through those hundred days together. It was a time of sudden new regulations restricting what we could do and how we interacted with one another, supermarket shelves being ransacked and builders rapidly constructing new Nightingale hospitals for fear the NHS, like the medical services in Italy, would be overwhelmed with COVID patients. We saw the government scrambling around for more ventilators and protective clothing which we became used to referring to as PPE.

We heard from scientists that the absence of large scale testing was making it difficult to identify how widely the virus had spread. We absorbed the inexorable daily increase in the number of COVID infections (almost certainly understated because of the imperfect information), hospitalisations and, sadly, deaths. Then the heart stopping drama of Prime Minister Johnson himself in hospital fighting for his life with the severe breathing difficulties experienced by so many affected by COVID-19. On top of all this, we witnessed the devastating impact the pandemic had on the economy and government finances with massive state support being handed out to the millions working in or running businesses forced to close by the new restrictions.

But these 100 days we lived through together also saw us clapping for the NHS and other frontline workers, the celebration of VE Day, the wonderful uplifting efforts of Captain Tom Moore pushing his walking frame around his garden and our gradual emergence from this first wave of the coronavirus as the hot days of summer and relaxation of restrictions gave hope for a return to spending time on beaches, in parks and more normal living.

And so the 100 days of my *Coronadiary* came to an end on Wednesday 24 June 2020 on a sunny day, like the day in March when I started the diary. Similar weather but, in the intervening hundred days, over 42,000 people had died from COVID-19. Losses borne by family, friends, colleagues. This was more than twice the figure of 20,000 deaths which Parliament had been advised at the outset would be a "good outcome." In addition, as many as 11 million people were receiving some sort of government financial support, whether this was having most of their wages paid by the furlough scheme or receiving grants if self-employed.

It is these 100 days that are described in Part 1 of this book: *Coronadiary: 100 days that changed our lives.*

There were fears that the winter months, when the public would spend more time indoors where the virus could more easily spread between people, could herald another wave of COVID hospitalisations during the busiest period of the year for the NHS. It would have been alarming in June 2020, as the *Coronadiary* ended, to have glimpsed the future. That, when writing this introduction, in March 2021, on the anniversary of the start of the first lockdown, COVID-19 deaths would have risen to over 126,000. Three times as high as they had been in June 2020 as the *Coronadiary* ended and we appeared to be recovering from the worst effects of the virus. Health and Social Care Secretary Matt Hancock's assertion at that time that "coronavirus is in retreat across the land" was temporarily accurate but in the longer term sadly over optimistic.

We all shared, albeit in different ways, the stresses and fears of living through the COVID-19 pandemic. We were all sailing though the same storm but each in our own boats. Because of this shared experience we have all formed views on the way that the government handled the arrival of the coronavirus pandemic in the UK. Millions of words have been written about this in the newspapers we read; millions of words have been spoken on news programmes by scientists, medical experts and other commentators.

When my *Coronadiary* ended in June 2020 I wanted to write some form of commentary on the passage of events which the diary had described. But I had nothing to add to what had already been said. And we all await the official public inquiry which will be held at some future date. So I accepted that my *Coronadiary* would remain a private record of the events we all lived through during the early months of the pandemic.

I did not therefore expect to be writing this introduction to an account of COVID-19 which others would read. The discovery that there might be something to say which had not been raised in previous analysis and discussion came after I posed myself a question. The question I thought warranted further consideration was:

Were there any links between the apparent shortcomings in the UK government's response to the COVID-19 pandemic and issues the government had been told to address as a result of its previous activities?

I felt able to try to answer this question as, for ten years between 2004 and 2013, I had been a Director of the National Audit Office, the auditor of government. In that role I had led over 50 reports to Parliament examining whether the government's development of large projects, such as the building of new hospitals, had been managed to produce the best value and outcomes for the public. That meant I was familiar with official reports which had made recommendations on improvements the government should make to its approach to large complex projects. So I set about researching recent reports from the National Audit Office and Parliament's Public Accounts Committee to see in which direction their recommendations had been focussed prior to the start of the COVID-19 pandemic. I also considered the output of organisations such as the Institute for Government and various "think tanks" which regularly reviewed and opined on government activity.

As it became increasingly clear that certain aspects of the government's pandemic response could have been handled better, I sought to assess whether there was any linkage with areas of decision making the government had previously been told to improve.

Part 2 of this book *And three skills government had been told to improve* focuses on three key issues which are relevant to all complex government situations: planning, data, risks. The disturbing key finding of the analysis presented in those pages is that the government's approach to planning, data and risks had been repeatedly highlighted in recent times as needing improvement; yet, despite these warnings, these three same issues were also major contributors to what are now widely seen as the main shortcomings in the government's response to the pandemic.

It is as if the same problems which had beset so much of previous government activity reappeared during the pandemic and were magnified by the pressures and urgency facing Ministers and officials as they desperately sought appropriate strategies for dealing with the impact of COVID-19. If you tend to make mistakes when driving on quiet local roads how much more dangerous those mistakes may be if you are driving for the first time in the middle of a pulsating, crowded, fast moving, motorway.

I am not ignoring the huge challenges those in government faced making decisions during the pandemic. None of us would have found that easy. But in this type of intensely pressurised situation you need the wheels of government to be moving with maximum efficiency. Anything less in a pandemic and lives are in danger. But the chances of failing to identify the best possible decisions when faced with complexity will inevitably be higher if the important techniques of effective planning, making good use of data and managing risks are not applied to the very best effect.

As I write this introduction on the anniversary of the first lockdown, Chief Scientific Adviser Sir Patrick Vallance was asked at today's Downing Street press conference what his greatest regret was. He said the absence of reliable information on infections in the early stages of the COVID-19 pandemic. Chief Medical Officer Chris Whitty had previously said "We were unable to work out exactly where we were and we were trying to see our way through the fog."

The absence of accurate information on how widely the virus was spreading was indicative of all three skills government had been told to improve: planning, data, risks. Better advance *planning* for a pandemic arriving in the UK would have put in place the capability for large scale testing which could have been quickly mobilised at the start of the

COVID-19 outbreak; large scale testing would have generated more accurate *data* on the extent to which the virus had spread in different areas of the UK; with that data, the *risks* to the nation's health, our NHS hospitals and care homes could have been properly assessed to inform decisions on when and how to enter lockdown.

Professor Neil Ferguson, whose modelling projected the course the virus might take in different scenarios, has said that if the first lockdown had been imposed a week earlier half of our COVID deaths at that time would have been avoided. But that depended on having the reliable information on the spread of the virus which Patrick Vallance acknowledges was not available in the early stages of COVID-19 in the UK.

It all comes back to the application of skills in these three areas: planning, data, risks. Doctors treating COVID patients used those skills every day but it is less obvious that the government's response to the pandemic demonstrated high standards of skills in those critical areas. The very skills which government most needed to manage the COVID-19 pandemic effectively were skills it had been repeatedly told to improve.

As you read Part 1: *Coronadiary: 100 days that changed our lives* there are a number of days where it now seems very apparent the government was having to put things right when events had moved much faster than their preparations. A Peter Brookes cartoon in The Times showed Prime Minister Boris Johnson running breathlessly after a bus loaded with COVID problems but unable to keep up with it. Insufficient earlier attention to planning, data and risks was a repeated factor in the problems that emerged. For example, although care homes had been sent guidance bulletins on how to deal with the virus, it was only on 8 June 2020 that the government announced a task force to fully develop a plan for keeping staff and residents safe in care homes. By this time more than ten thousand care home residents had died from COVID-19, deaths which were not even recorded in the government's daily statistics until the end of April, two months after the first virus wave had arrived.

It is a natural reaction to say that lessons will be learned from our experiences over the past year. But the analysis set out in Part 2 *And three skills government had been told to improve* points to previous lessons aimed at improving the way government would deal with complex situations not having been fully addressed in those key areas: planning, data, risks. It is concerning that repeating previous failings is very likely to have played a part in the outcomes we experienced which left the UK with COVID-19 deaths around 15 per cent higher than any other European country.

You cannot continually say lessons will be learned if that does not happen. There must be questions as to why the recommendations of the National Audit Office, Public Accounts Committee and other parties that government should improve its approach to planning, data and risks had not been more rigorously and urgently followed up. It was only after the COVID pandemic had done its worst in the UK that the government announced in late 2020 a new National Data Strategy and plans to overhaul its approach to the training of those who work in government with a major new programme entitled Better Training, Knowledge and Networks. These are welcome initiatives which will improve government decision making. But they had been under consideration for some time following earlier warnings that action was needed; adopting these new initiatives earlier would have brought a higher degree of professional skills to the government's response to the pandemic which could have avoided some of the adverse outcomes we experienced.

Another issue explored in Part 2 *And three skills government had been told to improve* is that Ministers, who come from different backgrounds, have received little or no training in making decisions in complex situations. In periods of relative calm they can rely on civil servants to put forward carefully researched advice; but in a national emergency, such as the COVID-19 pandemic, Ministers are under pressure on a daily basis to use their judgement on complex decisions involving huge consequences. As our Ministers had not been trained to a common standard in understanding the importance that planning, data and risks play in complex decisions this must inevitably have increased the possibility of errors in decision making during the COVID response.

This book then has its two parts:

> Part 1: *Coronadiary:100 days that changed our lives*, a record of those early days of the coronavirus arriving in the UK, the sudden changes it made to our daily lives and the ever present fear of the serious illness which the virus could bring. You may want to dip into different parts of the *Coronadiary* to remind yourself of those early COVID days.

> Part 2: *And three skills government had been told to improve*, an analysis of how the apparent shortcomings in the government's response to the pandemic appear to have repeated failings in the management of previous projects, failings which the government had been repeatedly told to improve, most notably in those three key areas of planning, data, risks.

This book concludes with six recommendations for placing greater emphasis on planning, data, risks in future government decision making. I hope that the content of this book will generate a debate on the skills which Ministers and public officials need to make the best possible decisions on our behalf in the many complex situations which government faces today.

We must all hope for a safer, brighter future.

David Finlay
London, 23 March 2021

PART 1

CORONADIARY: 100 DAYS THAT CHANGED OUR LIVES

1 THE CRISIS UNFOLDS
Days 1 to 20: 17 March to 5 April

DAY 1: TUESDAY 17 MARCH: *UK stats*: 1,543 confirmed cases 35 deaths*

Today the coronavirus illness known as COVID-19 became serious. The world feels different. Strange and anxious. Not normal. Yesterday Prime Minister Boris Johnson introduced drastic "social distancing" measures as identified cases and deaths began to increase at a faster rate than had been expected. "Social distancing," apparently, means having hardly any interaction with our fellow beings. The front page of The Times had a picture of a nearly empty Waterloo Station in the rush hour. Someone was standing on the clock face painted on the floor of Waterloo Station which says "Meet me under the clock." Except that would not be allowed under "social distancing."

I went for a walk to Golders Hill Park. It was strangely quiet with only a few people out and about. But it was reassuring that the café with the terrace, that is normally a magnet for people wanting to meet friends or sit in the sun, was open. A handful of the locals were outside drinking coffee. With so few of them there, most had taken the precaution of sitting well away from other human contact, but a few brave souls were actually

*statistics quoted are as at the start of each day as announced at that time sitting at the same table. They were the ones who valued conversation more than health guidance.

Local poet, the late Dannie Abse, would have been here on a day as sombre as this, scribbling a new poem on a napkin. The papers carried the observation of Neil Ferguson of Imperial College, London, that "hopefully tens of thousands" would die. Perhaps what he meant was that he feared worse, or perhaps he had identified those he would be pleased to see taken away by this new plague. It brought to mind Abse's line in his poem, Portrait of an old Doctor: "That's how it was in The Theatre of Disease."

The sudden realisation that illness and death are likely to be our constant companions for months to come, whilst we wait to see if a vaccine can be developed to combat the virus, makes one see the world in a different light. On the banks of the small lake in the park newly growing purple and white crocuses and miniature yellow daffodils now seem even more beautiful than normal. A party of primary school children pass by talking and laughing excitedly to each other. Their grandparents have been told to stay indoors for the foreseeable future to ward off infection. Like the children I prefer being in the park.

Despite the prospect of doom descending on us spring is making an appearance, regardless, in the park. A white haired man surely near to retirement is driving a tractor mower across the damp grass and as he does so takes the last puffs from a rolled up cigarette. Has no-one told him that the coronavirus particularly seeks out those with respiratory diseases? A girl sits alone texting on a park bench. Without realising it she has been social distancing every time she talks through a screen rather than face to face.

In the afternoon I dial into a teleconference with my colleagues on the regional NHS Board for Cambridgeshire and Peterborough. There is now a major incident room where plans are being made for how they will cope with the influx of patients expected as the coronavirus, COVID-19, takes a grip. Extra beds will have to be requisitioned from nursing homes and care homes in case our hospitals reach capacity to treat those stricken with the disease. With the virus hunting down with a particular enthusiasm those who choose to live in the capital, Cambridge awaits the arrival of wheezing Londoners unable to find a hospital bed nearer home. Existing patients will need to vacate beds to make way for the new COVID arrivals. What started out as a virus affecting thousands of people in the province of Wuhan in China has raged across Italy, and also Spain and France, as Britain inexorably succumbs to what is officially now termed a worldwide pandemic.

Meanwhile, in Westminster, Jeremy Hunt, he who once stood against Boris Johnson to be premier, is chairing the Health and Social Care Select Committee and questioning Sir Patrick Vallance, the government's Chief Scientific Adviser about the coronacrisis. Twenty thousand deaths would be a good outcome the scientist says before adding, "Of course that would still be horrible." Simon Stevens, urbane head of the NHS, is pressed by Hunt on why doctors have written to him complaining of a lack of face masks to shield them from coughing patients. Stevens reassures Hunt that the NHS has large supplies of face masks and surgical gowns stored away, showing that the NHS has thought ahead like the public who have ransacked supermarket shelves for every last packet of toilet paper.

On Newsnight Emily Maitlis interviews Lord Jonathan Sacks, the former Chief Rabbi. Sacks says we are experiencing events akin to a biblical revelation, which shows our potential vulnerability as human beings faced with danger and an awareness of how interdependent we are on each other for support and co-operation.

DAY 2: WEDNESDAY 18 MARCH: *1,960 confirmed cases 71 deaths*

Walked to the newsagent to buy the Financial Times as well as my usual paper to read about the unprecedented £350 billion bailout for businesses announced yesterday by our new young Chancellor, Rishi Sunak. Without warning the income of businesses was decimated once the government told us to take part in this new "social distancing" arrangement. Restaurants and cafes have been turned overnight into Mary Celestes, suddenly bereft of both staff and customers. There was only one Mary Celeste with a crew of eight, but there are around 40,000 restaurants and cafes in the UK employing over 3 million people, about 10 per cent of the workforce. As I pay for the paper my newsagent is wearing thick white gloves to prevent the risk of his hand picking up the virus from the coins his customers have handled. His white gloves have now become black from the dirt on all the coins he has handled. Who knows whether anyone with the virus paid with these coins? The newsagent's black white gloves move forward to put change into my hands. I motion for him to put the change down where I can pick it up.

As I read the Financial Times it becomes clear that the £350 billion bailout is not actual cash, but rather a commitment by the government to guarantee to banks that most of the new loans, which they may give to businesses to keep them afloat as customers disappear, would be repaid by the government if the businesses are unable to do so. But even so it is very welcome news to the business community.

E-mails land in my inbox from theatres, concert halls and museums across the land all with the same wording: "The welfare of our patrons and staff is our priority" and all with the same message, that they will be closing their doors for the foreseeable future. Some ask for donations to replace their lost income. Others have brought our attention to their archive which can be viewed online for culture vultures needing an artistic fix to survive the current crisis.

As twilight came at 6pm I was aware of a noise in the garden of our block of flats. Looking out from my study window I was greeted by a surreal sight. Around twenty men in black suits were spaced out around the garden seemingly engaged in some ancient ritual. It took some time to grasp that these were Charedi men, the most strictly Orthodox of Jews, who had decided to hold their evening prayers outdoors now that an indoor service involving close proximity with fellow worshippers had been stopped under social distancing. As they arranged themselves around the garden, with large spaces between each other, it felt as if I was watching a rehearsal for a strange new ballet, The Men in Black.

Jonathan Sacks, whose wisdom seems in great demand in these unusual times, was being interviewed again, this time on Radio 4's the

Moral Maze. Tonight he preferred optimism, noting the examples of people who have been helping others with small acts of kindness, to pessimism about people acting out of self-interest as they emptied the supermarket shelves depriving others of household essentials. Other speakers voiced the impact of globalisation, which had allowed this new coronavirus to spread so easily across borders.

DAY 3: THURSDAY 19 MARCH: *2,626 confirmed cases 103 deaths*

Today the newsagent was wearing a green mask as well as his white gloves. He did not look comfortable in either. Now the papers were full of the government's decision to close schools from the end of this week except for the children of key workers, later defined as medics, police, teachers and transport workers, and those children classified as vulnerable. So the primary school children who were walking happily through Golders Hill Park two days ago will not be doing so as a group next week.

The strain on essential shops was beginning to show: in the middle of the day Waitrose shelves were not just empty of toilet rolls and cleaning materials but also most other items including bread, fruit and vegetables. Boots was temporarily closed due to "staff shortages" and even the local butcher was closed awaiting deliveries. But the fresh fish shop had an abundance of fish: plaice, lemon sole, salmon, halibut, haddock were overflowing in their trays. If Jesus fed the five thousand with two fish it seems that, unlike other items, with fish we have a more than adequate supply to meet our current needs. Based on Jesus's performance three thousand six hundred fish would be sufficient to feed London's population of nine million so we should be able to survive on fish alone for some time.

I received an e-mail from my regional NHS Board in Cambridge that there would be an urgent teleconference at 5.30pm. Whilst preparing for this call a delivery man arrived with a huge plastic sack containing 24 kitchen rolls which looked like, and if needed would feel like, toilet rolls if these continue to be in short supply in the shops. I quickly took them inside lest it appear that I was stockpiling, but actually they were a job lot of 24 rolls which had appeared on the internet for just £9. So I have reasonable confidence that my single item purchase will gain the approval of the ethics committee overseeing kitchen and toilet roll purchasing.

Our emergency Board meeting is to approve the purchase of an additional 380 beds in a care home for the next six months to enable the NHS in Cambridgeshire and Peterborough to meet the additional demands the coronavirus may create. If the virus places large pressures on our hospitals most people allocated to the NHS beds in care homes will be there for end of life care with NHS hospital beds used for the intensive care of patients with a chance of recovering from the virus. What everyone fears is that the NHS will be overwhelmed in the way that the health services in the Lombardy region of Northern Italy have been; patients dying in makeshift field hospitals as the number of people needing treatment far outstrips the capability of Italian doctors to respond to everyone's needs.

In his now daily press conference Prime Minister Boris Johnson says that "we can turn around the virus within 12 weeks." One hopes we can. This from the man who said we would leave the EU by 31 October 2019 come hell or high water.

Former England cricket captain Mike Atherton notes that even during the two World Wars some recreational cricket continued to be played. But now, when professional cricketers would normally be getting ready for the new season which was due to start in April, there will be no leather on willow even on the village green.

DAY 4: FRIDAY 20 MARCH: *3,269 confirmed cases 144 deaths*

By 11am Waitrose was ransacked even after an early morning delivery. Now, not only no toilet rolls, but no fruit, vegetables, bread or eggs. All gone in a couple of hours. Dawn Bilbrough, a critical care nurse in Yorkshire, pleads on YouTube with shoppers to be sensible and leave things for others: "It's people like me who will be looking after you when you are at your lowest." A long queue built up outside my local Boots as it only allowed two people to be in the store at any time for the safety of both staff and customers.

Having seen the great collapse of the catering sector in recent days I recalled that it was only three weeks ago that I sat in my favourite Thai restaurant in Cambridge looking out on the serene beauty of Parker's Piece, the large area of open grass much frequented by students and other young people living in Cambridge. The restaurant was under new management and the owner told me of his plans to put tables outside during the summer months to build up trade, after sinking a large amount of money into a refurbishment of the restaurant when he took it over. Now he will be scrambling for the promised government financial support like so many others in the catering sector.

This afternoon children left school which, for most of them, will be for the last time at the start of a period which has no identified ending. To be off school for a few days can be greeted as a wonderful adventure, but most children feel anxious and uncertain about the open ended nature of this particular vacation.

And now the vice like grip on the nation's activities tightens still further. Cafes, pubs and restaurants must close from tonight, except for take-aways, to tackle the coronavirus. These are the new orders from Prime Minister Boris Johnson, a man who has been known to enjoy his food. All the UK's nightclubs, theatres, cinemas, gyms and leisure centres have also been asked to close as soon as they reasonably can. The government has promised to pay 80 per cent of the wages of employees who are not working, up to £2,500 a month.

The Prime Minister added: "The more effectively we follow the advice we are given, the faster this country will stage both a medical and an economic recovery in full." But already many experts were doubting Boris Johnson's assertion yesterday that we could turn around the virus in 12 weeks. Even if it is possible to slow the spread of the virus until a vaccine is produced, which could take a year, the threat of further serious outbreaks of COVID-19 remains.

Am I the only one who recalls at this time the words of the American 1960s songwriter, Tom Lehrer, singing about another unpleasant social disease: "I got it from Agnes, she got it from Jim, we all agree it must have been Louise who gave it to him, she got it from Harry, who got it from Marie, and everybody knows that Marie got it from me"?

DAY 5: SATURDAY 21 MARCH: *3,783 confirmed cases 171 deaths*

The weather was fine and I felt a desperate need to escape the gathering gloom and restrictions of corona London. I drive the two and a half hours journey to Aldeburgh on the Suffolk coast. The moment I drive down to the familiar sea road alongside the stony Aldeburgh beach, on which I once saw a wonderful live performance of the seafaring opera Peter Grimes, I feel at peace. Compared to London, life seems remarkably normal here. Not a mask in sight. Just the familiar scene of parents with young children walking along the beach. People were wrapped up against the cold wind but there was also beautiful sunshine and the world seemed at ease with itself.

But the effects of the virus were having an effect here in Suffolk. A notice outside Aldeburgh's smartest hotel, The Wentworth, advised customers that the restaurant and bar had now been closed because of the current health concerns. My hotel was still serving meals for those staying at the hotel but the tables where you could sit in the restaurant were spread out to facilitate social distancing. The Maltese waitress who served me said that she had just been told that after tonight there would be no more work for her at the hotel. Malta was no longer accepting people back into the country because of the virus situation, so she could not return to her family. She did not know whether the hotel would allow her to stay in its staff accommodation.

DAY 6: SUNDAY 22 MARCH: *5,018 confirmed cases 233 deaths*

It was a brilliantly sunny morning in Aldeburgh. The fishing boats on the pebble beach looked out over the grey rolling waves as if to say, "If there is a God then this is how he would wish to be remembered, not by a virus spreading fear throughout the land." In the newsagent on the High Street the lady who served me took my London money but warned, "Someone in Southwold has just died from the virus and it has been traced back to a Londoner with a second home in the area. You people coming here from London say, "I'm alright Jack." Actually, I never use that phrase but I understood her concerns. I felt well and didn't believe I was causing a health risk by coming to Aldeburgh. But should Londoners stay together away from places of beauty which can, for a few moments, lift their spirits in these dark times?

On checking out of my hotel they said that by mid-day the doors of the hotel would be closed and locked. So I had been one of the last of the customers the hotel looked after before the shutters went up as the coronavirus continues to ravage the hospitality sector.

With all the restaurants closed I joined the queue in the street outside Aldeburgh high street's famous fish and chips shop. We politely observed social distancing in the queue before diving inside to order our fishcakes and haddock and chips. The man behind me in the queue said that his wife, a nurse, may have been one of the first to experience coronavirus as she had had the symptoms of a cough and fever back in January.

Back to London to watch the television news. At 233 deaths as of yesterday 21 March we are at the same figure as Italy was on 7 March. Are we on the same trajectory that saw the health services in Lombardy, Northern Italy, overwhelmed?

In one of many religious services delivered online, now that places of worship have shut their doors, the Archbishop of Canterbury, Justin Welby, said that in a crisis the temptation is to look after ourselves but only by looking outwards, to care for others, will we find comfort and consolation. To illustrate this, many people are developing initiatives to help their neighbours. Some have started schemes where cards are put through letterboxes asking if those at home need any help. In Scotland, a young Muslim couple running a corner shop are making up food parcels for local people living alone.

DAY 7: MONDAY 23 MARCH: *5,683 confirmed cases 281 deaths*

Finding somewhere to have my hair cut seems impossible. My friendly hairdresser in Victoria said his salon had closed, and going to the hairdresser I sometimes use near where I live, I found the same. I read that cutting hair is almost impossible in gloves and hairdressers will typically touch a client's head or face 1,000 times during a haircut. Never before has having a haircut been a health risk. What will I do if all hairdressers remain closed? What will everyone else do? Only Samson would be pleased with the current situation.

The son of the Indian shopkeeper where I buy stationery asked me where all the money would come from to fulfil the Chancellor's pledge to support businesses with loans, and to pay the wages of those whose jobs were at risk. I did my best to explain quantitative easing; this method which always sounds like a mathematical laxative. I tell him that the Bank of England will buy bonds which investment funds and other large organisations may hold, thus giving them cash to further invest in the economy. The son of the Indian shopkeeper was impressed by my apparent knowledge but I am hardly an expert.

As the numbers of confirmed cases of COVID-19 and deaths from the virus in the UK continued to rise, many people queried why planes were still landing at Heathrow from Italy and China where the coronavirus has been particularly prevalent.

Seven year old Josephine from Stubbington, Hampshire writes to Boris Johnson saying that she understands why her birthday party may have to be cancelled ("I am staying at home because you told us to") and hopes the Prime Minister is washing his hands regularly. Johnson sends a hand written reply wishing her a happy birthday, and confirming he is washing his hands for as long as it takes to sing Happy Birthday twice.

The papers reported that, whilst I made my soul calming trip to Aldeburgh in Suffolk at the weekend, record numbers of people had been out in the sun in Snowdonia, the Lake District, the Yorkshire Dales and seaside beaches without due regard for the seriousness of the virus outbreak and the need for social distancing. "A national emergency is not an excuse for a holiday" said Cumbria Assistant Chief Constable Andrew Slattery. But where do you draw the line between public safety and disruption of our normal way of life? Nicholas Bevington, in a letter to the Times, said "I see the need to isolate and protect the elderly and other vulnerable adults. However, shutting down the economy for everyone else and threatening livelihoods on a massive scale troubles me then the human costs are likely to be far worse than anything coronavirus throws at us."

At 8.30pm we were given the answer on where to draw the line between public safety and leading a normal way of life. In a special address to the nation a rather frenetic looking Boris Johnson, clenching his fists, said that this was a national emergency. We all must stay at home except for a small number of clearly defined reasons to be outdoors: essential shopping and collecting medicines, exercising once a day and going to work, but only where working from home is not possible. Shops selling non essential items such as clothing or electrical goods would close, and police would have powers to break up any gathering of more than two people. Did George Orwell in 1984 ever foresee anything as stringent as this from those who stand in power over us? And why only exercising once a day? Why not twice a day if we are exercising on our own and not coming into virus spreading proximity to other people?

Rowan Williams is the next theologian to appear on Newsnight. All suffering makes you question your faith, the former Archbishop of Canterbury confesses.

DAY 8: TUESDAY 24 MARCH: *6,650 confirmed cases 335 deaths*

Today it feels as if we are taking part in a science fiction film about the world being devastated by a mystery illness, and it seems incredulous that it is actually happening for real. After Boris Johnson's instruction that we should all stay indoors except for a very limited range of reasons to be outdoors, the day began in beautiful spring sunshine, but no-one outside enjoying it. From my bedroom window just two cars and one van passed by during a five minute period. I saw the earnest man who runs our local hardware shop hurrying to his premises head down, the only person walking in the street. I thought he was going to put up a notice that the shop would now be closed for the foreseeable future, but it turned out that hardware stores were one of a few types of shop that were allowed to stay open. So the hardware shop will continue selling their strange mix of pots and pans and brooms and light bulbs.

It was seven days ago, last Tuesday, that I watched primary schoolchildren walking excitedly hand in hand through Golders Hill Park with the crocuses and daffodils, on a sunny morning heralding the start of spring. Even though that day was the start of the "social distancing regime" when life began to stop being normal it now seems a lifetime ago, in an innocent world where schools were open and cafes were happy to receive those who were still venturing out.

But the world is different now. Boris Johnson, fists clenched again, giving his address from the Downing Street study last night, was the picture on the front of all the papers. There was a sense of drama to what was unfolding, that we had now entered a new and severe period in the response to trying to slow the spread of this new and threatening virus. A world that just a few weeks ago would have seemed unthinkable.

Following the government guidelines that collecting essential supplies was one of the few reasons permissible for being outdoors I ventured out to buy a paper and pick up some much needed groceries from Waitrose. The packed supermarkets having their shelves stripped bare last week had given way to a new and starkly different experience. Today a marshal, as they are to be known, stood outside Waitrose, only allowing a few customers into the store at any time with those of us waiting outside standing two metres apart to honour the social distancing rules. Once in the store I felt a minor triumph in picking up the last available packet of porridge oats, but at least tomatoes and most fruit and vegetable were available. Did I make a mistake in paying the girl on the checkout till rather than using the self service checkout? Staff working in supermarkets are at the forefront of keeping basic life going whilst being exposed to an above average risk of catching the virus from customers. How would I know if the checkout girl was herself carrying the virus?

Went for a cycle ride on a sunny afternoon around the peaceful blossom filled roads of Hampstead Garden Suburb. This was my one daily piece of outdoor exercise allowed under the new stay at home instructions. In a game of exercise I-Spy I spotted all three of the forms of exercise which Boris Johnson had mentioned: running, walking and cycling. I also heard a fourth, a game of ping pong, to give table tennis its old name, being played in a garden hidden from view by a hedge, one hopes by members of the same family in a world where now no visitors are allowed.

At 3pm a telephone conference call with my regional NHS Board colleagues in Cambridge. As we waited for the discussions to start one of my colleagues on the call could be heard to have a very bad cough. Difficult not to wonder if that was an innocent cough or something more concerning. Can you catch the virus taking part in a conference call? Seems unlikely but everyone is on edge about being in contact with anyone who may have the virus.

Now the situation being discussed with my NHS colleagues shows a first real sign of urgency and the looming reality of an NHS system that could be overwhelmed in a few weeks time. Three hundred critical care beds have been made available in our region but that is in relation to a population of one million people. If one per cent of our population were to become seriously unwell with the virus that would be 10,000 people. They may not all become unwell at the same time but it is still thirty times the number of critical care beds available. We are also told that 80 per cent of the critical care beds are in the south of the region, near to Cambridge, so that patients who live in our large rural areas stretching up to the border with Norfolk may have to be transported over long distances to reach a critical care bed. And more doctors may have to be assigned to caring for those in the north of our region.

There are two deeply concerning issues. Firstly, 85 per cent of our GPs do not yet have adequate Personal Protective Equipment to reduce their risk of catching the virus when interacting with patients. We are told the NHS does have sufficient supplies of protective equipment, now being referred to as PPE, but there have been problems in rolling this out to local areas. Secondly, we only expect to have 300 ventilators available whereas at the height of the storm which is coming we may need as many as 1,400. We are currently at Week One of a calendar which may see us increasingly overwhelmed from Week Four with more patients with the virus needing urgent treatment than we can manage. The message is stark but spelt out: patients assessed as having a low chance of survival will be moved out of the critical care beds to receive palliative end of life care in the community, to free up the critical care beds for patients who have a greater chance of responding to treatment. This is the storm cloud which is about to envelop us.

It's clear that the situation that is expected to unfold in the area around Cambridge is anticipated more widely. The main news story of the day is that the government will build a vast emergency hospital, capable of treating 4,000 patients, at the Excel convention centre in Docklands, East London. All the signs are that, despite the total clampdown to stay at home that has now been imposed, the health experts still anticipate the dams will break and the flow of patients needing urgent treatment in three to four weeks will be overwhelming. If that happens will history say the measures to stop people moving freely were introduced too late?

Meanwhile, alarming images of people still travelling in London on jam packed underground trains. It seems that although much fewer people are travelling into work, a large reduction in the number of tube trains running has caused the overcrowding in carriages that we are used to from normal life. It has led to cross words between the Prime Minister and his successor as Mayor of London, Sadiq Khan. Johnson wants more trains running; Khan, who reduced the trains running to discourage people from travelling, is also struggling with a depleted workforce with many isolating at home either ill with the virus or experiencing virus symptoms. It was also unclear whether construction workers, who would find it difficult to keep two metres apart, should continue working.

A photo of a two year old girl with cancer smiling at her father outside her window is a reminder of how those with cancer need particular protection from the virus because treatment will have reduced the effectiveness of their immune systems.

DAY 9: WEDNESDAY 25 MARCH: *8,077 confirmed cases 422 deaths*

This is Day Two of the instruction to stay at home. The weather remains sunny and the trees continue to blossom calling us to be outside. But most people are obeying the instruction to stay indoors. My newsagent, he with the white gloves and green mask, who was still open yesterday, is now closed. Only three people ahead of me in the queue waiting to enter Waitrose. Small experiences like that can feel like major triumphs. I took home the one remaining packet of breaded haddock sitting alone at the back of the fridge cabinet, but more worryingly, still no disinfectant or olive oil (though nut oil was available).

As worldwide cases of coronavirus topped 400,000 India's 2.6 billion inhabitants, around a third of the world's population, went into total lockdown.

In our commissioning group overseeing the response to the pandemic in Cambridgeshire and Peterborough, business continuity arrangements were now in place. We now have a list of how key positions will be covered in the event that members of the senior management team became ill or otherwise required to self-isolate. In the event of our tireless Chief Executive Officer, Jan Thomas, herself once a nurse, being out of action her role would be split into two and covered by other designated managers. Similar arrangements had been made so that two people would step into any of the main management roles if the postholder was absent.

Spain has become the Italy of two weeks ago with the largest one day coronavirus death toll anywhere in the world, as 738 succumb to the virus. I visited Spain for the very first time only six months ago and enjoyed its history and its sunshine. Now this. Meanwhile Italy has the most deaths of any country with 6,820.

DAY 10: THURSDAY 26 MARCH: *9,529 confirmed cases 463 deaths*

Is it a sign of optimism or sadness that the number of UK deaths from coronavirus increased yesterday but at a lower rate than the previous four days? Are the drastic stay at home measures beginning to slow the rate of deaths, or is the worst still to come?

But a wonderful response to the request from the government for volunteers to take some of the pressure off NHS staff. A remarkable 500,000 people had signed up in a day to be NHS volunteers helping in hospitals, or keeping in touch with the elderly or others self-isolating at home, or delivering groceries or medicines to them.

In Waitrose today, where staff have been promised screens at the tills which have yet to arrive, a bizarre malfunction of the automatic checkout asked for confirmation of my age when I scanned a bottle of still water. "Keep your distance," ordered the Waitrose lady as she came to investigate. I backed off fearing that I would be tasered for not complying. She was able to confirm I was old enough to buy a bottle of still water.

Most of the people living near me seem to have adapted to the restrictions in movement which would have been unthinkable even a week ago. The few people walking in the nearby streets were careful to step out of the way of others walking in their direction. My cleaning lady sent a text offering to come tomorrow if I was happy with that. A difficult issue. I sent a text back to ask her to leave it for the time being; all the government guidance says the restrictions are about reducing the risk of the virus spreading between households.

Linked up by Skype to the daily briefing from senior NHS colleagues involved in the response to the coronavirus in Cambridgeshire and Peterborough. Today we were told that 60,000 additional staff would be available through a combination of retired doctors and nurses returning to work with medical and nursing students also stepping forward to support the caring effort. Thirteen tactical operation cells had been established covering different aspects of the organisation required behind the scenes; for example, one cell would focus on the need to discharge patients from hospital who did not have the virus as quickly as possible, once they were deemed well enough to return home.

I was suddenly alerted this evening at 8pm to the sound of clapping and whistling in my road. The applause that had been requested to thank our brave and caring NHS workforce. Maybe not as vigorous as the similar applause we have seen on television from Italians standing on their balconies but in our usually quiet road it was a good effort. Doctors and nurses have been putting themselves at risk. They all want to put patients first but need more PPE; they also want to be tested for COVID-19 so that they don't have to self-isolate if they have flu like symptoms while not knowing whether they actually have the virus.

Meanwhile Boris Johnson is criticised for missing the opportunity to join in a European order for more ventilators to deal with the need that will arise when the virus is at its peak. We have 8,000 ventilators but may need as many as 20,000 more in two to three weeks, when the effects of the virus peak. A consortium of manufacturers, including vacuum cleaner inventor James Dyson, are working on producing ventilators to meet the shortfall.

Having previously announced packages to help businesses and employees who might otherwise lose their jobs, Chancellor Rishi Sunak now unveils financial help for the self-employed. They may be eligible to up to £2,500 a month if they are earning under £50,000 and self-employed income is the majority of their take home pay.

DAY 11: FRIDAY 27 MARCH: *11,658 confirmed cases 578 deaths*

The 25 March decrease in the rate of UK deaths from the coronavirus was a false dawn. Yesterday a further 115 had died, the largest single day figure and the first time this grim century had been reached. But this was what had been expected because all the scientific evidence suggested we were still going up the curve, not coming down it.

A casual glance at my computer screen during the morning brought the dramatic news that Prime Minister Boris Johnson had tested positive for coronavirus. In a video posting he said that he was only suffering from mild symptoms, a cough and a high temperature, and was self-isolating as was appropriate. With the wizardry of modern technology he said he hoped to continue leading the country through the crisis. But somehow this unwelcome news ratcheted up the drama of the story we are all living through.

In our lunchtime Skype update from Cambridge the statistics of those being treated in hospitals in the Cambridgeshire and Peterborough region is, relative to London figures, low at under 100 but the whole health system is gearing up for an increasing surge of cases with a peak expected to occur between 15 and 17 April. Bed occupancy rates in the region's hospitals, which are normally around 90 per cent, have been reduced to 70 per cent as patients, where feasible, are sent home to free up beds for the expected COVID-19 patients. We are told the region wants 230 intensive care beds with ventilators but currently only 150 are available. Doctors and nurses who normally work in operating theatres and acute care are being trained to take on roles in intensive care. Even so the expectation is that, whereas normally each intensive care nurse looks after one patient, each nurse will have to look after four to six COVID patients, all needing critical care. Some senior doctors and nurses will not be assigned specific patients so they can respond to any urgent situation that may arise. Still 85 per cent of GPs say they have not got sufficient PPE to see patients with symptoms of the virus.

Outside the blossom on the trees continues to develop in what has been a run of spring sunshine throughout this week that no-one has been allowed to enjoy. People have savoured their permitted once a day exercise with a few minutes to enjoy the sunshine while they may.

And then more dramatic news. As if to prove how easily coronavirus spreads between people who spend time together Secretary of State for Health and Social Care, Matt Hancock, has now tested positive for the virus after the news this morning that the Prime Minister had become, it is believed, the first leader of a country to succumb. I met Matt Hancock in his first junior Ministerial appointment in charge of skills and enterprise. He was a fresh faced young man starting out in his Parliamentary career. Now he has to carry the responsibility for the health of the entire nation on his shoulders.

DAY 12: SATURDAY 28 MARCH: *14,543 confirmed cases 759 deaths*

The weather was cooler but still nice enough for me to go for a 30 minute walk around the quiet tree lined roads of Hampstead Garden Suburb.

But elsewhere the virus was ravaging on. Two days ago the daily deaths from COVID-19 reached a hundred for the first time. Now, suddenly, the daily figures are much higher. At the end of the day it was announced that 260 had passed away from the virus in the last twenty four hours, people with family, friends, work colleagues. This took cumulative COVID-19 deaths above the thousand mark. Is this the surge that the NHS has always known was coming?

Meanwhile in America, where New York and the surrounding areas of New Jersey and Connecticut have been in lockdown, predictions that between 100,000 and 200,000 may succumb to the virus.

Last Saturday I walked along the beach at Aldeburgh in lovely sunshine just before going out for leisure trips and staying at hotels was prohibited. That now seems a last moment of freedom from a different lifetime.

One has to try to find some humour in the world we are now living in. I liked the joke that Cluedo would be easier to play as Miss White is the only person allowed in the house.

DAY 13: SUNDAY 29 MARCH: *17,089 confirmed cases 1,019 deaths*

It occurred to me today that whilst car journeys are now off limits we are in danger of becoming a nation of flat batteries. So decided to give my car a once a week exercise and drove around local streets for twenty minutes to get the engine warm. But who knows when I will actually be allowed to drive anywhere meaningful in the car?

Every death from this new coronavirus is a personal story, a tragedy for those who knew the victim. And now the risk to NHS staff is clear, with the news of the first UK surgeon and consultant to die from the virus. Adil El Tayar, a 63 year old Sudanese doctor who had carried out life saving operations around the world, and who had volunteered to help on the front line treating COVID-19 patients. Now he had become one of the statistics himself after dying from the virus in West Middlesex Hospital, London. And 55 year old Amged El-Hawrani, an ear, nose and throat consultant, who had been working in A&E in Derby and Burton, had also died, almost certainly from contracting the virus from one of his patients.

The nation is told to brace itself for a possible six months before life returns to normal. It is likely to be two to three months before there is any relaxation of the current stay at home measures, and even then the NHS will be concerned not to cause a sudden new surge in virus cases by taking the brake off too quickly.

DAY 14: MONDAY 30 MARCH: *19,522 confirmed cases 1,228 deaths*

It is now coming up to two weeks since this diary started and the statistics of confirmed cases and deaths in the UK continue to increase. 1,193 men and women who were alive as I started these daily notes have now left us as a result of this virus for which there is no vaccine. And the business life of the nation has been brought to almost a standstill; some estimates say the economy will contract by 15 per cent whilst the stringent social distancing we are implementing stays in place.

I have noticed that, whilst most people politely stand approximately two metres apart in the queue waiting to go into Waitrose, as soon as they come out ready to scurry home to replenish their store cupboards and freezers, they walk by almost within touching distance of those of us waiting to go in. Perhaps the government needs to instruct us to observe horizontal distancing as well as vertical distancing. I may appear rude but I now turn my back to prevent a rogue germ from those departing shoppers infiltrating my defences. I wish everyone would follow the BBC's advice that we should imagine their beanpole health correspondent Hugh Pym lying on the ground to help us measure the distance we need to be apart from each other.

Today's triumph was the return of crunchy peanut butter to the supermarket shelves. How one savours the prospect of enjoying something which had gone missing from the shops in recent days. And when I get home a package arrives with three small bottles of pine disinfectant from a British company I have never heard of called Zamo. Who or what is Zamo? But with the supermarket shelves still bare underneath the labels marked disinfectant one is grateful to those still able to supply cleaning products.

An apology from an academic highlights the dangers of assuming all scientific estimates of how this virus may pan out must be correct because they have been produced by experts. Tom Pike, from Imperial College, London, had predicted last week that Britain would suffer 5,700 deaths from the virus which, whilst still grim, would be considerably lower than previous estimates. But now Professor Pike acknowledged that the latest data on how the virus was affecting us suggested that his calculations of last week were a significant underestimate and that currently Britain was "in a very dangerous state." Pike's previous calculations had assumed that Britain would follow a similar trajectory to Wuhan in China where the virus originated. His paper had predicted that Britain would have 260 deaths a day at the peak of the virus. But this number of deaths had been reached two days ago when all the evidence indicated we still had a long way up the curve to travel before the rate of people testing positive and the number of deaths would begin to slow. Other scientists warned that all the indications were that fatalities would continue to double every three days for at least another two weeks. All the work of the NHS to prepare large numbers of intensive care beds may not be an over-reaction at all, but the reality of what will be needed.

The tendency for predictions from arithmetic models to be believed only for actual results to reveal errors in the predictions is a topic I have some familiarity with. In previous work reporting on large government projects, cost estimates have often proved to be wrong when flaws are subsequently revealed in one of the key assumptions. "Pseudo scientific mumbo-jumbo" was a phrase coined to describe the worst of such cases.

Others have also cautioned against pinning too much faith in the predictions produced by excel spreadsheets. Only a few months ago Mervyn King, Governor of the Bank of England during the 2008 financial crisis, and economist John Kay argued in their new book, Radical Uncertainty, that arithmetic models could often give far too great a sense of confidence about likely outcomes when they were used to predict events which were unusual. By definition, events which are unusual will have little or no previous data on which to build up probabilities of likely outcomes. In these situations initial estimates prove to be wide of the mark when subsequently compared with the actual result. Perhaps a copy of this book should find its way to Professor Pike.

Tuned in again to what is now a daily ritual, the lunchtime update from my NHS colleagues in Cambridge. Our numbers are still relatively low compared to the national picture. To date we have 121 confirmed coronavirus cases and have suffered four deaths. But we all know that we may be lagging some way behind the experience in London and the worst is yet to come. Like other parts of the country consideration is being given to where possible temporary field hospitals might be located. There is also some concern that the number of people referred for new cancer treatment has dropped significantly against normal levels. Is this an example of the possible adverse effects focussing on COVID-19 patients will have on other areas of medicine? Are there members of the public who are not getting the early diagnosis of cancer and the opportunity for treatment they would receive in normal times?

As many as 9,000 people are now in hospitals around the country with complications from being infected with the coronavirus. But on the news Patrick Vallance, the government's Chief Scientific Adviser, has cautious optimism that although the number of confirmed cases and deaths continues to rise, they are not accelerating. This suggests that the stringent stay at home rules are beginning to have some effect on slowing the rate at which the virus is spreading. Meanwhile, the Nightingale Hospital in East London, as the newly constructed overflow hospital is now known, has been kitted out in a matter of days and will be ready to care for the first 500 of its potential capacity of 4,000 intensive care patients. The main concern at present is that it is estimated that as many as one in four doctors are away from work either with coronavirus symptoms or isolating because a family member has the virus. Doctors are still waiting for more testing to be available so those at home can know whether they are able to return to work.

DAY 15: TUESDAY 31 MARCH: *22,141 confirmed cases 1,408 deaths*

The latest rescue package from the government is literally a rescue. Arrangements are being made to bring back to Britain up to 300,000 Britons believed to be stranded abroad in countries as diverse as India, Peru, the Philippines, Morocco and Cyprus. They will be flown back on commercial airlines where they are still operating, or alternatively, by planes the government will charter, at a cost of £75 million.

I am watching a number of webinars which various organisations are running to provide training and a sense of community to business people working at home, away from their usual networks and sense of camaraderie. In the webinar I watched today those of us participating online were asked to send in a comment about the challenges we were experiencing in this corona crisis. The emotions which united many of the comments were uncertainty and a feeling of losing control. How long would this go on for? What would the effect be on the participants' jobs and livelihood? Richard commented that he had been self-employed for less than a year, so probably wouldn't qualify for the new government support for those who work for themselves, but meanwhile all his work had dried up. Others were concerned about partners whose job future was now at risk. A second webinar I listen to concludes that above all we are dealing with a human crisis and that we must listen to the problems that our staff and business contacts are experiencing.

Joined my NHS colleagues in Cambridge by Skype for the first Board meeting we have run in this brave new world, where colleagues appear onscreen in front of the pot plants and untidy bookcases that are their home environment. Today a new problem has emerged. Hospices in our region are contacting us for financial support because the donations and charity shop income which they largely rely on have been hugely reduced in recent weeks. We in the NHS aren't exactly flush with money but we agree to help the hospices rather than seeing their unique and sensitive work curtailed at this critical time. We are experiencing the same problems as have been highlighted at a national level. We need around 200 more ventilators to cope with the expected peak of the pandemic but do not know where these ventilators are coming from. We also have a local problem. Littlehey Prison, near Huntingdon, a Category C prison with 1200 prisoners, mostly of an older generation, is a potential enclosed community at risk of a widespread coronavirus outbreak. We discuss what arrangements will be made for prisoners who contract the virus.

Later in the afternoon a recruitment agency contacts me about a possible position as Chair of a well known charity helping young people. The charity sector faces a double bind in the current situation: demand for their services has increased but most charities are losing large parts of their income as donations evaporate and fundraising events are cancelled. Some estimates say charities may in aggregate face a £4 billion income shortfall.

Still the main concern is the failure to ramp up, a new term for accelerate, the number of daily tests for coronavirus. At least 25,000 tests a day are needed to build up a more accurate picture of how many people may be carrying the virus and how many have built up antibodies to prevent a recurrence of the virus symptoms. More testing is also needed to enable NHS staff isolating at home to return to work if they test negative for the virus. But at present only 8,000 a day are being tested. The government blames a lack of supplies of the chemicals needed to make the tests.

The day ends with the news that 381 more people have died from the virus, far outstripping the previous largest number of daily deaths of 260. This, after two successive days where the death count dropped. Imperial College estimate that one in 40 people in Britain have had the virus although Spain with one in 7 and Italy with one in 10 are both suffering worse than we are, at least for the time being.

George Aligiah, the BBC newsreader, who has been treated for bowel cancer since 2014, reveals that he is recovering from being infected by the coronavirus. He noted that being a cancer sufferer had given him the mental strength to fight the virus.

DAY 16: WEDNESDAY 1 APRIL: *25,150 confirmed cases 1,789 deaths*

A new month. On 1 March, a Sunday, I took part in a gardening group in Battersea Park with a dozen other volunteers and then went to a book festival attended by hundreds. What a difference a month makes.

So, a question many people are asking is: could the government have done more to prepare for the COVID-19 coronavirus pandemic hitting the UK? Minutes of a key meeting of the government's leading scientific advisory group, SAGE, on 21 February, which have just been released, reveal that this new form of coronavirus was then judged by the advisers to be a moderate risk to the UK. Only one dissenting voice, John Edmunds of the London School of Hygiene and Tropical Medicine, judged the risk to be "high." Was this complacency by the experts or a genuine belief that we would not replicate the experience of thousands of deaths that had occurred in China where the virus began?

The long queue of businesses asking the government for financial support is joined by bus companies who have suffered an 80 per cent reduction in passengers, and garden centres which have had to close leaving millions of bedding plants to be destroyed.

Despite the government's instructions that people should not travel unless it is essential for them in the course of their work, two cars crash this morning in the quiet residential road I live in. I note that the drivers are not observing social distancing when they have the customary argument in the road about whose fault it was. On closer inspection I can see that cars unusually parked down both sides of our road in daytime, because so many people are at home, may have played a part in making the road more difficult to navigate by the two protagonists.

In our lunchtime Skype briefing from NHS colleagues in Cambridge a moment of light relief amongst all the serious business for discussion. There will be prizes for those displaying good style on screen when making their Skype input. Various categories are announced including "best desk arrangement", "best backdrop" "best Covid haircut" and "best workmate" (as in child or pet sharing your home workspace). I don't think I will qualify for any of these.

Contacting my friendly IT man, who fixes all sorts of problems I encounter with my laptop and other devices, I am sorry to hear that he and his partner have been laid up with the virus. One of the perils of providing any type of service indoors to the rest of the public.

The day ends with sombre news. The daily coronavirus death rate is beginning to lift off into the peak phase which the government and the NHS have known was coming. After yesterday's announcement that daily deaths had risen for the first time to over 300, today's figure is 563. This takes Britain's total deaths from the COVID-19 virus to 2,352.

There is growing criticism of the government for still not stepping up virus testing to meet its promise to significantly increase the rate of testing. Still NHS workers complain they are isolating at home when they may be well enough to return to work, but don't know for sure, as they have not been tested. And the absence of mass testing of the public means vital information about the spread of the disease and how many people may have built up immunity is unknown.

DAY 17: THURSDAY 2 APRIL: *25,150 confirmed cases 2,352 deaths*

The front page of the Daily Telegraph, that most Conservative of papers, carries the headline "Questions without answers." It poses three key questions the government has been unable to answer: Why does Britain's testing strategy lag so far behind other nations? Why are so few medics being tested? And what is the government's strategy for exiting from the lockdown?

The Guardian front page headline says, "Just 2,000 frontline NHS staff out of half a million have been tested." Difficult not to agree with those who feel the government has mismanaged this vital part of the response to the pandemic. President Trump, viewing us from the other side of the Atlantic Ocean, says Britain's early strategy for addressing the coronavirus crisis has been "catastrophic."

Also, to the puzzlement of most of us, the papers carry pictures of an almost deserted testing centre at Chessington, Surrey, which NHS staff found difficult to find. And, like other testing centres, many of those who did locate the testing centre were turned away because they had not made an appointment.

The government now aims to involve private sector laboratories in the testing. Public Health England says the intention is to test hundreds of thousands in the coming weeks. But will that be too late to manage the situation that is going to emerge in the next few days: vastly increasing numbers of patients and possibly not enough doctors and nurses at work to take care of them.

Even seagulls are suffering from the lockdown. They are getting less food to eat because of the absence of people coming to the seaside to feed them.

An interesting insight into the challenges pharmacies are facing is given in our lunchtime NHS briefing from Cambridge. Pharmacies are the lifeblood of our health service. In aggregate they receive 657 million visits a year compared with the 300 million visits that GPs receive. The pharmacies often work with just two or three members of staff. In the current coronacrisis some of those staff may be at home isolating at a time when the public's demands for prescriptions have rocketed. We are told there has been a four fold increase in the number of prescriptions pharmacies are dealing with.

The scale of the effect that the response to the pandemic has had on the economy is startlingly clear. One million new people have applied for universal credit benefit in the last two weeks compared to 100,000 that would normally apply in that time period.

Mervyn King, former Governor of the Bank of England, raises the moral dilemma which other commentators have mentioned. Is it right to saddle the younger generation with a wrecked economy and uncertain future work prospects in order to safeguard the lives of the elderly whose lives are at most risk from being infected with the coronavirus? Perhaps we should have a referendum on that, except we do not have enough time to wait for the results and, based on previous experience, the time to implement the results of such a referendum would be calamitous in the current situation.

Meanwhile two of Britain's most iconic summer events, Wimbledon and the Edinburgh Festival, have both been cancelled. Very frustrating for the thousands of fans who normally attend these events.

Finally, some good news. The man who looks like a diligent sixth form student, Health and Social Care Secretary Matt Hancock, is back, after his seven days of isolation following his positive test for the virus. He has emerged with a five point plan to massively increase the virus testing rate. He says the testing will increase tenfold to 100,000 people a day by the end of April. A heroic promise which one thinks will make or break his reputation. But the number of virus deaths continue to climb; today was another 500 plus day. And around the world the number of those who are known to have been infected with the coronavirus has now reached one million.

DAY 18: FRIDAY 3 APRIL: *29,474 confirmed cases 2,921 deaths*

I wake with a clear thought. What would have happened if the government had, much earlier, told old people and those medically at risk, to stay indoors without visitors and if all other people had been advised to reduce their socialising? Would that have contained the virus without the devastating impact on businesses and the economy which has now arisen? Perhaps businesses could have been told that half of their staff should work at home with the other half remaining in their normal place of work. Could that have been a solution which both saved lives and avoided economic meltdown? A poll says that 56 per cent of Britons believe the government's enforcement of social distancing was too late. That was when drastic action was needed to curtail the spread of the virus. Was there another road we could have travelled which would have been more effective at limiting the spread of the virus?

Two nurses have died from COVID-19 showing the tragic selflessness of those who are at the frontline of caring for patients who have contracted the virus. Areema Nasreen, aged 36, a mother of three children, died at Walsall Manor hospital, where she had worked for 16 years, initially as a housekeeper, achieving her life's ambition of becoming a nurse only last year. Aimee O'Rourke, aged 39, also with three children, died at the Queen Mother hospital in Margate.

And amongst those who have died from the virus a well known name to some of a certain age. Comedian Eddie Large, the rotund permanently cheerful larger half of Little and Large has died, sadly for a clown who liked to entertain, alone, after contracting the coronavirus whilst being treated in hospital for a heart attack.

His formal title may be Secretary of State and his responsibilities include social care but I have just noticed how the description Health Minister Matt Hancock has a satisfying symmetry. The initials, like a palindrome, reading the same going forwards and backwards. Perhaps he was born to become Health Minister.

Health Minister Hancock may have looked like a diligent sixth former yesterday but today he was a stern headmaster. In the government's daily press briefing he tells us the weather will be fine this weekend but tells us not to be tempted to venture outside to enjoy it. "The advice is clear. Stay indoors. This is not a request; it is an instruction." Can something that is advice, which implies the recipient is free to decide whether or not to follow the advice, also be an instruction? Please discuss amongst yourselves.

Unlike Hancock, Prime Minister Boris Johnson has still not emerged from his self isolation period after contracting the coronavirus. He has been looking pretty groggy in the video messages he has been issuing to the nation. As the temperature rises around the coronacrisis his own temperature has remained high, forcing him to spend further time indoors.

The new Nightingale Hospital, amazingly built from scratch within just a week inside the Excel Conference Centre in East London, has opened but will not be treating patients yet, as hospitals in London have sufficient intensive care beds to cope with the coronavirus patients currently needing to be hospitalised.

DAY 19: SATURDAY 4 APRIL: *33,718 confirmed cases 3,605 deaths*

The weather, as we had been promised, was fine, a real feeling of spring and renewal in the white blossomed trees I can see from my window. But still the death toll from the virus mounts. A further 684 deaths in figures announced yesterday. Most people found reserves of self-discipline to avoid the temptation to go out and enjoy the lovely weekend weather. But not everybody. Brockwell Park in South London will be closed tomorrow after 3,000 people descended on the park today to enjoy the spring sunshine.

The first Saturday of April last year also had beautiful sunny weather. I arrived then at Euston station at 6am to join a happy group boarding the Orient Express style Northern Belle train for the journey to Aintree, to watch the Grand National, won for the second year running by Tiger Roll. Today the Grand National will be televised as a "virtual race" with the field of fearless equines replaced by computer generated horses moving in ways determined by complex algorithms based on recent form. Not wishing to miss an opportunity, bookmakers will be taking bets from punters happy to have a flutter from the comfort of their armchairs at home.

I fear that television weather forecasters have not changed their style of delivery to fit these sombre times. The forecast that the fine weather is set to last the whole weekend is brought to us with an enthusiasm that makes the idea of flocking to the seaside and parks irresistible. "How can one not miss out on enjoying this lovely weather?" they seem to be saying. Surely they should be dressed in black, and mourning that, on days when we are instructed to remain inside for nearly all the time, there is an awful forecast of sunshine. Whereas overcast and rainy days should be brought to us cheerfully as "ideal weather for remaining indoors."

In London the union Unite announces that five London bus staff have lost their lives to the virus. Another example of those who have been innocent victims whilst enabling essential public services to continue.

In the last twenty four hours there have been a further 708 deaths, the highest daily figure so far.

Tomorrow night the Queen will address the nation in a televised broadcast. We wait to hear what comfort Her Majesty can bring.

DAY 20: SUNDAY 5 APRIL: *41,903 confirmed cases 4,313 deaths*

It was, as promised, a beautiful sunny morning. On a normal Sunday I would rush off to Battersea Park where I am a member of a gardening group working in the enclosed beauty of the Old English Garden, a hidden jewel in this much visited Victorian park by the river. But to follow the government's instructions I have to curb the enthusiasm of my green fingers and follow government instructions by staying indoors. My hour of exercise comprises a walk round Hampstead Garden Suburb taking photographs of the white painted houses in the afternoon spring sunshine, whilst zig zagging across the roads to avoid others also taking an afternoon walk.

I am not the only one taking photographs. Sophie Raworth, the BBC newsreader, posts photos of an eerily empty central London, the familiar sites of Trafalgar Square, Leicester Square, Oxford Circus all virtually devoid of any human life. She mentions that the only sound she can hear in a central London normally teeming with people is a flag fluttering above a closed cinema. One of her photos looks down on the empty chairs and tables of an outdoor café in Covent Garden, which seems to symbolise the emptiness of this world that has been imposed upon us.

And so, at 8pm the Queen addresses us. One of the rare times the Queen has made a televised address, and the first since the death of the Queen Mother in 2002. Speaking from Windsor Castle, it is an assured performance from our 93 year old monarch. The Queen acknowledges that the coronavirus has caused an increasingly challenging time bringing grief to some, financial difficulties to many and enormous change to the daily lives of us all. She thanks the NHS, care workers and others continuing to deliver essential services. And those of us staying at home. Then the message that the public wants to hear which the Queen can deliver far better than any politician; "If we remain united and resolute we will overcome it." There is a hint of Britain in wartime: "Those who come after us will say that this generation of Britons was as strong as any."

The Queen's wartime analogy is further expressed as she recalls her first broadcast in 1940 reading with her sister, Princess Margaret, a message to children who had been evacuated from their families as the Second World War took hold. We, too, are living in a period of separation. But the Queen assured us with words evocative of Forces Sweetheart, Vera Lynn, "We will be with friends again, we will be with family again, we will meet again." The Queen had given us all hope in these dark hours which is what the Queen does best.

In Scotland the Chief Medical Officer Doctor Catherine Calderwood is photographed at her second home in Fife breaking her own official guidance to stay at home unless there is an essential reason not to. She apologises for this error of judgement and First Minister Nicola Sturgeon says she should stay in the job, but later Calderwood resigns.

As the UK death toll from the virus rose to nearly five thousand the day ends with dramatic news. Prime Minister Boris Johnson, who had not re-emerged after seven days from his self-isolation after having the virus confirmed, had been taken to St Thomas' hospital, London, a short drive from Downing Street, on the advice of his doctor, for precautionary tests. Robert Peston speaking from his North London home, says it is "profoundly shocking" news. Foreign Secretary Dominic Raab stands by to lead the nation if Johnson is unable to do so.

2 THE PEAK OF THE STORM ARRIVES

Days 21 to 40: 6 April to 25 April

DAY 21: MONDAY 6 APRIL: *47,806 confirmed cases 4,934 deaths*

It is a difficult editorial judgement: which is the bigger front page story, the Queen's address to the nation, or Prime Minister Boris Johnson being admitted to hospital with his ongoing coronavirus condition? I think the Daily Telegraph has it right. A picture of the Queen taking up three quarters of the front page but the lead story, "Johnson taken to hospital for coronavirus treatment." In days gone one cannot imagine The Times' front page would have got past the sub-editor's gaze, the Queen is relegated to a postage stamp size picture whilst Boris Johnson's photo is spread across three columns.

The son of the Indian owner of the shop where I buy stationery is taking the first step into home deliveries having left a phone number glued to the shop door. I buy more than I normally would to make his visit worthwhile and I now have enough pens and notepads to survive a prolonged lockdown.

In the queue to gain entrance to Waitrose this morning a London ambulance races by with lights flashing. Is this yet another coronavirus patient needing urgent care, or are people still becoming unwell through other causes? How do they prioritise which patients are most in need of an ambulance?

Calculations by the Centre for Economics and Business Research show the devastating effect on the economy of the lockdown. They estimate it is causing a reduction of economic output of 31 per cent per day, a daily hit of £2.4 billion. The Institute of Fiscal Studies notes that women and those under the age of 25 are being particularly hit by the economic downturn because of the collapse of the hospitality sector.

In our daily briefing from Cambridge on how the coronavirus situation is being managed in our region, which covers the county of Cambridgeshire and Peterborough, we are told that modelling currently suggests hospital admissions will peak around 13-14 April at just under 150 a day. Arrangements are still being made to start the testing of NHS staff which everyone has been waiting for. A drive through centre is being set up but is still three days away from opening. We are told that the test will have to be sent to laboratories in Germany as UK laboratory capacity is being used for the tests of patients in hospital with symptoms of the virus.

The news that seven bus drivers have now died from contracting the virus makes me think of the cheerful lady who often drives the morning bus down the Finchley Road who greets each and every passenger with a personal "Good morning." Just decent people doing a job which serves the public. Now drivers are asking for the front of buses to be closed to give them greater protection.

It was two weeks ago this evening that Boris Johnson gave a televised address where, with great earnestness, he told us that we must stay at home and only go out for essential purchases, one period of exercise a day and going to work if work could not be done at home. The death rate from the COVID-19 coronavirus was then just over three hundred but the Prime Minister's medical advisers knew that the virus was spreading to an extent that the number of fatalities would increase dramatically in the coming weeks. Only a lockdown keeping most people at home would avoid the NHS being overwhelmed. In these two short weeks five thousand more families have lost loved ones who have died in hospital from the effects of the virus, an unquantified number of others have lost their lives in care homes and the community, and the economy has been brought to a standstill from the lockdown.

But now a twist in this ever changing drama which no-one can have anticipated. An announcement at 8pm that Boris Johnson's condition in hospital worsened during the afternoon and he has been moved to intensive care. Again, this is described as being a precaution but there is now serious concern for the Prime Minister's wellbeing. An unprecedented situation that, in the middle of a national emergency to deal with a life threatening virus, the Prime Minister himself is now a victim of the disease he was leading the response to. In the words of BBC political editor, Laura Kuenssberg, "power is no protection from harm." Foreign Secretary Dominic Raab, who is also First Secretary of State, has been asked by the Prime Minister to deputise for him as and when required.

DAY 22: TUESDAY 7 APRIL: *51,608 confirmed cases 5,373 deaths*

It was another beautiful sunny morning in what has been a remarkable run of warm spring weather. But meanwhile Prime Minister, Boris Johnson, is seriously ill in the intensive care unit of St Thomas' Hospital. And most of the rest of us are only allowed out of our homes for very limited periods to enjoy this fine weather. It feels as if the fates are taunting us with the situation we find ourselves in. That the Prime Minister, who had been trying to lead us through this crisis, should himself succumb so seriously to this awful virus seems to underline that we are all in danger at this time. Any one of us could become ill.

Historians recall parallels with September 1918 when, two months before the end of the First World War, Prime Minister David Lloyd George became seriously ill, during the Spanish Flu epidemic which raged across the world killing at least 50 million, but recovered after hospital treatment.

With deaths from the virus now past 5,000 many are querying whether the government was right to have allowed, a month ago today, the

Cheltenham Racing Festival to have started, bringing 200,000 spectators into close proximity to each other over the four days of the festival. Was the coronavirus circulating freely there despite the organisers' safety steps such as hand sanitising points in the viewing enclosures? Did those ardent racegoers, many from other parts of England and Ireland, catch the virus and then take it back to their home communities?

My good friends in Canterbury, Ian and Alyson, both former medics have joined the large army of those recently retired from the health service who have signed up to help support NHS staff in the current crisis. Ian was a much respected leader of clinical trials for new medicines and is hoping he might join one of the teams trying to develop a new coronavirus vaccine. Alyson is a former GP and is ready to assist wherever her experience can help.

In recent times I have become a collector of coincidences which seem as if they have a hidden significance, perhaps indicating a greater power influencing our lives. Just a few weeks ago, but before the coronavirus had taken hold in this country, I met Parvov, a young American woman, who was on a short research visit to England with the worldwide medical charity, Medicins Sans Frontieres. I offered to introduce her to my NHS colleagues in Cambridge. And now, on my desk at home, is a newspaper appeal from the same charity urgently seeking donations to support their international work bringing medical aid to treating people stricken with the coronavirus. Just a coincidence or something more profound? I also wonder if Parvov made it back to America which is itself facing alarmingly large numbers of those affected by the virus.

Still there is much anxiousness about the rate that both NHS workers and the wider public are being tested for the virus. Matt Hancock's aim that testing would be scaled up to 100,000 people a day by the end of April looms over him like a sword of Damocles. Testing of NHS workers is increasing as part of the programme, which is now allowing just under 15,000 people a day to check whether they have the virus. But it is still not clear whether there are going to be enough testing stations, and enough laboratory capacity to analyse the tests, to enable the Health Secretary's ambitious target to be met. The plans for tests to identify whether individuals have developed antibodies which would indicate a person has had the virus but is now immune have also stalled. The government had sourced 17.5 million antibody tests from China but UK medical experts are not satisfied they work. Caveat emptor comes to mind. Now the government is looking to UK companies to develop these finger prick tests which are key to identifying who may be well enough to return to work based on evidence that they are not capable of transmitting the virus to others.

Even the government has acknowledged that there should have been a better strategy for testing large numbers of the population at an earlier stage in this unfolding drama. Germany is held up as the model of a country which seems to have organised testing effectively. The German health authorities immediately mobilised 170 test laboratories when the outbreak began and are currently testing between 35,000 and 50,000 a day, around three times our rate. All the indications are that this has helped contain the number of COVID-19 fatalities in Germany. Britain has a death rate of around 106 per million people whereas in Germany their rate is just a quarter of ours, at around 26.

But as Boris Johnson faces his own battle against the coronavirus in the intensive care unit of St Thomas' hospital, the day ends with the feeling that events have taken a serious turn which no one could have foreseen.

DAY 23: WEDNESDAY 8 APRIL: *55,242 confirmed cases 6,159 deaths*

In the daily government press briefing, Chancellor Rishi Sunak tells us that whilst Boris Johnson remains in intensive care, his condition is improving and he had been sitting up in bed and engaging with his medical team. The nation breathes a collective sigh of relief.

The Chancellor also unveils a further financial support package, this time £700 million to support charities which are facing a twofold challenge: drastically reduced fundraising income at a time when there is increased demand for their services. The charities say the Chancellor's package is a welcome first step but is unlikely to be enough to stop many smaller charities folding.

Earlier, in our lunchtime briefing from NHS colleagues in Cambridge, our chief executive, Jan Thomas, takes us through her working day in the daily command and control response to managing the coronavirus situation in our region. The morning starts with an 8.30am Skype call with her leadership team. Today they discussed: the plans to make more testing available for our staff and other NHS colleagues in the areas; the progress on sourcing the additional ventilators which we still require; and the need to ensure that those patients with urgent cancer conditions are being seen by our hospitals despite the demands of treating virus patients. Then at 11.30am Jan joins a Skype call with the strategic commands across our region: the fire service, police, ambulance services and a recovery group considering the impact on Cambridgeshire and Peterborough when we finally emerge into the post-COVID world. The afternoon goes in following up the actions agreed in the morning before a further leadership group discussion at 5pm to talk through how the day has gone and any issues for follow up the next day.

Patients with serious non-COVID 19 conditions face a dilemma. Will the treatment they have been waiting for be deferred because staff and beds are needed for taking care of virus patients? Or will they be called in for treatment and then face the increased risk of contracting the coronavirus within the hospital environment at a time when their immune systems may be vulnerable and less able to fight off the virus? Despite great efforts by the NHS to arrange for the most urgent non-COVID treatments to be continued some cancellations are inevitable. Newspapers report 72 year old James Byrom has had potentially life saving surgery for a recently diagnosed brain cancer cancelled by Addenbrookes Hospital in Cambridge, an unfortunate victim of a virus which has created risks to the treatment of patients not infected by the virus but who are equally in need of urgent care.

But the grim news is that the UK has now experienced by far its worst daily deaths, 938 dying from the virus in hospital in the 24 hours ending at 5pm yesterday, 7 April. We are now moving relentlessly towards the top of our "peak." There is, though, some comfort that the social distancing rules are beginning to dampen the increase in the numbers contracting the virus and those needing hospital treatment. The government says that the NHS expects to have sufficient beds to deal with those who will need hospital treatment for the COVID virus.

And in Wuhan, China, where the coronavirus outbreak started, the lockdown was lifted today after 76 days; evidence that eventually this virus which has brought the world to a standstill can be contained.

DAY 24: THURSDAY 9 APRIL: *60,733 confirmed cases 7,097 deaths*

There is a seeming paradox in the stats of infections, admissions to hospitals and deaths from coronavirus. The daily number of deaths is soaring as we move into the phase the government knew was coming, the critical period when the NHS would be under the most pressure as hospital admissions reached the high levels expected in early to mid April. Yet pandemic experts are now saying there could just be some good news, in that new cases and hospital admissions may be reaching a plateau. The Oxford English Dictionary defines a plateau as an area of fairly high level ground or a state of little or no change following a period of activity or progress. If we are on high level ground then the view below is anything but serene. You can hardly say that activity has stopped when there are around 5,000 new confirmed cases of the virus a day. But if the optimism is that the situation we are living with may not get even worse than it is now, then most of us would be grateful for that.

For our NHS staff in Cambridge, who have been working flat out, some seven days a week, there is time for a little humour before the Easter break. Many of those joining our Skype link up show off funny coffee cups and hats, the best of which will be winning prizes when the judges assess the many entrants. Most staff will get some time with their families over the coming long weekend whilst our regional oversight of the response to the coronavirus outbreak will continue to be worked on round the clock, including the bank holidays. Everyone knows that when we finally emerge from this pandemic there will be a public inquiry looking at how well-prepared we were, and why we took the decisions we did. We are told to keep notebooks and even post-it notes as an evidence trail for our decision making.

There has been widespread approval of the government's scheme to pay 80 per cent of the wages up to £2,500 a month of those staff who would have otherwise been made redundant to enable their employers to retain them until business picks up. As many as nine million are expected to benefit from this support. But the government scheme to encourage banks to make loans available to both small businesses and larger businesses up to an annual turnover of £500 million has had a faltering start. Many businesses claim that, despite the government guaranteeing that 80 per cent of the loans will be repaid, banks are applying lengthy application processes so that it is not the fast injection of new cash which the businesses need to survive.

Meanwhile Tesco which has, with all other supermarkets, been keeping the nation fed as it stays at home, and in recent days has taken on 35,000 extra staff, many made let go from their previous jobs, has come under criticism for taking government rates relief of £585 million and paying a dividend to its investors of £635 million. Has the government's support gone straight out to investors? No, Tesco argues, the dividend was already justified from the profits the business had earned over the past year.

And just as the nation prepared for its weekly clap to celebrate all those who work in our NHS, the news that Boris Johnson, the unexpected beneficiary of NHS care this week, has been moved to a general ward in St Thomas' hospital after his three night stay in intensive care. Our larger than life Prime Minister may attract both supporters and critics in equal measure but everyone felt buoyed by this welcome news.

DAY 25: FRIDAY 10 APRIL: *65,077 confirmed cases 7,978 deaths*

Good Friday. And also the second day of the festival of Passover. What can we learn from these religious events as we sit in our homes, anxious and uncertain about the coronavirus world we now all live in? Easter brings its message of life continuing after the darkest of days. Passover celebrates freedom from oppression. Both are welcome spiritual stories to comfort us in these troubled times.

People often question where God was during the Holocaust and one could ask the same question now. Has this pandemic been some sort of lesson to us that we are not as able to control the world we live in as we may have thought? Is this God's retribution on materialistic globalisation?

And in this pause for reflection what can we now see about the situation we have arrived at? There are questions which could be posed to the World Health Authority which oversees medical issues at a global level. Once it became known that there was an outbreak in China of a life threatening virus, why didn't the World Health Authority ask China to apply stringent rules about travelling out of China to other countries where the virus could then spread and flourish? And why wasn't Britain's pandemic plan clearer and applied more speedily as soon as the first cases of the virus were confirmed in the UK? It seems haunting in retrospect that on 23 January Matt Hancock, as Secretary of State for Health and Social Care, told MPs there was an increased likelihood that the new coronavirus would arrive in the UK but said the authorities were well prepared and would remain vigilant. Hancock also said that we were one of the first countries to have a world leading test for the new virus. Although the Chief Medical Officer Chris Whitty revised the risk to the UK population from the coronavirus upwards this was only from "very low" to "low."

Reasons to be cheerful on this Good Friday were that Boris Johnson is continuing to make progress in his recovery, taking some short walks from his bed in a general ward at St Thomas' hospital. And Keith Watson of Worcestershire was one of the smiling faces we are now seeing daily giving the thumbs up sign to applauding doctors and nurses as those recovered from COVID-19 leave hospital. Keith Watson is 101 years old. All the more remarkable.

We are told that it is most likely that 10 per cent at most may have had the virus but it is difficult to know whether to cheer or feel concerned by this figure. Does this demonstrate that social distancing and the stay at home message have significantly contained the spread of the virus? Or perhaps that the virus was never being transmitted as widely as was feared? Or does it highlight that there are many more of us who may be at risk of contracting the virus, particularly if the current restrictions on our daily lives are lifted?

A paradox is revealed by a study by University College London. Despite being more at risk to serious illness from the virus, people over 60 are reporting a higher level of self-satisfaction than young people aged 18 to 24, who are suffering most from loneliness and feeling down as they see their futures put on hold, with uncertainties over jobs and finances. Young people, though, may be allowed back to work first when the lockdown is lifted; a generation of baristas, waiters and waitresses are waiting to return to their cafes and restaurants to serve their cappuccinos and Pret baguettes.

One of the coping and reasonably happy older people is the 86 year old Joan Bakewell. Like many of her generation she is having to become familiar with new ways of working. Attending her first "Zoom meeting", the online platform we are all getting used to for our computer meetings, she wondered why her fellow Labour peers were not reacting to her earnestly made points only to find that she had not "unmuted" her microphone.

The evening news on what would, in normal circumstances, have been the start of a sun-filled happy Easter weekend, is overwhelmingly grim. 980 people died in hospital from the coronavirus in the 24 hours ending at 5pm on 9 April, the UK's largest daily death rate as we continue the accelerating ascent of "our curve." Not only is it our highest number of fatalities in one day from COVID-19 but it exceeds the highest daily death rates recorded in Italy and Spain, the two countries we watched on television being ravaged by the coronavirus when our daily deaths were at a far lower level. China, where the coronavirus outbreak started, had much lower daily death rates than we are experiencing. Only America and France have recorded higher daily death rates than the UK.

With this deeply concerning virus death rate in the UK, and with worldwide coronavirus deaths now past 100,000, the public are reminded to stay at home this bank holiday weekend as the continued fine weather continues to taunt us.

DAY 26: SATURDAY 11 APRIL: *73,758 confirmed cases 8,958 deaths*

On the Jewish Sabbath three strictly Orthodox Charedi Jewish men stand in a socially distanced triangle in the gardens of my block of flats reciting the Sabbath morning prayers, their black and white prayer shawls draped over their black suits in the warm spring sunshine.

The papers carry the encouraging news that Sarah Gilbert, professor of vaccinology at Oxford University, is 80 per cent confident that a successful vaccine against the coronavirus will be ready by September.

Further reassuring news is that Prime Minister Boris Johnson is continuing his recovery at St Thomas' hospital and has been watching films and playing Sudoku. Later he issues a brief message of thanks to the NHS, "I can't thank them enough, I owe them my life." His father, Stanley Johnson said his son's cavalier attitude had almost done for him. "To use that American expression, he almost took one for the team. We have got to make sure we play the game properly now."

On my afternoon walk I watch an elderly man and woman walking ahead of me, their arms linked as if in defiance that they will not bow to the virus, the woman with a sunhat embroidered with a flower, the man moving forward with the aid of his stick. I zigzag across the road to ensure I am keeping my proper distance from them and other walkers coming towards me. I smiled as I thought of the news that Sheffield council has been using blown up images of the late entertainer Bruce Forsyth saying "Nice two metres, two metres nice."

But the sad news is never far away. Another 900 plus daily deaths as we move towards the peak of our curve with cumulative deaths closing in on the 10,000 mark. These include 19 NHS staff who have given their lives in the cause of saving others. And after the earlier concerns that there was not enough PPE for NHS and care home staff, now doctors, nurses and carers are saying that the protective equipment that has been provided by the government is running out. The one sense of better news on the horizon is that the daily numbers of new cases of the virus and hospital admissions are beginning to fall a little suggesting that the numbers dying from the virus each day will, at some not too distant point, also begin to fall. But we are not there yet.

DAY 27: SUNDAY 12 APRIL: *78,991 confirmed cases 9,875 deaths*

The Queen's Easter message yesterday, "Coronavirus will not overcome us" in the long run will most likely be true, but still remains a daily prayer for each of us.

The fine weather continues. Most people have been stoically staying at home and being reasonable in maintaining social distancing when going out for their daily walk or bike ride. But a small minority, urged on by the good weather, are less careful. On a balcony of the block of flats next to mine a hippy like party of young people drinking and laughing in the sunshine was in full swing. The police have issued over 1,000 fines to people like this who have breached the government instructions not to meet with people outside our own household.

On Easter Sunday Pope Francis says Mass in an empty St Peter's Basilica watched by millions online. Archbishop of Canterbury, Justin Welby, brings innovation to his Easter address, speaking in white robes from the temporary cathedral that is his kitchen.

But today's day of holiness will go down in Britain as the most sombre of days. A further 737 deaths took the UK past 10,000 deaths in hospital from coronavirus. Many others are known to have died from the virus in care homes, where elderly residents have been particularly vulnerable, or elsewhere in the community. With already nearly 20,000 coronavirus hospital admissions the fears continue that we will experience the highest COVID-19 death rate in Europe. Amongst those who have perished more than 30 NHS staff are now believed to have given their lives to the virus in the care of others. These now include Sara Trollope, a 51 year old nurse with Hillingdon hospital, who last year was pictured with Prime Minister Boris Johnson. As they posed for their picture they would not have thought then that a worldwide virus pandemic would, within a year, leave one of them dead and the other seriously ill in intensive care.

But the abiding image of this Easter Sunday is that of Boris Johnson himself. To everyone's great relief he has been discharged from St Thomas' hospital after a week which has included three nights in intensive care.

About to continue his recovery at Chequers with his pregnant fiancée, Carrie Symonds, he gives a moving address saying that "the NHS has saved my life, no question." He acknowledges that "for 48 hours things could have gone either way" and then goes on to thank the team of doctors and nurses who cared for him. In particular he mentions the two nurses who were at his bedside throughout the night keeping him under observation and making sure he had oxygen: Luis Pitarma from Portugal and Jenny McGee from New Zealand, In Johnson's words "they were watching and they were caring and making the interventions I needed." Boris Johnson may not be the son of God but on this Easter weekend we, the people, are delighted that he has returned to us.

DAY 28: MONDAY 13 APRIL: *84,279 confirmed cases 10,612 deaths*

Is coronavirus particularly targeting our comedians? After the death of Eddie Large earlier this month yesterday we lost that most affable of clowns, the much loved Tim Brooke-Taylor of The Goodies and 'I'm sorry, I haven't a clue' fame. It seems particularly grievous that two people who brought us together through so much humour and laughter should end their lives in hospital alone, victims to this awful illness.

The nation is bracing itself for what is to come. The daily death rates have fallen over the last two days from the 980 high reported on 10 April. But we are told that the peak may be a week away so the slightly lower figures of the past 48 hours may not be indicative of a real improvement.

There are two serious ongoing problems. Firstly, the problems that have been experienced with PPE continue. For many days the initial problems were difficulties in distributing face masks, gloves and gowns to all the NHS staff and carers who needed them. Now the problem is that many doctors, nurses and care home staff say they are running out of the PPE stocks which they had. The Royal College of Nurses has said nurses should not compromise their own safety, and the risk of becoming infected and passing the virus to others, by treating patients if they do not have the right equipment. The second serious problem is the spread of the coronavirus in care homes where elderly residents, often with health problems, are particularly at risk. Around one in eight care homes have reported deaths of residents from the virus and some have experienced an internal COVID-19 pandemic of their own. The care home at Stanley Park, County Durham has suffered 13 deaths out of its 72 residents. There is a growing feeling that care homes were vulnerable to this sort of tragedy, with support and equipment mainly being directed towards hospitals and GPs.

Meanwhile, those with businesses grow ever more frustrated at not being able to access the new loans the government promised to help them stay afloat during this sudden and dramatic economic downturn. £4 billion pounds of loans applied for are still stuck in the bureaucracy of paperwork that has to be submitted and approved before the banks will open their tills to help businesses desperate for financial support.

On television a three part serial written by young playwright James Graham starts. Called Quiz, it tells the story of the so called "Coughing Major" Charles Ingram who was convicted of fraudulently winning the top prize of £1 million on TV's 'Who Wants to be a Millionaire'. A shade ironic that a story about coughing should be the big draw this Bank Holiday, when the world is gripped by a virus for which repeated coughing is a key symptom. Any member of a television quiz audience repeatedly coughing would now be politely asked to go home and isolate.

DAY 29: TUESDAY 14 APRIL: *88,621 confirmed cases 11,329 deaths*

Today we learned the shocking effect that closing down large parts of the economy to manage the coronavirus pandemic will have on the financial wellbeing of millions of UK businesses and households.

As the government decided to extend the stay at home lockdown ("Stay at home, protect the NHS, save lives") for a further three weeks, the maximum allowed under the emergency coronavirus legislation, the Office of Budget Responsibility (OBR), those nerdy officials who pore over economic data, dropped a bombshell. According to their estimates the economy may contract by a staggering 35 per cent in the three months up to the end of June. Even if the economy recovers quickly when we leave the current lockdown, which some economists believe is unlikely, the OBR still predicts a 14 per cent loss to the economy over a full year. That would be more than double the 6 per cent recorded after the banking crisis of 2008 and the worst since the Second World War. Meanwhile public borrowing, the extent to which government spending exceeds its income from taxes and other sources, is estimated to reach £273 billion in the current financial year, another downturn not recorded since the Second World War. Historians tell us that we are on course for the deepest decline in the economy since 1709 when the worst winter for 500 years was followed by floods, flu and crop failure.

The words Zoom and Peston seem at odds with each other, one a fast modern way to communicate, the other one of the slowest forms of speech known to man, each word elongated and stressed forcing us to listen carefully to every syllable uttered by the financial and political guru. Speaking by Zoom, from his North London bookcase lined lounge, Peston says these alarming figures will mean politics will move to the left. He argues that even a Conservative government will have to focus on supporting those on low incomes who, without financial reserves to fall back on, have been hit the worst by the economic downturn.

And on the medical front figures emerge today to show that there were an all time high number of UK deaths from all causes in the week to 3 April of over 16,000, six thousand more than in a normal week, but only half of the additional deaths have been attributed to the COVID-19 virus. This raises the concern that large numbers of deaths are occurring because people with non-COVID conditions, including strokes and heart attacks, are not going to hospital for fear of contracting the coronavirus there. In addition, the number of GP referrals for cancer tests are down by 70 per cent compared to a month ago, creating worries that some cancers will go untreated for longer than usual, reducing the chances of a successful recovery.

In these troubled times we hang on to any good news story. Today's was the picture on the front page of The Times of five-month-old Amelia Woodger of Suffolk, who has been released smiling from hospital after contracting the coronavirus.

DAY 30: WEDNESDAY 15 APRIL: *93,873 confirmed cases 12,107 deaths*

The headlines in the papers tell the story of the world we now live in. The Daily Mail, in large black print, says "4000 may have died in care homes." The daily deaths figures reported by the government are for hospitals only. It has become increasingly evident in recent days that there has been a rapid transmission of the coronavirus in many care homes. We await work by the Office of National Statistics (ONS), based on the cause of death which doctors have inserted onto death statistics, for information on the true number of COVID-19 deaths outside hospitals. If the Daily Mail headline is right then the total number of coronavirus deaths is already over 16,000 and rapidly approaching the 20,000 fatalities which Chief Scientific Adviser Sir Patrick Vallance had told Parliament would be the upper limit of "a good outcome."

Other papers focus on the huge downturn in the economy expected by the Office of Budget Responsibility. The Daily Telegraph's front page leads with "Biggest economic shock in 300 years" beneath a picture of Chancellor Rishi Sunak superimposed on a graph with a blood-red line moving downwards at an alarming rate. The Financial Times headline is "Virus threatens to hit economy harder than war and flu in 1918"

At our lunchtime briefing from NHS colleagues in Cambridge, GP Doctor Tom Shackleton talked about his work with care homes. Many of the residents he needs to speak to he can contact through video calls which the care home nurses arrange. But if necessary, he will don full PPE (visor, mask, gown, gloves) to attend to the care home patient in person. Doctor Shackleton notes that there are no oxygen supplies in these homes, which can be a problem if serious coronavirus symptoms are experienced by residents. Even though care home residents may be in the later stages of life GPs and care home staff will have often known residents for several years, so losing a resident, particularly if this is prematurely because of the coronavirus, can still feel like a loss of a family member.

Each day brings further tragic stories of NHS staff who have lost their lives after being infected with COVID-19 in the course of treating patients. Today we learn of Gareth Roberts, a 65 year old nurse in Cardiff, who had come out of retirement to help with the current crisis but had his life put at risk, his family say, because of inadequate PPE. And Mary Agyeiwao Agyapong, a 28 year old nurse from Luton, becomes another NHS fatality just days after her own father died from the virus, but not before doctors deliver the baby she was expecting. What will that child in due course know of her mother, a nurse who gave her life so others might live?

There is widespread approval of the acknowledgement by French President Macron that "Mistakes were made. Were we prepared for this crisis? On the face of it, not enough." With 15,000 coronavirus deaths, around the same as Spain, Macron accepts that there have been shortages of protective clothing such as gowns and masks. Meanwhile America with 25,000 deaths and Italy with 20,000 lead the gruesome league table of those countries who have experienced the highest numbers of COVID deaths.

Today's good new story is that of 99 year old retired Army Captain, Tom Moore, two weeks short of his 100th birthday who has been pushing his walking frame each day for ten laps of his garden. He initially aimed to use his daily walks to raise £1,000 for wellbeing packs and rest rooms for NHS staff in Berkshire where he lives. But after film of the proud Captain wearing his army medals became an internet sensation the public have been enchanted by Captain Tom, as he is now known, and have donated a remarkable £4 million to help his causes.

Amidst the continued sad litany of the number of coronavirus deaths reported each day, some glimmers of hope that we may soon be over the worst. For the fourth day running the UK deaths are in the 700 to 800 range compared to the 900 plus of previous days. Chief Medical Officer Chris Whitty says we are probably reaching the peak after which the government will be able to consider how some of the stay at home restrictions can start to be eased.

DAY 31: THURSDAY 16 APRIL: *98,476 confirmed cases 12,868 deaths*

Still, many of those running businesses await the precious guaranteed loans the government were so keen to announce last month. Only 6,000 out of 28,000 loan applications have been approved, with as many as 300,000 having made enquiries. And in the background, the question that will be asked now and for many years ahead: was it really necessary to wreck the economy and push thousands of businesses to the wall in order to save lives threatened by the coronavirus?

One of our hardworking GPs in Cambridge, who spends a lot of his working week attending to the elderly in local care homes, reports that every resident of one home has COVID-19 symptoms. The great concern that has arisen in the last few days is the ease with which the virus can spread through a care home full of elderly residents; the government has told older men and women living in their own homes to stay indoors away from other people but inside a care home they are all vulnerable together. In our update from Cambridge we also hear about hospitals in our region lending each other staff and equipment, a new spirit of collaboration that has specifically come out of the coronacrisis. At a more local level, consideration is being given to how 200 fruit pickers, who have flown in from Eastern Europe to work in orchards near Wisbech in the north of our region, can be tested to ensure they are free of the virus.

Although sadly thousands of older people have lost their fight against the virus it is heartening to see pictures in the papers of 106 year old Connie Mitchell leaving hospital after successfully recovering from the virus after three weeks treatment.

As Boris Johnson continues his own recovery at Chequers after his intensive care treatment for the virus, First Minister Dominic Rabb, confirms what had been expected, that the lockdown keeping most of us at home for most of the day will continue for at least the next three weeks. Raab warns that we are in "a delicate and dangerous stage" of the virus outbreak. This is evidenced by a further 861 deaths as the latest daily statistic and care home deaths, not included in the daily statistics for England, would have added to this figure.

Rabb goes on to outline a new five point plan of conditions which will need to be met for the lockdown to be eased: the NHS must be able to cope with the number of people who need hospital treatment; there must be a sustained and consistent fall in the daily death rate; the number of new cases of infection must fall to manageable levels; there must be enough testing and PPE to meet the demand; and there must be no risk of a second peak of patients requiring hospital treatment which would overwhelm the NHS. How long must we wait for all five of those conditions to be met?

DAY 32: FRIDAY 17 APRIL: *103,093 confirmed cases 13,729 deaths*

Today global deaths from the coronavirus pass 150,000, a huge human tragedy from an illness which has spread across the world and for which there is no ready medicine to provide immunity. President Trump announces that America, which, with 34,500 lives lost to the virus has contributed nearly a quarter of the worldwide deaths, will now start to come out of lockdown. Trump believes, at least for the time being, America is over the worst and needs to restart its economy which already has 22 million out of work as a result of the coronavirus outbreak.

With UK deaths, including those who have died in care homes and the community, almost certainly now in excess of 15,000 there will always be, amongst all these deaths, people you know; either because they were your own family members, they were your friends, they were people you knew in your wider social circle or because they had become well known to the population at large through their particular skills. In this last category, Leeds United football club sadly announced the death at 76 of legendary defender Norman Hunter whose aggressive tackling brought him the nickname "Bites yer legs," though he was a good enough player to represent England on 28 occasions.

At 11am bus drivers in London stood and remembered the 26 London Transport colleagues who have died from the virus, as Transport for London now requires passengers to board buses in the middle to give further protection to drivers.

The problems with availability of PPE, which have been repeatedly raised by doctors, nurses and carers, continue. Now the problem is that the availability of new gowns is running out. New guidance from Public Health England says that if necessary gowns should now be washed and reused after their initial use. Matt Hancock appeared before the Health and Social Care Select Committee meeting through video conference and reassured Jeremy Hunt, chairing the meeting from his booklined study, that there was "a plan." As indeed there always is.

Better news was that the government has an order with a UK consortium for 15,000 additional ventilators. And those in business welcomed the government's announcement that it will continue to pay 80 per cent of wages, up to £2,500 a month, of staff who have been furloughed for an additional month up to the end of June. Furlough, this strange word to describe staff, who might otherwise have been made redundant, receiving state support to stay with a business. None of us knew this word before the lockdown in March; now we all look to use it when playing Scrabble.

The wheel of history comes full circle as Hilda Churchill, who lost a sister a century ago to the devastating Spanish Flu pandemic, becomes, at 108, the oldest person to die in the UK from COVID-19. Could she ever have imagined as a child, losing the sister who was her friend and playmate, that, one day, many years into the future, she herself would be mourned for losing her life to another terrible fast spreading illness?

DAY 33: SATURDAY 18 APRIL: *108,692 confirmed cases 14,576 deaths*

The Daily Mail headline three days ago that 4,000 may have died in care homes from the effects of the coronavirus was shocking. Today the front page of The Daily Telegraph told us that Care England, a representative body for care homes, estimates that 7,500 care home residents have lost their lives from the virus, with many more care home residents at risk. As these figures for deaths in care homes are not included in the government's daily statistics for coronavirus deaths, this means that probably now over 20,000 people have lost their lives to the virus in the UK, nearly all in the last five weeks.

This is a human tragedy of huge proportions and the death rate now appears to have exceeded government scientific adviser, Sir Patrick Vallance's previous double edged assessment that less than 20,000 deaths would be "a good outcome." On a sunny Saturday afternoon I recall many happy similar days watching Portsmouth Football club play at their famous Fratton Park ground. The maximum crowd capacity there now is just under 20,000. I try to imagine a packed cheering ground gradually falling totally silent as every single person there, one by one, succumbed to the virus.

Curiously, relatively speaking, we are not suffering as much as Belgium, a country which has not featured in television or newspaper reports of the toll the virus has been taking. Belgium, with total coronavirus deaths of just over 5,000, has suffered 445 deaths per million people, the highest rate of COVID deaths in relation to the size of population of all countries. They are followed by Spain 419, Italy 376, France 286 and then the UK, fifth in this ranking, with 215. But can one draw any comfort from these statistics when we know that around 20,000 families in the UK have lost loved ones?

A new phrase has entered the lexicon of the coronavirus. The Captain Tom effect. This is now increasingly used to describe the many acts of fundraising and other altruism to help NHS workers, those in other frontline services and individuals or families isolating or in distress in these difficult times. Captain Tom Moore, just short of his 100th birthday, completed his painstaking walking frame assisted 100 laps of his Berkshire garden to great acclaim, the promise of a Spitfire flypast on his birthday and the satisfaction of having raised a monumental £20 million from the public's donations with more money still coming in each day.

Very few business sectors, other than supermarkets and the producers of food and cleaning products, have not been hit by the effects of the government's instruction to us all to stay at home. During a prolonged period of sunny weather, which included the Easter weekend, garden centres would normally have been enjoying their busiest period of the year as people bought plants to prepare their gardens for summer or to give as presents. Now garden centres are having to throw away, or turn to compost, as many as 500 million plants which growers had been carefully nurturing so that they would be ready for us to enjoy. Garden centre owners point to the Netherlands and parts of Germany where garden centres remain open, recognised for the life affirming role they can play at times of public stress and ill health.

Publishers of newspapers and magazines are now the next in line to highlight the financial difficulties they are facing. Less people going out to shop, most newsagents being closed and less advertising revenue have caused a dramatic downturn in copies sold and cashflow needed to stay in business. We are urged to continue buying newspapers when we do go to the shops.

The Radio Times runs an interesting article on how our well known radio and television presenters have adapted to presenting from their spare rooms, studies and kitchens. Radio 4 Today presenter, Justin Webb, still gets up at 3.30am every morning as the time spent in the taxi to the BBC studio is now replaced by the time to set up broadcasting equipment in his lounge. But he still dresses smart to make sure he feels at his best. Blue Peter's Lindsey Russell, hosting the programme from her parents' conservatory, thinks it is important for children to see presenters having to adapt to new ways of doing things as all families are at the present time. Steph McGovern, presenting Channel 4's The Steph Show, is used now to filling in if her expected guests fail to appear, due to technology failing. And Robert Peston, whose North London lounge has become a familiar sight during coronavirus news programmes, misses going out after a turn in the studio for a coffee shop flat white, but senses that journalists may in future be more flexible in how and where they broadcast, having experienced these new ways of working.

But even a sunny Saturday cannot get us away from the human tragedies of the pandemic. Another 800 plus reported deaths takes us over the 15,000 deaths reported in the government's daily statistics; these figures, as we are now constantly reminded, do not include the large numbers who have sadly died from COVID-19 in care homes. or in the community. Recent deaths include 37 year old childminder, Salina Shaw, who gave birth to her third daughter on 7 April but died from the virus on 12 April having posted a Facebook message, "Feeling anxious bringing a child into this mess." And 68 year old Barbara Sage, who had devoted her working life with the charity Marie Curie to comforting those with terminal illnesses, dies alone in hospital, before the government's recent change to allow relatives, suitably dressed in protective clothing, to visit COVID-19 patients during their final hours.

DAY 34: SUNDAY 19 APRIL: *114,217 confirmed cases 15,464 deaths*

Here, on another sunny day, some evidence of families wanting to be close to each other despite the lockdown. A young couple arrive in a car to show their young baby off to relatives in the small garden of a nearby house, no social distancing here but what would normally be a natural act of family interaction. And relatives come to talk through an open ground floor window to their elderly parents in the block of flats where I live. A cry goes up from the window of another flat, "Stay indoors and close the window." "We meant well" the visitors standing outside reply.

Last night I enjoyed watching again on television the film, "The Sense of an Ending," based on the Julian Barnes Booker prize winning novel of that name. The title of this book describes what everyone is seeking at the present time. Some evidence that there is a plan which will bring us to the end of this prolonged period of isolation and suffering.

To enjoy my hour of exercise I cycle once again through the pretty country-like roads of Hampstead Garden Suburb, where the philanthropist Henrietta Barnett created, at the start of the twentieth century, this quiet place, devoid of shops, with small homes for artisans alongside larger houses for those who could afford them. Stopping for a moment to take in the peaceful view I overhear a twenty something girl talking, as she walked, on her smartphone to her best friend. She complains about her dilemma of not being able to meet up with her new boyfriend because of the lockdown. Probably low down the scale of misfortunes caused by the coronavirus pandemic, but part of our new world nonetheless.

The debate goes on within government on how soon some of the lockdown restrictions can be loosened. Boris Johnson, making occasional calls to the Cabinet from his recuperation at Chequers, has cautioned against coming out of the lockdown too soon for fear of triggering another wave of the virus. Chancellor Rishi Sunak is concerned about the impact on the economy of prolonging the lockdown. Sir Jeremy Farrar, director of the Wellcome Trust, tells Sky News that the lockdown is affecting the health, wellbeing and mental health of all of us but disproportionately affecting the most vulnerable. Hospital doctors are reporting an increase in emergency admissions for attempted suicides, domestic abuse and alcohol related conditions.

The daily deaths in hospital figure of 596 is the lowest for two weeks but no-one is celebrating; it is still high and we need to see a consistent trend of falling daily deaths to be convinced we are well past the peak. The government squash the hope that schools might re-open soon; they want to see more evidence that the worst is over and also need schools to work out how social distancing would be applied before children return.

Still the shortages in PPE continues to be reported. Shadow health secretary, John Ashworth, says that a number of small firms have told him they contacted the government to say they could produce more equipment but have had no answer.

DAY 35: MONDAY 20 APRIL: *120,067 confirmed cases 16,060 deaths*

The Resolution Foundation says that as many as 11.7 million people in the UK could be furloughed or unemployed; in other words, no longer working. As I go for my morning walk past coffee shops now shuttered and closed, I wonder how many of those are baristas. And what are those baristas doing now; making lovely coffee for themselves at home? Perhaps they could show us online how to make the perfect cup of coffee.

If those who are furloughed do continue in their jobs once restrictions are eased, then that will be a welcome success for the government's scheme to protect jobs during the lockdown. But it comes at a price. The cost to the government of paying the wages of perhaps as many as eight million employees is expected to be as much as £40 billion. Concerns for our long term finances grow as Treasury modelling now suggests that there will be long term damage to the economy, not just the short term 35 per cent crash estimated last week by the Office for Budget Responsibility. If that happens then more of those baristas and others, whose jobs and wages have been temporarily protected by the government furlough scheme, are likely to find they will eventually be out of work.

In America, such has been the slump of demand for oil because no-one is travelling anywhere, that the price of oil has incredibly turned negative. Oil producers have so much unsold oil that they have run out of storage space and are prepared to pay to offload their unwanted oil supplies. And in America now the first signs of civic unrest. Thousands take to the streets to say the lockdown must end because the alternative is unemployment; uncomfortable reminders of the Great Depression of the 1930s. "Give me liberty or give me COVID-19" reads one banner although, of course, both may be possible simultaneously. There continues to be tension between President Trump, who seems keen to end the lockdown, and state governors, who believe it is their call when and how to ease the restrictions.

On the medical front Matt Hancock's promise that by the end of April 100,000 people a day would be tested for coronavirus currently looks like a bold and perhaps unrealistic pledge. Latest figures show 19,000 a day are being tested. No-one envies Hancock's job but how will history judge him when we all look back at these unprecedented times?

It is the strangeness of the times we have been accustomed to live in that the huge tragedy that 449 people died yesterday from coronavirus is seen as good news, because it is the first day with less than 500 deaths for a fortnight.

DAY 36: TUESDAY 21 APRIL: *124,743 confirmed cases 16,509 deaths*

Lord Lamont, former Conservative Chancellor, makes the point that many of the public will have been anaesthetised from the full pain of the economic downturn because of the furlough scheme and other government support packages. But if some sectors, like hospitality, remain closed for a long time then either the government must repeatedly extend the furlough arrangements at an additional large cost to the taxpayer or risk mass unemployment and more business failures.

In our daily briefing from NHS colleagues in Cambridge we are shown graphs which demonstrate that the incidence of coronavirus infection and hospital admissions, which had been increasing, now appears to be flattening. We currently have 286 COVID-19 patients in our hospitals and, if there is some good news, it is that our "peak" has been at a lower level than had been anticipated, with daily deaths in recent days averaging around ten.

In our weekly Board meeting later in the day the trials and tribulations of video meetings are there for all to see; one Board member appears upside down to others watching the meeting and our esteemed Chair appears to have acquired an oriental fez as an overhead red lamp shade sits onscreen above his head. But the discussion is serious as we are given a draft of a paper setting out ethical issues which doctors, nurses and carers may have to consider in dealing with COVID-19 patients. It is good that skilled minds have focussed on these important issues. But the paper does not directly address the two big dilemmas that doctors, nurses and carers could face: whether to continue to treat patients if there is insufficient PPE, and how to decide which patients should receive ventilator support if there are not enough ventilators for all who need them. Maybe it is only God who can answer those dilemmas.

In the evening the daily deaths in hospitals have increased again, up to 828, taking the total UK hospital deaths to over 17,000. Currently, some 8,000 more people are dying in a week than would normally be expected. A third of the additional deaths are from the coronavirus. But that means over 5,000 of the excess deaths may be from non-COVID 19 causes. That raises serious concerns that either the coronavirus figures are understated or many people with other conditions have sadly been dying because they have not been seeking medical assistance for fear of catching the virus inside a hospital, or their treatment has been delayed.

However, in the Downing Street daily briefing today graphs are revealed showing that the UK "peak" in terms of coronavirus illness and deaths may have been two weeks ago on 8 April. This implies we are, albeit very slowly, now improving from the worst virus days we have experienced. Robert Peston is the latest to demonstrate the Bakewell effect. Like Baroness Joan Bakewell before him he forgets to switch off the mute button on his laptop with the result that his earnest beautifully crafted question to Downing Street disappears into the walls of his lounge and is completely missed by everyone else.

A senior civil servant becomes embroiled in a war of words with the government. Giving evidence to the Science and Technology Committee, Foreign Office Permanent Secretary, Sir Tom McDonald, says it was a "political decision" by the government not to join an EU procurement for PPE and new ventilators, only to retract his words in writing a few hours later. The government maintains it was an administrative error due to EU e-mails going to a defunct Downing Street e-mail account. But as Matt Hancock is rather pleased to explain, "We have not lost anything because nothing has been delivered yet through the EU procurement." Sounds like the language of "Yes, Minister."

Hancock assures us that the government is "straining every sinew" to procure new PPE. He is a man who likes athletic phrases. "Herculean effort" is another recent one, as is "throwing everything at it." A career in sports journalism awaits Hancock if he ever leaves Parliament.

DAY 37: WEDNESDAY 22 APRIL: *129,044 confirmed cases 17,337 deaths*

Still the debate goes on as to whether schools should be re-opened, both for the benefit of children and also to allow their parents to return to work. New data reveals that less than one per cent of children have continued schooling under the government's rule that vulnerable children may continue to attend school; 10 per cent had been expected.

The daily number of tests for coronavirus continue to be just under 20,000. Matt Hancock now says his previous promise that 100,000 a day would be tested by the end of April will be achieved because there will be capacity to test 100,000 a day by then. But some testing centres are under-utilised, partly because they are situated a long way from the homes of people who want to be tested. What is the value of capacity if it is not being used?

In Cambridge our CEO, Jan Thomas, is already looking ahead to how health services may be delivered after the worst of the pandemic is over. Jan outlines a "recovery plan" of five key issues the providers of

NHS health services in our region will have to consider. They are: Do we have enough PPE to deal with non COVID-19 illnesses? Have we worked out how we will use our NHS buildings to ensure that those with non COVID-19 conditions can be treated safely, minimising the risk that they will contract the virus? Are there some services we may have stopped to deal with those suffering from COVID-19 which should remain stopped when we return to more normal times? What is the model of care we will return to, taking account of the new ways of working we have adopted in the last few weeks? How do we programme the actions which need to be taken over three timescales: the short, medium and long terms?

Later, in the Downing Street daily briefing, as another 783 deaths takes us to over 18,000 in total, government chief medical adviser, Chris Whitty, brings the sombre news that we will be living with social distancing for a very long time. He warns us it would be wrong to assume life will return to normal in the foreseeable future. He is starkly realistic that, for each vaccine that may be tested, the chances of success are "incredibly small" and that, even where a vaccine passes the proof of concept stage, there is still a very long timescale for testing to be completed and manufacturing of the vaccine to be carried out. Until we have a vaccine, or drugs to treat the COVID-19 illness, the government must continue social distancing to prevent the spread of the virus. So, this new world we are living in, unable to interact face to face with friends, work colleagues and family members outside our own household, seems here to stay, possibly for a very long time into the future.

Parliament moves into the Zoom age that most of the rest of us have now embraced. With a small number of MPs sitting spread out in the House of Commons chamber other MPs join in from the comfort of their own homes. Most of the men have consciously worn a suit and tie to reassure the public that they are taking it seriously. With Zoom only one person at a time can speak which may at least cut out the usual raucous heckling across the green benches.

DAY 38: THURSDAY 23 APRIL: *133,495 confirmed cases 18,100 deaths*

Concern grows over the impact that focussing NHS attention on treating COVID-19 patients is having on the treatment of other conditions. Cancer charity, Cancer Research UK, estimates that there are currently more than 2,000 undiagnosed cancer cases each week. Their estimate is derived from a fall of around 75 per cent in patients being referred urgently by their GP for a cancer assessment which is supposed to take place within two weeks of a referral. Leading oncologist, Professor Karol Sikora, says that in April normally around 30,000 new cancer cases would emerge; this month it will be down to around 5.000. He underlines the point that early referral and diagnosis is essential to enable treatment to start before cancers have a chance to grow.

The good news on the medical front is that in Oxford today the first trials on humans of a possible coronavirus vaccine began. Elisa Granato and Edward O'Neill became the first to be involved in the trials. But it will be a long path from these initial trials, involving analysing the trial results and widening the testing, before the medical experts will know if they have produced a vaccine which can prevent COVID-19 illness without causing unwanted side effects.

The debate on when and how the lockdown should be relaxed continues. Sir Charles Walker MP, talking of the fears of business owners from a prolonged lockdown, says "There has got to be an economy to go back to." A spokesman for the hospitality sector warns of the "catastrophic effect" that extending the lockdown will have on the sector. Andrew Beale, the owner of the excellent West Lodge Hotel in Hadley Wood, to the north of London, sends an e-mail to his loyal customers showing photos of the beautiful arboretum in the hotel grounds alongside the news that the hotel is closed for the first time in its history. 150 staff have been placed in the government furlough system for paying most of their wages. Beale hopes in his message, as we all do, that the days of happy family lunches in the hotel will return.

With Prime Minister Boris Johnson still recovering at Chequers from his brush with COVID-19 the government line is that we must continue to focus on observing the lockdown and that it is too early to begin talking about how the lockdown may be eased. But in Scotland First Minister Nicola Sturgeon is applauded for producing a 26 page paper about the trade-offs between health and economic risks and saying that she wants "a grown-up conversation" with the public about how the restrictions may, in some ways, be reduced.

DAY 39: FRIDAY 24 APRIL: *138,078 confirmed cases 18,738 deaths*

Let us start with some good news today. Last night's Big Night In, a collaboration between Comic Relief and Children in Need, was a big success raising over £60 million to help support causes involved in fighting the coronavirus outbreak. A galaxy of stars took part including the Doctors, that is those who have been Doctor Who, providing a message of support to the NHS, care homes and hospices. Stephen Fry has a Blackadder themed bantering conversation with the Duke of Cambridge before the Duke and Duchess stepped outside with their children to lead the weekly applause for front line workers.

Today saw the start of a new government website to enable key workers to book tests for the coronavirus as the government tries to pull out all the stops to meet Matt Hancock's ambitious target of 100,000 tests a day by the end of the month. There is such a demand to book these tests that the new website has to close for a while, but re-opens later.

Still the virus death rate climbs. Another 768 deaths are announced. This means the official UK COVID deaths total, which exclude deaths in care homes and the community in England and Northern Ireland, is now within 500 of the 20.000 mark which was considered to be the top end of what would represent a satisfactory outcome from this pandemic. And still the human tragedies behind the statistics, each day bringing new stories of loved ones cruelly taken from their families before their time. Today, 37 year old identical twin sisters Katy and Emma Davis, both popular nurses at Southampton General Hospital, die within three days of each other leaving a heartbroken third sister Zoe.

Former Cabinet Secretary Gus O'Donnell, now Lord O'Donnell, suggests the government should compare the trade-offs between continuing the full lockdown to minimise the chances of the virus spreading, with the resulting risk of severe damage to the economy. He says the comparison could be done by using the common currency of a "wellbeing" score. But can one compare lives and money through a common measure? What would those who have lost loved ones to the virus say about that? O'Donnell also thinks that Prime Minister Boris Johnson, expected back at work next week, may reflect on his own brush with mortality during his three nights in COVID-19 intensive care to err on the side of protecting lives, even if it means further economic hardships.

Two remarkable examples of the power of music to inspire us through these troubled times. Captain Tom Moore captured the hearts of the nation last week when he completed his fundraising challenge of a hundred laps, pushing his walking frame around his garden, just a few days short of becoming a centurion; he has now become the oldest person to have a Number One record with the highly appropriate You'll Never Walk Alone. And a video appears of beautiful scenes at Northwick Park Hospital in London of Doctor Maxton Pitcher on violin and Katherine Fawcett on piano playing Ave Maria as their colleague A&E sister Alicia Borja is wheeled through the hospital corridors having recovered from a long battle with COVID-19.

DAY 40: SATURDAY 25 APRIL: *143,464 confirmed cases 19,506 deaths*

In the Jewish community the weekly reading from the Old Testament this week is the section from Leviticus setting out that, in the event of an outbreak of leprosy, those infected should stay apart from the community for seven days or, if not cured, fourteen days. So we are not the first to have had to self-isolate.

The weather remains warm and sunny. This has, without doubt, been a truly wonderful spring. But we are confined to our daily hour of government approved exercise. Despite the fine weather picnics in the park and trips to the coast are just memories of what we used to do.

We realise just how much we have had to give up in order to ward off the virus.

But the reasons why the government has imposed such stringent restrictions are underlined by today's update on deaths from the virus. Hospital deaths from the coronavirus in the UK have now passed the 20,000 mark. It is a startling and tragically large number and has come in under two months. The first UK death was announced on 5 March at which point there were 3,000 deaths worldwide. Today, just seven weeks on, we in the UK are past 20,000 out of 200,000 worldwide deaths. And, as we are constantly reminded, the UK figures exclude COVID-19 deaths in care homes and the community in England and Northern Ireland. So the true figure is most likely somewhere between 25,000 and 30,000.

With another 813 deaths in the last twenty-four hours it is also becoming clear that, whilst the top of our UK peak may have been reached, we are going to linger near the summit for some time. So, sadly, coronavirus fatalities are going to get considerably larger in the coming days before there is real evidence that the impact of the virus is receding. NHS National Medical Director for England, Stephen Powis, is asked by the BBC at the Downing Street press conference about the implications of the UK passing the 20,000 coronavirus deaths mark given the government's chief medical and scientific advisers had said at the outset that limiting the outbreak to less than 20,000 deaths would be "a good outcome." Doesn't this suggest, Stephen Powis was asked, that the government's strategy for dealing with the pandemic had not been successful? Powis did not answer this but spoke about the continued importance of the social distancing measures to contain the number of deaths.

There can, though, be no doubt that we, and indeed most countries worldwide, allowed the virus to get too much of a head start before we chased after it with measures to restrict its spread. South Africa, which carried out house to house checks and imposed a lockdown when the first cases of the coronavirus were found, has experienced less than a hundred COVID-19 deaths.

3 THE STORM CONTINUES AND QUESTIONS ARE ASKED

Days 41 to 60: 26 April to 15 May

DAY 41: SUNDAY 26 APRIL: *148,377 confirmed cases 20,319 deaths*

The peace of a lovely sunny Sunday morning was interrupted for an hour in mid-morning by the sound of the whirring blades of a police helicopter stationary in the skies above nearby Hampstead. The timing of this disturbance was clear. A visible and audible warning that we shouldn't even think of going out for a picnic on this beautiful day as we would be under surveillance. There is a line between expecting the public to act in a responsible manner, and putting us in a police state where personal actions are monitored. It is in danger of being crossed.

The nation awaits the return to work of Prime Minister Boris Johnson who, having recuperated at Chequers after being hospitalised with COVID-19, is expected back at Downing Street tomorrow. The key issue which requires his immediate attention is whether to allow some easing of the lockdown restrictions. But if there is to be an easing then this must be done in a way which avoids another surge of virus infections and hospital admissions. It is a most delicate balance to get right.

Those over the age of 70 wait to hear what any changes may mean for them. It is possible they will be told to remain behind closed doors whilst the rest of the UK, in gradual stages, returns to work and a more normal life. But for those over 70 who are reasonable fit and well the idea of prolonged confinement is not at all welcomed. Well known septuagenarians make their views known. Michael Beurk, 74, host of Radio 4's Moral Maze and a former BBC news presenter, says, "I'll be the best judge of what's in my interests as long as I don't adversely impact others," whilst fellow former news presenter Angela Rippon, 75, says, "Those who are fit and healthy will say why are you making this decision on age?"

We grasp at any hint of a silver lining. The daily deaths from the virus are announced as 413, the lowest this month. But figures released over a weekend are often lower than they should be, as some information has yet to be collected.

But let us be grateful for small mercies. Asteroid 1998 OR2, about to pass within four million miles of the earth, appears to be observing social distancing rules, with a little to spare.

DAY 42: MONDAY 27 APRIL: *152,840 confirmed cases 20,732 deaths*

Today was a day of moving into different phases. Most significantly it was the return of Prime Minister Boris Johnson to official duties after a three week absence, following his admission to hospital on Sunday 5 April, as a victim of the virus he had been seeking to wage battle with on our behalf. In an early morning address at the familiar lectern in Downing Street he tells us we are moving into a second phase of battle. "If the virus were a mugger, then this is the moment when we have begun to wrestle it to the floor." He acknowledged the impatience of businesses who wanted to see restrictions eased and pledged to "begin gradually to refine the economic and social restrictions to fire up the engines of this vast UK economy." But he also expressed caution saying we were at a moment of "maximum danger" and he did not want to throw away all the sacrifices that had been made, only to risk a second wave of infections. He could not say now when and how the easing of restrictions would take place. He did, though, promise to say more about the government's plans "in the coming days."

This then is the test that will define Johnson's premiership. Can he steer the country a course which avoids adding large numbers to the already tragic scale of lives lost in the UK to the coronavirus, whilst, at the same time, preventing a devastating collapse in the economy which will add further human misery and social unrest through large scale unemployment and poverty? This is the Rubik cube of coronabritain. Somewhere there may be a combination which gives the right answer. But there are scores of possible solutions which may end in failure.

The daily deaths from the virus fall again to 360, the lowest for a month, tempting a belief that we are on the down slope of these dark days and that we can soon return to the world of cafes, restaurants and shops, a world which, two months ago, we never questioned. But, as Chief Medical Adviser Chris Whitty reminds us, it all depends on the R factor, the rate at which the coronavirus infection is passed on to others. Whitty estimates it has reduced from around 3 (each person with the virus passes it on to three others) to about 0.7. Keep the R factor under 1 and the virus will eventually die out. But loosen too many social distancing restrictions and the moment it goes above 1 the virus may spread exponentially.

Meanwhile Johnson's colleague, Health Minister Matt Hancock, faces his own day of reckoning. The number of frontline workers being tested for the coronavirus at centres, or through home testing kits, is now significantly increasing. But, having promised 100,000 tests a day by the end of April, with just three days left the latest daily figure of 37,000 tests looks like Hancock may be a long way short of his target at the month end.

Chancellor Rishi Sunak unveils another package for businesses promising small enterprises loans of up to £50,000 within 24 hours and with the lenders protected by a 100 per cent government guarantee. This as a response to the many businesses who were finding it hard to access the previous emergency loan scheme.

And in the garden of my flats this afternoon a little girl with a magnifying glass looks with her mother at the formation of flowers, no doubt as part of home education as schools remain closed. Whilst on television Jamie Oliver, speaking to us from the unvarnished family chaos of his kitchen at home, shows us how to whisk up frozen spinach and peas to make pasta with a green sauce. Tomorrow the sales of frozen vegetables will soar.

DAY 43: TUESDAY 28 APRIL: *157,149 confirmed cases 21,092 deaths*

The weather broke today. The seemingly continuous days of warm sunshine were replaced by a significant drop in temperature, overcast skies and morning rain. How much easier it might have been to follow social distancing in the last few weeks if there had been continuous rain. Why didn't the government arrange that in its pandemic plan?

As the number of COVID-19 cases in hospitals falls, the NHS wants to make sure that those with other conditions who have stayed away from hospitals, for fear of catching the virus or adding to the work of overstretched NHS staff, will now attend for treatment. In our regional NHS Board meeting we are told how our hospitals will arrange completely separate areas for treating COVID-19 patients and patients with other conditions. We also approve additional financial support to care homes to help with their additional costs such as PPE.

The travel sector was in the news today. British Airways announces that, as a result of the almost total collapse of international travel, it is laying off 12,000 of its staff, a quarter of its workforce. And thousands of the public are waiting for refunds of pre-booked holidays which have been cancelled. Travel companies are encouraging consumers to accept credit notes rather than a refund but many worry about losing their money if their travel company was to go out of business.

Alarming statistics today highlight the devastating effect that the coronavirus is having in care homes where, once an infection is introduced into the home, it can quickly spread through vulnerable elderly residents. Figures from the ONS show that in the week ending 17 April, deaths in care homes from all causes were 7,316, three times the number at the end of March. It is likely that, as hospital deaths from COVID-19 begin to fall, those occurring in care homes are still on an upwards curve and could exceed those in hospitals.

Teachers and parents are still grappling with home learning. There is wide variation between schools on the amount of online learning they are providing. There are concerns that children who come from poorer backgrounds will be adversely affected as they may be living in homes with less space to study and with fewer computer devices than children from wealthier homes.

My final thought of the day is when will we enjoy café society again, that hubbub of conversation over the flat whites and cappuccinos? Many owners of businesses in the hospitality sector fear that, even when they are finally allowed to re-open, imposing social distancing will mean accepting fewer customers with the loss of revenue leaving the businesses worse off than when they were closed. Perhaps we should all purchase two skinny lattes rather than one to help them survive.

DAY 44: WEDNESDAY 29 APRIL: *161,145 confirmed cases 21,678 deaths*

In the early hours of this morning Boris Johnson who, a month ago was in hospital fighting for his life, was now in hospital again, looking at life from the other end of its spectrum, to keep his fiancée, Carrie Symonds, company as she gave birth to a baby boy. Bounding up the stairs of 10 Downing Street on his return Prime Minister Johnson looked himself like a big version of a baby boy, smile beaming across his chubby face, ready to get on with his other challenge of the day, talking to Cabinet colleagues about whether to announce plans to ease the lockdown.

The alarming effect on businesses of the lockdown continues with fashion chain Next announcing a 41 per cent reduction in profits. And so many other sectors are profoundly affected by the current events. Theatre producer, Cameron Mackintosh, says that all he sees in front of him are the millions of pounds he will be losing in the coming months as theatres remain dark. The idea of reopening with half full auditoriums to comply with social distancing restrictions is anathema to him. "Social distancing and theatre don't go together" he observes.

But still the tension exists. How do you prevent a new wave of deaths from the coronavirus if you ease some of the lockdown restrictions?

Germany, which had been doing very well at controlling the virus, may now have to re-introduce their lockdown as deaths have been increasing following the easing of restrictions.

At the Downing Street press conference new statistics are unveiled. For the first time the daily reported figures of deaths from the coronavirus give the full picture, including deaths in care homes and the community across the whole of the United Kingdom. As a result, the total deaths figure increases by nearly four and a half thousand to over 26,000. There are fears that the UK will experience the largest fatalities in Europe from the virus. Our rate of deaths per million people is now only exceeded by Belgium and Spain.

A discussion on Newsnight considers whether cities will change beyond recognition when the virus finally passes. If remote working from home becomes the norm, then few people will need to come into city centres. John Vincent, the founder of the fast food chain Leon, says it will be a sad society if we only connect with each other on a computer. Others comment that it is the noise of the city, with people of many different backgrounds in close discussion with each other, that is the catalyst for many new ideas. Some Newsnight guests, however, have found new pleasures from the stay at home world. Actress Tracey Ann Oberman is enjoying the stillness of life the lockdown has brought, whilst journalist and former MP Matthew Parris is delighted by all the receptions he no longer has to attend.

DAY 45: THURSDAY 30 APRIL: *165,221 confirmed cases 26,097 deaths*

Today Captain Tom Moore, he who walked 100 laps of his garden and has raised over £30 million for the NHS, celebrated his 100th birthday. Except that he is no longer Captain Tom. He has been made an honorary Colonel. A hugely popular promotion as evidenced by a sea of 140,000 birthday cards sitting on the floor of his granddaughter, Georgia's school hall.

I was asked to write a piece today on the future of government projects in an economic downturn. I wrote that it isn't all doom and gloom. Government will always want new infrastructure to stimulate business activity. But with the public finances hugely in debt because of the government's various support packages any new projects will really have to demonstrate that they can deliver a high level of relevant benefits. And the priorities for which projects to take forward may now change. Will new transport projects still be important if people are wary of travelling, and have become used to having video meetings, rather than face to face discussions? Will there be a greater demand now for health and social care projects? And will there be a greater need for new IT projects which help us to connect with each other online?

My NHS colleagues in Cambridge continue to discuss how the hospitals in our region can create COVID free areas where patients with non-COVID conditions can come to be treated. This, so the backlog of operations, scans and other procedures which have been put on hold during the peak of the pandemic, can now be reduced. The concern is that part of the increased death rates in recent weeks have been people who put off going to their GPs or hospitals because they did not wish to be at risk of contracting the virus.

Boris Johnson gives his first Downing Street press briefing since before his week in hospital with his own struggle with the coronavirus. The Prime Minster says it is too early to lift the restrictions we have been living with, but says next week he will outline a "menu of options" for how the restrictions may be eased in due course. The R factor, the rate at which the virus reproduces itself through transmission to other people, gets another mention. The government's advisers now believe the R factor has dropped to between 0.6 and 0.9 which means the number of new cases of the virus should be declining. What is less certain is to what extent the R factor will increase once any of the current restrictions are withdrawn. This is the uncertainty which is underlying the government's caution about lifting the restrictions.

And so, as the public applaud the NHS and other front line staff for a sixth successive week, April draws to an end. At the start of the month under 2.000 coronavirus deaths had been reported in the UK. Now we have over 26.000. It has been a grim month. Health Minister Matt

Hancock promised 100,000 tests a day for the virus. Has he achieved his ambitious target? We will have to wait until tomorrow to hear the answer.

DAY 46: FRIDAY 1 MAY: *171,253 confirmed cases 26,711 deaths*

The effect on businesses of the lockdown continues to be felt. Those in the hospitality trade are deeply concerned that they will be amongst the last businesses which are given the government go ahead to reopen. And even then, if social distancing rules are still in place, they will face greatly reduced levels of clientele. I had sent a sympathetic letter to Andrew Beale, owner of the much loved West Lodge Park Hotel and two other hotels on the outskirts of London. He writes back describing the current situation as "a nightmare."

A new study shows that the virus is having the worst effect in economically deprived areas where the death rate from the virus is as much as two and a half times higher than more affluent areas. This may be due to many factors: those on lower incomes are more likely to be having to go to work and use public transport, increasing their possible exposure to the virus; they may be living in more crowded housing conditions; and those living in deprived areas are more likely to already have underlying health conditions which can make them more at risk of severe illness from the virus. Professor Sir Michael Marmot, who has made studies of so called health inequalities, confirms in a television interview, that, whilst anyone can be infected with the virus, you are more likely to suffer badly from COVID-19 if you start with a poor hand in respect of income and living conditions.

Like a contestant on Who Wants to be a Millionaire the nation waits with baited breath to hear if Matt Hancock has delivered the right answer: in his case his promise of 100,000 tests a day by the end of this month. Remarkably, given how distant the target seemed to be for much of the month, a late surge of sending out home testing kits means Hancock has given the right answer, 122,364 being tested in the last twenty four hours. The home testing kits may have helped him get over the line, but it has been a noteworthy achievement to significantly increase in a few weeks the capacity for testing staff working for the NHS and care homes, and those with symptoms of the coronavirus.

DAY 47: SATURDAY 2 MAY: *177,454 confirmed cases 27,510 deaths*

A weekend is often an occasion for a trip to an interesting museum or other place of historical interest. But even if this seemingly endless lockdown is eventually eased there are risks that some of our most important visitor attractions may not be able to re-open because of financial losses they have suffered during the lockdown. Stewart White, Chairman of the trustees of Brading Roman Villa on the Isle of Wight says, "We're not subsidised so we need lots of visitors during the summer. Now it is likely that we'll be reopening as the season is ending." Across the Solent in Portsmouth Helen Bonsor-Wilton, in charge of the Mary Rose Museum, which houses Henry VIII's warship lost in 1545, and recovered from the depths of the sea in 1982, says a £2 million shortfall in income means its mission to preserve the 500 year old flagship is in "mortal peril." Places of historical interest join the long queue of sectors asking for government support.

In The Times Philip Collins outlines the concept of tragic choices, as initially described by Guido Calabresi and Philip Bobbitt, where either option in a choice gives an outcome you do not want. Boris Johnson and the government face a tragic choice in deciding whether to save the economy by allowing more people back to work or to continue the lockdown to minimise loss of life to the virus. The skill will be in planning a route which does not have too tragic an outcome from the tragic choice.

After British Airways announced this week 12,000 job losses, now Rolls Royce says 8,000 jobs out of its 20,000 workforce are at risk. Yet another example of the knock on effect of the economic downturn. With less new planes likely to be needed there will be less demand for Rolls Royce's famous engines.

Those self-employed entrepreneurs, owners of flower shops, cafes and many other High Street businesses who chose to be tax efficient by taking their annual income as dividends from a company, rather than as a salary, had been excluded from Chancellor Rishi Sunak's financial support for the self-employed. But now they are campaigning for their share of the government bailout as their only hope of staying in business after months of being closed to customers.

For those women, and perhaps some men, who saw one small blessing from the lockdown as the end of live televised football matches, the relief has been short lived. It merely created a vacuum which had to be filled. Armchair fans can now watch endless reruns of great matches from the past. Today the friendly tones of Brian Moore (remember him?) could be heard as ITV reprised the 1987 FA Cup Final when Coventry, who had never played in an FA Cup Final, pulled off a memorable victory beating Tottenham, who had never lost an FA Cup Final, 3-2 after extra time. BBC meanwhile continues to fill the Match of the Day slot with Gary Lineker, Alan Shearer and Ian Wright, debating from their homes their top ten lists including such highlights as the ten most bonkers moments in the Premier League. Essential viewing? Only for those who can't live without football.

DAY 48: SUNDAY 3 MAY: *182,260 confirmed cases 28,131 deaths*

Boris Johnson tells the Sun on Sunday that it had been 50/50 whether he would be put on a ventilator during his days in intensive care with COVID-19, the coronavirus illness, and that doctors had discussed a contingency plan for how to deal with the situation if he should die.

But in the here and now the recovered Prime Minister is still treading this tightrope of giving the public hope that there are plans for easing the lockdown, but not wanting to rush in to lifting restrictions for fear of creating a new surge of infections which take the virus reproduction R factor above one, after which a new lockdown will be needed to prevent the virus from growing exponentially. Today Michael Gove says that there will be an announcement by the government next Sunday about creating an environment whereby schools might re-open and some people can return to work. This is likely to involve guidance to businesses about how they can re-open in a way which will make their workforce safe. It is possible that businesses will be asked to stagger the working times of their staff to avoid overcrowding on buses and trains.

Also, today the government announces plans to trial on the Isle of Wight an app for those with smartphones, which will enable anyone who tests positive for the coronavirus to send an alert message to other people who have the app who they have been in close proximity to. It needs a 50 to 60 per cent take up to be successful. In addition, 18,000 people are being recruited to be contact tracers for people who do not have the app or in situations where contact tracing may be complicated.

On a lighter note, three pole vaulters hold a "virtual" pole vaulting competition, each soaring over the high bars they have put up in their gardens. What about throwing the javelin? Well, perhaps not if you have neighbours.

DAY 49: MONDAY 4 MAY: *186,599 confirmed cases 28,446 deaths*

The week starts with former US President George Bush striking a biblical tone in commenting on the coronavirus pandemic saying, "We are all human beings, equally vulnerable and equally wonderful in the eyes of God."

But for many people the week starts with worries about the future. Virgin Atlantic is the latest business to announce job losses as it prepares to cut a third of its 10,000 workforce and to close its Gatwick operations, warning it will take up to three years to return to 2019 levels of air traffic. Meanwhile 27 million people in total are being supported by the state in some way. This includes over six million who are having 80 per cent of their previous wages up to £2,500 a month paid by the government furlough scheme. But how much longer can the government continue this scheme which is already costing the taxpayer £8 billion a month, an amount which is closing in on the NHS budget of around £11 billion a month? And many businesses, particularly restaurants, cafes and hotels will find that they will have to reduce their staff complement, as complying with social distancing requirements will mean less customers. So many in the hospitality sector, who are currently being financially supported by the government, will wonder if there will be a job waiting for them when restrictions are eased.

Even well-known people are suffering the same types of drops in income that their more anonymous peers are experiencing. For classical musicians most of their income disappeared the night that concert halls around the world were closed. No more Concertgebouw in Amsterdam or Sydney Opera House or Royal Festival Hall, all closed, concert plans abandoned. Even Sheku Kanneh-Mason, the prodigiously talented 21 year old cellist who performed at the wedding of Prince Harry and Meghan Merkel, is suddenly without bookings. At his family home in Nottingham with his six musician siblings, he takes turns with his brothers to sleep on the floor and joins impromptu family concerts which are then available on Facebook for the millions who like to follow this wonderful musical family.

At least in Italy, for so long at the centre of pandemic storm, life is now getting a little better. Four million are back at work, visits to relatives are allowed and cafes have reopened for takeaway cappuccinos.

The plans to introduce the tracing app, which will allow smartphone owners who download the app to self report if they have the virus, and for other app users they have been in contact with to be traced and isolated, gathers pace. Some say it is an invasion of privacy and have concerns that their medical data will no longer be private. But GCHQ, the home of intelligence information, says whilst the app "may appear scary" it has built in protection to safeguard data security. We live in a new world where the government needs our data to plot its way out of the lockdown by identifying and isolating those who have the virus.

DAY 50: TUESDAY 5 MAY: *190,584 confirmed cases 28,734 deaths*

Those who have fought the virus long and hard and have pulled through are heroes in this pandemic war. None more so than former explorer, Robin Hanbury-Tenison, who is used to surviving in the rain forests of Borneo, but is now a survivor of an even more challenging environment, the coronavirus infection. One is never too old to feel that surge of elation at being restored to health after illness. Hanbury-Tenison will no doubt recount his recent experiences, a month in hospital much of it on a ventilator, at his 84th birthday party this Thursday.

At our regional NHS video Board meeting today colleagues in Cambridge talk of "the recovery phase." This is about moving back to a situation where members of the public return in large numbers for the treatment of non-COVID-19 conditions, and do so in an environment which is safe for both patients and NHS staff. There is a consensus in our discussions that the good ways of working which have been developed under pressure during the virus pandemic should stay, as we enter the recovery. One innovation, which hopefully will be continued as we move forwards again, has been the great growth in video consultations between GPs and their patients, We discuss the opportunity for extending this so that there could be three party video calls linking up patients with both their GP and a hospital consultant where a referral for hospital treatment was being considered.

We also discuss the situation in care homes. Like other areas we have had some care homes which have had severe outbreaks of the coronavirus and resulting fatalities. It is a delicate area as most care homes are privately managed and local authorities have the primary responsibility for their oversight. But increasingly the NHS is being drawn into ensuring that residents of care homes are being safeguarded during the pandemic.

It has become a feature of the daily televised Downing Street briefings that slides are presented of graphs showing multi coloured lines rising and falling as the virus storms its way through different countries. Today there is the further grim news that the UK has overtaken Italy to become the country with the highest number of coronavirus deaths in Europe, now second only to the United States. Dominic Raab makes an attempt to explain that there are differences between countries in the way they compute their deaths statistics. But even so, the thought that we might perhaps have the highest death toll in Europe is harrowing. Having a city as big and dense as London, three times the size of Italy's largest city, Rome, was not in our favour in trying to contain the virus. But Italy had its own problems; its love of family life with households of different generations living together also allowed the virus to spread more easily.

On Newsnight, Professor Debbie Sridhar, Chair of Public Health at Edinburgh University says that a virus like the coronavirus spreads whilst you are waiting to make decisions. Early to mid-March was a critical time where it is clear now we allowed the virus to spread whilst we delayed the restrictions on social contact which the full lockdown later introduced. We also did not have sufficient capacity for testing for the virus to enable those who had been infected to be isolated, to prevent further cases. Is this being wise after the event or were these really serious misjudgements by the government and its advisers?

South Korea is now often mentioned as an example of a strong approach to containing the coronavirus. An early lockdown and a ready to use system of testing and tracing contacts of those infected by the virus, which had been developed previously when trying to stop the spread of SARS from neighbouring China. South Korea's approach has produced an outcome of just 250 deaths so far in a population of 52 million.

DAY 51: WEDNESDAY 6 MAY: *194,990 confirmed cases 29,427 deaths*

If you are a person in the public eye then you carry the risk that the slightest error in the way you conduct your life may attract media attention. Think Cecil Parkinson, think Jeffrey Archer, think John Major (yes, John Major) all of whom fell from grace due to personal acts they would have preferred to remain private. Professor Neil Ferguson of Imperial College London, the government's leading adviser on the modelling of possible death rates from the coronavirus, has also found that what he does in his spare time is every bit as much of interest as his professional input to the current crisis. Unfortunately for Professor Ferguson, the man whose modelling persuaded Boris Johnson that it was essential that the government imposed a full lockdown to contain the virus, the Daily Telegraph found that, contrary to the social distancing rules which he had so strongly espoused, he had entertained a female friend at his London flat on at least two occasions. Professor Ferguson resigns from SAGE, the scientific committee advising the government, acknowledging an error of judgement and reaffirming the importance of the social distancing measures. His departure from SAGE has echoes of the resignation on 5 April of Doctor Catherine Calderwood, Scotland's Chief Medical Officer, falling on her sword after being found by the media visiting her second home, an unnecessary journey under the lockdown rules.

And on the theme of human weaknesses, we all have addictions, whether Sudoku or McVities hobnobs. Chancellor Rishi Sunak is concerned we may have become addicted to his generous furlough scheme paying, 80 per cent of the wages of workers who would otherwise have been made redundant in the sudden economic downturn following the lockdown. With a total expected cost already around £40 billion it cannot be sustained; also, the government does not want the scheme to be a disincentive to getting people back to work to refire the economy. It is likely that the amount of government support under the furlough scheme will be gradually reduced as the government allows different sectors to return to work.

Former Prime Minister, Theresa May, enters the debate about the response to the coronavirus, writing in the Times that there should be more joined up collaboration between countries to fighting what has become a global pandemic. She queries how much mutual cooperation between countries has taken place, and the effectiveness of organisations such as the United Nations and World Health Organisation in marshalling an international response to the pandemic.

And at the daily Downing Street press conference more grim statistics as the UK total deaths from the coronavirus pass 30,000. We are now 50 per cent more than the 20,000 deaths the government's chief scientific adviser, Sir Patrick Vallance, said in March would represent "a good outcome." So, what type of outcome is 30,000 deaths? Disappointing? A middling outcome? A disaster? Overseas journalists are forming their own opinions. Commentators from Italy to Australia accuse Britain of a complacent approach "massively underestimating" the gravity of the coronacrisis. Italy's leading newspaper, Corriere delle Sera, says the UK's situation has been "like a nightmare from which you cannot awake but in which you landed because of your own fault or stupidity." Are they right?

At least the Royal Horticultural Society has some good news, telling us that those of us lucky enough to have gardens are twice as likely to feel very satisfied with life during the pandemic, than those with no outdoor space. Sales of seeds for growing indoor plants and vegetables have been soaring as the nation looks for something they can watch grow, which will be a symbol of hope for the future.

DAY 52: THURSDAY 7 MAY: *200,101 confirmed cases 30,076 deaths*

As confirmed cases of the coronavirus pass 200,000 a study by Glasgow University shows that 49 per cent of COVID-19 patients they monitored were discharged alive, 17 per cent are continuing to receive hospital care and 33 per cent have died. But they also found that patients with COVID-19 who met the clinical definition of obese (a BMI, body mass index, of over 30), were dying in hospital at a rate which was 37 per cent higher than for COVID-19 patients who were not obese. It would be interesting to know how the population's weight has changed during a lockdown where only one hour of exercise a day has been permitted. If the allowed exercise period remains at an hour perhaps we should all increase the intensity of our exertions.

Gavin Barwell, Theresa May's former Chief of Staff, makes the point that, whilst the official number of deaths from the coronavirus has already passed 30,000, we do not know the total number of deaths which may have arisen as a result of the pandemic. He draws attention to those who have died because treatment for non-COVID-19 health conditions has been deferred, or because they died as a result of increased poverty and other problems attributable to the pandemic and the related economic downturn.

The tension between "health and wealth" remains front of stage. The government formally extended the lockdown today for another three weeks, the maximum period allowed under the legislation passed to deal with the coronavirus outbreak. With total UK deaths from the virus the highest reported in Europe, and the spread of the virus within care homes continuing to cause concern, Prime Minister Johnson is said to be very cautious about easing the lockdown restrictions. But the longer shops, restaurants and other businesses remain closed the greater the costs to government of its financial support to businesses and individuals; and the greater the chance of high levels of unemployment and business failures which may lead irreversible damage to the economy.

The wealth side of this almost impossible dilemma is brought into stark focus by a new report by the Bank of England. The new Governor of the Bank, Andrew Bailey, can never have envisaged, when he took up his appointment on 16 March, just as social distancing was being introduced, that he would immediately be plunged into trying to help the country deal with what he now describes as the most severe recession for over 300 years. The new Governor reveals the most disastrous set of projections the Bank of England has ever published. Gross domestic product (GDP), the key indicator of economic activity, is on course to be 30 per cent lower than it was in December. The projections show the economy, as the OBR had suggested previously, shrinking by 14 per cent this year, over twice the damage caused by the banking crisis of 2008 which caused a 6 per cent contraction. As many as two million people may lose their jobs this year taking unemployment which had been relatively low at 4 per cent to a 26 year high of 9 per cent. The Bank does, though, expect a strong recovery by the economy if the lockdown is ended in the next few months with 15 per cent growth projected for 2021 so that the economy and unemployment will be back to pre-COVID levels by 2022. A number of economic commentators, however, feel this is too optimistic and that the economy may suffer some level of permanent damage as a result of the current lockdown induced recession.

Who would want to be in the Prime Minister's shoes, seeking to find a balance between protecting health by keeping most people indoors and the terrible implications for the economy and many people's finances of prolonging this government imposed lockdown? The government formally extended the lockdown today for another three weeks but Boris Johnson will address the nation on Sunday to set out his plan for how the lockdown can gradually be lifted

At least the John Lewis partnership, which includes the Waitrose supermarket chain, is able to tell us what we are spending our money on as we live through these home based weeks. Eggs and egg cups apparently, sales of both having increased dramatically as most of the nation has time for a leisurely breakfast at home to start the day. Former Bakeoff judge Mary Berry's eggcups have sold out in John Lewis and egg suppliers are finding it difficult to keep up with demand as hens have suffered their own pandemic of avian flu in recent months. John Lewis also say that, in a throwback to a more leisurely age, sales of board games and ingredients for home made cocktails have also rocketed. One hopes the Monopoly values of Mayfair and Park Lane have not fallen too much in the economic downturn.

DAY 53: FRIDAY 8 MAY: *206,715 confirmed cases 30,615 deaths*

Today is the 75th anniversary of VE Day, the day that Victory in Europe was announced as World War Two drew to a close. At last an important news story that is not about coronavirus. This was the day in 1945 when Winston Churchill told the country that we were no longer at war after six years of waging what was, for much of the time, a terrifying battle against an enemy which had sought to gain total power throughout Europe, and to eliminate millions of people whom it considered inferior or blamed for its previous economic hardships. As Churchill's voice came over the radio that hostilities in Europe had ended there was an eruption of excitement and celebration. In London thousands danced their way down the Mall to Buckingham Palace and stood on cars, Army trucks or lampposts to gain a view of the King and Queen who repeatedly came on to the Buckingham Palace balcony accompanied by Churchill to acknowledge the cheering, singing crowds. Around the country, towns and villages, suddenly freed from the years of fear and anxiety, held impromptu street tea parties, children sitting at long tables filled with ration book made sandwiches and cakes, parents standing behind them, smiling, relieved, happy in that moment that heralded the return of peace and normal family life.

The celebrations now to mark the 75th anniversary of VE Day took on a new tone in our corona times. There was something of the war spirit of a defiant Britain 75 years ago in the way that events and street parties to mark VE Day were hastily re-arranged to take account of social distancing restrictions. People dressed up in 1940s clothes, cakes were made, singers performed the songs the nation sang all those years ago and yes, on a sunny day, there were blue birds over the white cliffs of Dover.

But what could never have been anticipated just a few months ago was that these celebrations were, for us, a pause in our own ongoing battle against another tyranny, one that the coronavirus is seeking to wage, not just in Britain but across the world. For the majority of us who were not alive in 1945 we felt some of the feelings that those smiling faces in the black and white photographs of VE Day had felt in the previous months and years: fear from being in a long ongoing battle where the outcome was uncertain and might be devastating, anxiety for the welfare of loved ones, the grief from losing many of those one has known and the knowledge that, whether the outcome was victory or defeat, the world would never be as it had been before the war began.

The Queen caught this mood of how our remembrance of the events of the Second World War struck a chord with the crisis the world was facing now when she addressed the nation this evening. Our monarch's reassuring voice told us, "Never give up, never despair, that is the message of VE Day."

At the end of the Queen's address a montage was broadcast of members of the public of all ages, some in the front line of caring for others during the battle against coronavirus, others just trying to make the best of their socially distanced lives, all singing the Vera Lynn wartime anthem "We'll meet again." Just as it had been then, the country was united in the belief that the dark days of adversity would eventually end.

DAY 54: SATURDAY 9 MAY: *211,364 confirmed cases 31,241 deaths*

What must it be like to be young living in this corona world? Concerned is one word which perhaps sums up how most young people are feeling. Concerned for the health of older members of their family and all those thousands of people who have already lost loved ones to the virus and concerned about their own future now that study and career plans have been severely disrupted.

Children of school age are waiting for the day when they will be allowed back into their schools but are uncertain what this will be like if classrooms can only take half the normal numbers of pupils to preserve social distancing. Those who would have been sitting exams this summer are anxious about what grades they may be awarded under a system which will be based on previous classwork. Those waiting to go up to university are uncertain whether their first year of study and the ancient rituals of Freshers Week will take place this autumn. And for those waiting to start their careers the stark reality that one in three have already had job offers withdrawn. Internship opportunities have also been put into the long grass. The big unknown for young people is what impact these disruptions will have on their lives in the longer turn. To what extent will they now struggle with careers and finances and just making sense of life? As some have observed, the burden of protecting the older generation, who are most at risk from the effects of the coronavirus, has fallen on the young.

Another unknown is how much the world will have changed when we finally emerge from the dangers of the virus. As we were drawing parallels on VE Day between Britain at war in the 1940s and our own situation now in lockdown it is worth remembering what happened as Britain returned to peacetime in 1945. There was great hope for a fairer society with less inequalities in the middle of significant economic hardship. But many struggled to find jobs as millions returned from the armed forces to life in "civvy street" and food rationing would continue into the 1950s. Most significantly, Winston Churchill, who had embodied the British fighting spirit in wartime and who had been cheered to the rafters on VE Day, was voted out of office by a public who, as peace returned, looked to a Clement Atlee led Socialist government to create a better world for the future, a world which would include a new welfare state and National Health Service. "Cheer Churchill, vote Labour" was the Labour Party's election message. When we come through this prolonged period of isolation will the British public see the calm persona of

Sir Keir Starmer, who has made a good start since taking over from Jeremy Corbyn as Labour leader, as the man to take us into the challenges of a changed world rather than the larger than life Boris Johnson who has led us through the eye of the storm? Will history repeat itself?

The country awaits Johnson's televised address tomorrow night where he has promised to outline his plan for taking us out of the lockdown. We shouldn't anticipate any great changes. The government's messaging through the media has now started to downplay the expectations Johnson himself raised on Wednesday, when he told Parliament that "we will, if we possibly can, get going on some of these changes on Monday." Now the government message is that coming out of the lockdown will be "a gradual process, not a simple leap to freedom."

DAY 55: SUNDAY 10 MAY: *215,260 confirmed cases 31,241 deaths*

The weather changed today. A sudden drop in temperature and overcast skies as if matching the country's mood about Prime Minister Boris Johnson's scheduled address to the nation this evening. It seems as if we are in for a long haul in this attempt to protect the nation's health from this virus for which there is no current cure.

As we await the PM's new advice it seems a suitable time to take stock of what has happened since we were plunged into this nightmare landscape of closing the economy in order to protect the public's health and preventing the NHS from being overwhelmed by the spread of the coronavirus.

We know that over 30,000 people in Britain have lost their lives to the virus and that this number is going to rise as we are not yet out of the first peak of cases, let alone what might happen if we experience further peaks in due course. So, this outcome is far more tragic than what might have been hoped for when the government's chief scientific adviser, Sir Patrick Vallance, said at the outset that limiting deaths to under 20,000 would be "a good outcome"; when he made that statement that number of fatalities sounded alarming rather than a source of satisfaction yet we are a long way past that number now.

We also know that, whatever plans the government and its advisers had made previously for dealing with a pandemic, in practice implementing these plans has been much slower than was needed to produce a fast efficient response to the virus and was full of difficulties which do not seem to have been properly anticipated. At a human level one sympathises with Ministers and public officials who were trying to grapple in real time and under great pressure with a widespread life threatening situation none of them would have experienced for real before. But in terms of government at an organisational level two months into the pandemic some of the shortcomings in the national response are becoming increasingly clear.

The initial plan to trace everyone who had contracted the virus had to be dropped when testing could not keep up with the number of people displaying symptoms of the virus, the introduction of the full lockdown appears to have been too late as the virus was by then circulating widely and crucial weeks passed before the government had a system which could test large numbers of people for the virus on a daily basis. Even then, there were still many frontline NHS and care home staff who were waiting to be tested.

It now seems clear that, whilst the government paused before introducing the full lockdown it initially wanted to avoid, the virus continued its onward journey of spreading across communities. So, when the lockdown was introduced on Monday 23 March the extent of the first peak of COVID-19 in Britain was already determined and inevitably considerably higher than it would have been if the lockdown had been introduced when coronavirus infections were first occurring in the UK.

There were the recurring delays to getting PPE to frontline workers in hospitals and care homes. Clearly the country's stockpiles of PPE, which were supposed to be ready to deal with a pandemic, were insufficient and we then became immersed in the competition with other countries for the finite resources of PPE that were being produced around the world.

And then there are the care homes. Privately managed, overseen by local authorities and outside the official boundaries of the NHS, there seems to have been little in the way of a government strategy for minimising the spread of the coronavirus amongst the elderly and infirm residents of care homes, who then became, quite literally, sitting targets for the virus. The Guardian newspaper highlighted this week a 2017 government report on a simulation exercise for a future flu pandemic which concluded that Britain was not adequately prepared for a flu pandemic's extreme demands. The report highlighted the challenges care homes would face from taking in patients discharged from hospitals, when hospital beds are needed for patients seriously ill during a pandemic, and recommended that care home capacity be increased to deal with this. The government maintains the recommendations of this report were acted upon but Martin Green, Chief Executive of the care home representative body, Care England, says that the sector's ability to deal with large numbers of patients discharged from hospitals and the need for the sector's large providers to increase capacity, had not been discussed by government with Care England's members.

The feeling that the response to the coronavirus pandemic could have been better organised here in Britain, and in other countries which have suffered large numbers of virus deaths, was echoed yesterday by former US President Barrack Obama who described the response as "an absolute chaotic disaster." All of these apparent shortcomings will no doubt be the subject of future public inquiries.

What has made this pandemic different from all other natural disasters of recent times is that nearly everyone has been adversely affected in some way, whether in relation to their health, emotional well being or financial prospects. This has driven the drama of these days we are now living through.

And so, at 7pm, Boris Johnson makes his Prime Ministerial address to the nation. He thanks us for all the efforts we have made to adhere to the stay at home restrictions of recent weeks. His address is brisk and firm. He refers to the coronavirus as "the most vicious threat in my lifetime" and that it "would be madness" to allow a second spike in virus infections. He recognised that the public are afraid, both for their health, and their financial wellbeing. "The time has come," he says "to restart the economy." He tells us that the easing of the lockdown has, however, to be conditional on the five tests he has previously set out being met regarding the spread of the virus and introduces a new scoring system which will influence the degree to which restrictions can be eased. On a scale of one to five where five is the virus at its most severe Johnson tells us we are currently at four and gradually moving towards three.

Given where we now are the Prime Minister unveils a three point plan for a gradual easing of some aspects of the lockdown. From tomorrow those who cannot work from home should return to work provided their employer can provide a safe socially distancing workplace; Johnson encourages those returning to work to travel by car, bicycle or foot to avoid overcrowding on buses and trains. In addition, also from tomorrow, we may take as much exercise we want each day and may sit or sunbathe in parks; driving to a location to take exercise is also permitted. Then in June, provided it seems safe to do so, there will be a gradual opening of schools starting with the return of primary school children, but those at secondary school are not expected to return until the autumn. Non-essential shops will be allowed to re-open if they can make suitable arrangements for social distancing. The third stage of the plan is that, from July, consideration will be given as to whether some businesses in the hospitality trade can re-open, for example outdoor cafes.

The tone of Johnson's voice and his frequent references to the stages of the plan being conditional on a series of "big ifs" leaves us in no doubt that even the small steps towards a more normal life which he has outlined are not certain. They are subject to the data regarding the spread of the virus supporting the case for allowing these steps away from a full lockdown to take place. As Johnson says, we may have passed the peak of virus deaths but "coming down the mountain is often more dangerous." If the now famous R factor, the rate at which the virus is spreading, appears to be rising "we will not hesitate to put on the brakes." The Prime Minister also introduces new plans to quarantine those coming in to Britain for fourteen days, a step some critics say should have been taken weeks ago.

Finally, Johnson drops the "Stay at home, protect the NHS, save lives" message and replaces it with "Stay alert, control the virus and save lives."

Leader of the opposition Keir Starmer says the Prime Minister's address lacks clarity and consensus amongst the four nations as Nicola

Sturgeon, the First Minister for Scotland and her counterparts in Wales and Northern Ireland make clear they are continuing with the "Stay as home" mantra for the time being.

Are we making progress? Only in a very small way it seems and subject to the data about the virus continuing to support the case for these limited changes. Increasingly, it feels as if, until a vaccine is available to overcome the virus, we will live in this world whereby only very small steps towards a more normal life can be made if the virus is to be kept in check.

DAY 56: MONDAY 11 MAY: *219,183 confirmed cases 31,855 deaths*

Boris Johnson's new message for the nation last night was "Stay alert, control the virus, save lives." But what exactly does "stay alert" mean in the context of the COVID-19 coronavirus? And can we really control it?

Staying alert is an instruction one could associate with driving on a motorway, the need to keep looking for visible dangers from other vehicles sharing the motorway space with you. But the virus is an unseen enemy. Presumably the government wants us to be conscious of how our actions can affect the health of others if we ignore the social distancing rules or fail to isolate if we develop COVID-19 symptoms. But in all other respects it is the government which is in control, or should be in control, of the extent to which the virus is spreading throughout the country.

"Stay home, protect the NHS, save lives" was a much more direct easy to follow message. There must be someone somewhere whose career specialism is creating three part instructions. I noticed today on the wall outside Waitrose "Protect yourself, protect others, shop alone." I have always tried to follow this sensible advice. It is the other people in Waitrose who make adhering to the last part of the instruction difficult. Our regional NHS Board in Cambridge has the following three clear objectives as we seek to manage the coronavirus pandemic on behalf of the one million people of Cambridgeshire and Peterborough: "Ensure there is the capacity (in terms of available intensive care beds and NHS staff); maximise survivorship (those who recover from COVID-19); and keep staff safe."

The Prime Minister's broadcast last night, on how we would be moving into what he described as phase two of dealing with the coronacrisis, left families, businesses, schools, manufacturing companies, the hospitality trade and everyone else trying to work out what it would mean for them. Locking down society was a big step but one that was relatively easy to impose. Unlocking the restrictions in the very gradual way that is needed to keep a tight control on the rate at which the virus spreads is a much more complex exercise.

Labour leader Sir Keir Starmer said last night that Boris Johnson's address provided more questions than answers. Today many of those questions became clear; the government sought to respond to some. Families with children were worried about the instruction to return to work, if they had children at home waiting to return to school; Boris Johnson said he accepted that the care of children should come first. Various manufacturing companies say their production processes required some of their staff to work in close proximity to each other; the government has set out guidance in a fifty page document but also wants businesses to adopt a common sense approach to the safety of their staff.

Many schools have concerns about their ability to impose social distancing on young primary school children who need the close contact of their friends and teachers. Some teachers feel they should wear protective clothing. The teachers' union, the National Education Union, brands the government's proposal for re-opening schools as "reckless." But the government says it is basing its strategy on scientific advice that working in a classroom with the same small group of children each day limits the virus risk. A lot of parents have yet to be convinced. A poll shows that a third do not intend to send their children back to school yet.

In the daily Downing Street briefing members of the public put their questions to the Prime Minister. Teacher, Natasha, asked why it is alright for people to go to work but not to mix with family members outside their own household. Boris Johnson said this was a legitimate question. This was one of many anomalies raised by people trying to understand the government's instructions. Johnson himself seemed to accept that the rules that had been introduced could not cover every eventuality saying that what was needed was "good solid British common sense."

With Scotland, Wales and Northern Ireland deciding to keep with the previous "stay at home" message there are mixed feelings about whether the government is right to attempt even the relatively limited easing of the lockdown measures in England. A You Gov poll finds 44 per cent support the relaxation; 43 per cent oppose it.

Back on the frontline, the BBC broadcast the first of two programmes filmed at the Royal Free Hospital in London showing how the hospital coped with the great inflow of patients with COVID-19. Doctors and nurses rushing around trying to free up beds to deal with further arrivals of COVID-19 patients, using so much oxygen to support patients with breathing problems that at one point the hospital's system for piping oxygen into the wards is almost overwhelmed. Then, in the midst of all this activity, the doctors finding a moment to make difficult telephone calls to the families of COVID-19 patients to update them on their loved ones' conditions. The programme showed the human side of doctors and nurses as they dealt with the stress, fatigue and sometimes fear from their continuous engagement with the seemingly never ending numbers of patients being admitted with COVID-19.

There is a delicate balance between easing restrictions to allow the economy to restart and doing so whilst still trying to severely limit the rate of new coronavirus infections. Germany, which has been so efficient at keeping the coronavirus low, is having to re-impose some lockdown measures as the number of new infections grows again after allowing people to move more freely. Sir David King, a former government scientific adviser, referring to the risk that new outbreaks of the coronavirus may occur as people return to the workplace says, "It is foolhardy to go back to work now." He is clear in his opinion that greater emphasis should have been put on test and trace to identify those who have the virus so they can be isolated.

On Newsnight Emily Maitlis sneezes. "Hay fever" she quickly informs us.

DAY 57: TUESDAY 12 MAY: *223,060 confirmed cases 32,065 deaths*

Coronavirus doesn't discriminate, we were told, in the early stages of the outbreak. But the evidence now shows that it does. The virus discriminates by sex; roughly two-thirds of deaths have been men. And the virus discriminates by occupation. The ONS has analysed the occupations of those who have died from the coronavirus illness. Women working in social care are dying from COVID-19 at almost twice the rate of all women. But for men it is work as a security guard which has had the biggest risk factor with deaths at a rate almost five times as high as all men. Male taxi drivers, chauffeurs and road transport drivers all have relatively high COVID-19 death rates compared with other occupations. Avoid working in enclosed spaces where you are in close contact with many different people on a regular basis, seems to be the learning point from the ONS data.

Francis Elliott, writing in The Times, makes the point that those most at risk from the virus are lower paid manual workers in manufacturing and construction who have been told by the government to return to work and who may have to use public transport to do so. Those in more lucrative jobs have a better chance of being able to remain working at home with a lower risk of contracting the coronavirus. This is a classic case of what the medical profession term 'health inequalities'. People on lower incomes face a greater chance of becoming ill.

In our weekly regional NHS Board meeting with colleagues looking after the one million people living in Cambridgeshire and Peterborough, concern is being identified at the capacity of local hospitals to treat non-COVID-19 patients in the coming months. Understandably, whilst our local hospitals were focussing on looking after COVID-19 patients, a significant backlog in other patients awaiting treatment was building up. COVID safety issues will also affect the throughput of other patients. Infection control will have to be applied to those areas of the hospitals treating non-COVID patients to limit new virus outbreaks amongst other patients and NHS staff. Unless a patient is known to have definitely tested negative for the virus, doctors and nurses will have to wear full PPE.

Surfaces will have to be cleaned after each patient is seen. This will all slow the number of non-COVID patients who can be treated; an initial estimate shows that, depending on the type of medical procedure, the throughput of patients could drop from between 25 and 70 per cent compared with normal levels. It is possible that some of the demand for treatment can be addressed by the NHS paying private hospitals to do the work. But it seems certain that many of the public will face significantly longer waits for treatment than before the pandemic so severely disrupted the NHS.

The current situation will also place a bigger burden on GPs as they see more patients waiting for hospital procedures, and more people experiencing mental health issues from the pressures, financial and emotional, of living with the restrictions and economic hardships of the coronavirus world. In our Board meetings we also pause to remember that today is International Nurses Day, an opportunity to appreciate the unstinting devotion of the thousands of nurses who have been caring for patients, as the coronavirus infection rate has risen and peaked. International Nurses Day is always held on the anniversary of the birth of pioneering nurse Florence Nightingale after whom the Nightingale hospitals, built at short notice to provide extra beds to deal with virus outbreak, have been named. This year is the 200th anniversary. "For the sick it is important to have the best," said Nightingale. Our nurses in Cambridge, and in hospitals across the land, have personified that philosophy in dealing with the dramatic and sudden influx of coronavirus patients.

All NHS staff are dealing with human stories. In the second part of the BBC's programme filmed at London's Royal Free Hospital the condition of retired accountant Stanley, who had been filmed talking to his wife on his phone to update her of his progress, deteriorated; sadly, this man we had only just begun to know became another COVID fatality, one of more than 30,000 people lost to their families and friends from this rapidly spreading virus which has invaded our lives.

Businesses in construction and manufacturing, which the government has encouraged employees to return to from tomorrow, are working quickly to try to make their workplaces safe for their returning staff. In some cases this will involve introducing shift work to reduce the number of workers travelling at the same time, and to make social distancing in the workplace easier to implement. But those in construction and manufacturing are concerned that a number of tasks can only be performed by members of their teams working together within two metres of each other, making social distancing impossible in all parts of their operations. The Health and Safety Executive will have a big role in inspecting business premises and construction sites to ensure the government's new safety guidance is being followed, and has been given a further £14 million to fund this work.

Chancellor Rishi Sunak, on his fortieth birthday, announces that the furlough scheme to pay for the salaries of staff whose jobs have been put on hold will be extended to October increasing the total cost of this support package to an estimated £80 billion. Businesses will though be required to contribute to the costs of the scheme from August.

The Chancellor also said that the total costs to the government of dealing with the coronavirus pandemic will be £300 billion, pushing the public finance deficit this year to a record £337 billion. Eventually we will have to pay for this through higher taxes, or public sector wage freezes or another austerity round of public spending cuts. But economists say the government must allow the economy to recover before it seeks to reduce the increased public finance deficit.

With people wanting something to look forward to, enquiries for holidays in France have soared after Boris Johnson agreed with President Macron that the proposed plans to quarantine those arriving into the UK from abroad would not apply to those returning from France. But the government says the public should not plan to have overseas holidays this year. So it is unclear whether the dreams of a week in Provence or a romantic break in Paris will be realised to provide an antidote to lockdown Britain. J'espere que c'est possible.

DAY 58: WEDNESDAY 13 MAY: *226,463 confirmed cases 32,692 deaths*

Today many people across the nation returned to workplaces they had not seen for almost two months, since the start of the lockdown. In London there were crowds on some buses and tube trains, raising concerns about how social distancing can be maintained if large numbers return to work. Transport for London had messages at underground stations which echoed the original lockdown by saying that the tube services were for essential workers only. Road traffic also increased with congestion on some routes.

But others saw the day as an opportunity to pursue leisure pursuits which had been in hibernation. It was a largely overcast day for the new freedom to play golf and tennis and, let us not forget, to go angling. Such is the enthusiasm for getting out on the golf course that some courses, which would normally have allowed players to just turn up and play mid-week, had all time slots for teeing off booked in advance. Sue Elliott, the club secretary of Henbury Golf Club in Bristol, said one player observed that it had been easier getting a ticket for Glastonbury last year.

But those of us who would normally be watching the opening matches of the county cricket championship in mid May cannot get our usual fix of that most elegant of games. I have to be content to read the players' averages from last season set out in my Playfair Cricket Annual, the handy pocket book, which has just arrived. Former Sussex captain John Barclay, who normally hosts one of summer's highlights, the annual county game in the grounds of Arundel Castle, e-mails to say that, without cricket, he has been walking his dog, Robert, and has enrolled in a fiction writing class.

Back in the coronavirus world our discussions in Cambridge return to the subject of care homes. Local authorities pay towards the costs of residents in care homes, with the residents also contributing to the costs based on their financial means. Local authorities, who have had severe cuts in their funding in recent years, had been asking if the NHS can help them support the additional costs that the private owners of care homes are incurring to provide the standard of care needed to manage the coronavirus pandemic. Now Boris Johnson announces a £600 million infection control fund to help care homes meet these additional costs.

At Prime Minister's Questions in Parliament Boris Johnson is challenged by Labour leader, Keir Starmer, on why, up to 13 March, guidance from Public Health England had said "it remains very unlikely that people receiving care in a care home would become infected with coronavirus." This leads to an angry exchange of letters between the two, with Johnson defending the guidance as having been drafted at a time when there had not been evidence that the virus was spreading within the community. A further concern is that until 15 April hospitals had not been required to ensure that patients tested negative for COVID-19 before releasing them into care homes as they sought to free up beds to treat coronavirus patients. This almost certainly would have resulted in some people going back to care homes with the virus and then spreading it to other residents. At the Downing Street press briefing Deputy Chief Medical Officer Jenny Harries says that care home residents returning from hospital are required to be put into isolation to prevent the risk of spreading the virus. The Prime Minister is, nevertheless, challenged to prove his assertion that there is now a system for testing patients discharged from hospitals into care homes.

The severity of the economic downturn caused by the lockdown is laid bare in new statistics today from the ONS. March recorded the largest ever one month drop in economic output with GDP falling by 5.8 per cent; over the first quarter of the year the economy contracted by 2 per cent. But most of March was before the lockdown was imposed so the figures are bound to get worse. The looming catastrophe to businesses from being in lockdown is revealed by the National Institute for Economic and Social Research estimates that the economy will collapse by 30 per cent in this quarter. If the estimate is correct it will, according to one economist, trigger "the recession to end all recessions". Can the economy really bounce back from that as the Bank of England suggested last week?

DAY 59: THURSDAY 14 MAY: *229,705 confirmed cases 33,186 deaths*

The problem we were discussing in Cambridge at our regional NHS level earlier this week comes centre stage today. Statistics released by the NHS show the enormous backlog which is building up of people waiting for treatment for conditions not related to coronavirus. The number of patients going to A&E in April dropped by 57 per cent compared with April last year. Emergency admissions to hospital dropped by 39 per cent. Head of the NHS Simon Stevens appeals to the public not to put off going to hospital for serious conditions such as strokes, heart attacks and cancer for fears about the virus, as they will be seen in areas of the hospital kept separate from COVID-19 patients.

But patients with less serious conditions face long waits. New estimates suggest that, after giving up space for COVID patients, observing social distancing and taking time for extra cleaning, the capacity of hospitals to treat patients with non-COVID conditions could reduce by 30 per cent. That could lead to a doubling of waiting lists so that up to eight million people may be waiting for NHS treatment by the autumn. The reality is that the public will have to adapt to an NHS which has been forced to work in dramatically different ways because of the coronavirus.

Hardly a day goes past when we do not hear of yet another fatality amongst the doctors and nurses who have given their all to caring for the public during the pandemic. Doctor Keramat Ullah Mirza came to England from Pakistan in 1966 and had worked continuously in the NHS since then without a day off from illness. The 71 year old from Clapton told his wife when the coronavirus outbreak began, "I can't sit and do gardening. I'm a doctor." Continuing on the front line he became another name on the list of those in the medical profession who have died from COVID-19 contracted whilst serving the public in these awful times.

One cannot get away from the grim news by going to the cinema, the theatre or a show because all venues are closed. Craig Hassall, Chief Executive of the Royal Albert Hall, says that they have lost £8.5 million of income since they closed their doors and there are serious doubts about how they could re-open; implementing social distancing would mean they could only use 30 per cent of the normal seating and such a reduction in ticket sales would not be viable when matched against the costs of putting on a concert. On the South Coast the Southampton Theatre Group is already in administration. The government says it will discuss with the arts sector how its future can be preserved.

One celebrity who is able to perform in the middle of the lockdown is the goat owned by Dot McCarthy of Cronkshaw Farm in Lancashire who is being hired out to make a guest appearance on other peoples' online Zoom get-togethers. The bookings have flooded in to have this unexpected face amongst the guests in the Zoom screen panel. It reminds me of a Private Eye cover which depicted every member of Boris Johnson's new Cabinet as a poodle.

DAY 60: FRIDAY 15 MAY: *233,151 confirmed cases 33,616 deaths*

One cannot help but have feelings for Kit and Sean, two young people in their thirties with terminal cancer, who spoke last night to the BBC's News at Ten. They both had found treatments they were receiving were being delayed because of the NHS's need to focus on COVID-19 patients. Sean, whose plan to be part of a new drug trial has been put on hold, said the coronavirus "had wreaked havoc with our treatment, our surgeries, our futures, our hope."

Is there anyone now who does not know that the R number is? It has become our constant companion. As if to challenge the Prime Minister's decision to ease some of the lockdown restrictions the R number has increased from somewhere in the range 0.5 to 0.9 to 0.7 to 1.0. This new data, which reflects how the virus was spreading two weeks ago, means we were then getting closer to the tipping point of R being more than 1.0 where the virus starts to spread rapidly. This increase in the R number may have been because of the increasing prevalence of the coronavirus in care homes. But, at a time when the government has introduced a very gradual easing of the lockdown, the higher R range shows how easy it is for the rate of the spreading of the virus to become concerning. The worst of the virus peak appears to have passed in London but is now seriously affecting the North East in areas such as Middlesbrough and Gateshead.

How words can be interpreted in different ways. On Wednesday Boris Johnson had defended Public Health England guidance in force until 13 March that it was very unlikely that anyone receiving care in a care home or the community would become infected with the coronavirus; his defence had been that the guidance had been drafted at a time when there had not been evidence that the virus was spreading within the community. Yet it now becomes clear that scientific advice to the government on 10 February said (at a time when there may not have been evidence that the virus was spreading) that there was "a realistic probability that there was already sustained transmission of the virus or that it will become established in the coming weeks." So, the Labour leader Keir Starmer seems to have been correct to pose serious questions to the government about why there hadn't been more urgent preparation for the possibility that the coronavirus would spread within enclosed care home communities.

The devastating effect of COVID-19 on the elderly continues. Lifelong sweethearts Margaret Emmett aged 97 and her husband Clifford, aged 91, who met at Blackpool Tower Ballroom on Easter Saturday 1952, die within ten minutes of each other after Mr Emmett tested positive for the virus.

4 AS THE DANGER SUBSIDES THE FULL COSTS ARE CLEAR

Days 61 to 80: 16 May to 4 June

DAY 61: SATURDAY 16 MAY: *236,711 confirmed cases 33,998 deaths*

On a lovely sunny Saturday morning the Orthodox Jewish men who live in my block pray individually, socially distanced from each other in the gardens of our block of flats. And in the Old Testament reading in the book of Leviticus for this Sabbath it says that if God's commands are not adhered to "I will appoint terror over you, even consumption and fever." Has this happened?

People down the ages have asked why God has allowed human tragedies to happen. Primo Levi, who survived to write about the horror of Auschwitz, wrote in 'If this be a Man' that "Auschwitz is outside of us, but it is all around us, in the air. The plague has died away, but the infection still lingers and it would be foolish to deny it. Rejection of human solidarity, obtuse and cynical indifference to the suffering of others, abdication of the intellect and of moral sense to the principle of authority, and above all, at the root of everything, a sweeping tide of cowardice, a colossal cowardice which masks itself as warring virtue, love of country and faith in an idea." Have our travails at the hands of a virus, for which there still remains no known cure, come about through indifference to the suffering of others and, in pursuit of individuality? Have we rejected human solidarity and how to protect our communities from the ravages of the coronavirus?

The longer the economic contraction caused by the lockdown to respond to the spread of the virus goes on, the more individuals and families will be experiencing financial hardship in a way many will not have known before. Food banks are having record levels of demand for the basic necessities they can provide. One woman, out of thousands who have had to rely on them in recent times said, "I never thought I would need help in this way but the financial strain resulting from Covid-19 pushed me into frightening and unfamiliar circumstances."

On an afternoon walk I hear a sound I have not heard for a long time. The sound of tennis rackets hitting balls across the net and cries of "Out" as some shots just clear the base line. Two men have taken the opportunity to play at Farm Lane tennis club as part of the government's allowance that we can now take as much exercise as we wish provided it is socially distanced exercise with one other person.

But still we can only meet one family member outside of our immediate household, and only if the encounter is socially distanced and in a public outdoor space. Robin Harmer of Yorkshire writing in The Times about some of the jobs which are now permitted says he would be able to visit his children if he could persuade them to put up a "for sale" sign or if he became their cleaner (of which he says he has previous experience).

Whilst locked indoors television programmers are allowing us to watch the best of sporting and cultural events from previous years where the lockdown has prevented these events occurring this year. Tonight, BBC brings us the best of the Eurovision song contest for those (are there really such people?) who simply cannot let a year pass without indulging their craving for "Nil points" and "Boom bang a bang."

DAY 62: SUNDAY 17 MAY: *240,161 confirmed cases 34,466 deaths*

Boris Johnson writing in the Mail on Sunday refers to the complexity of trying to ease the lockdown whilst balancing the competing needs of safeguarding health and protecting the economy. It is not just Prime Ministers who have these complex decisions to make. Parents up and down the country are wrestling with whether to comply with the government's directive that primary school children should return to school tomorrow (being in school better for education than home learning) or to keep them at home (to avoid the risk of their child bringing the coronavirus from school into the home). The nature of these complex decisions is that both alternatives have potential benefits which will be lost if the other option is taken; it is difficult to construct a common scale of benefits for each option, to enable them to be weighed against each other. There is a consensus that saving lives should be the overriding objective; once you have made that decision then alternative benefits must, of necessity, come second.

One decision that is easy to make is that making further finance available to help the search for a vaccine that will prevent infection by the coronavirus, is a priority. The government announces that it is giving a further £65 million to the Oxford University vaccine project which appears to be the project which may find a successful solution first amongst UK research centres. Without a successful vaccine there remains the possibility that we stay in some sort of lockdown for a greatly extended period of time. But, hedging their bets against the Oxford University project being the first research project to produce a vaccine, the government also gives £18 million to the Imperial College, London vaccine project.

Funding these two vaccine projects may be one of Prime Minister Johnson's easier decisions in this multidimensional web he has to oversee. It is clear from other countries that, if you are perceived to have made the wrong choice in your decision making, the voice of public opinion is a vengeful one. In Belgium, where the 9,000 coronavirus deaths continue to be the world's highest rate of deaths per head of population, medical staff turn their backs during an official visit by premier Sophie Wilmes to Saint Pierre hospital in Brussels. Belgian frontline staff are disappointed at the government's handling of the crisis including budget cuts and low salaries for the health sector. Whilst in America, still reeling from unemployment at levels reminiscent of the Great Depression of the 1930s, Barrack Obama makes another criticism of President Trump saying, "A lot of them aren't even pretending to be in charge," to which Trump brands Obama, "a grossly incompetent President." Thankfully one cannot imagine Theresa May and Boris Johnson having such an exchange.

Even though there is often under reporting of deaths at the weekend the news that there have been "only" 170 deaths from the coronavirus in the last twenty four hours, the lowest since the lockdown began, is welcome news to end the day.

DAY 63: MONDAY 18 MAY: *243,303 confirmed cases 34,636 deaths*

The question that many are asking themselves is, "Will I be able to have a summer holiday this year?" There is uncertainty both about holidays abroad, and also about breaks in this country as we await news of whether hotels will reopen. The government had said that a 14 days quarantine period would be imposed on those returning to the UK. This appeared to rule out overseas holidays until President Macron and Boris Johnson appeared to agree that there would be no quarantine rules for people travelling between Britain and France. The government has now stepped back from confirming that France will be open for business as a holiday destination this summer but has introduced the idea that there may be "air bridges" between countries with low infection rates. Greece, which has only experienced 166 coronavirus deaths, has said it is interested in creating "air bridges" with people from other countries who want to experience the Acropolis and the delights of the Greek islands.

On the other hand, if you are a lorry driver involved in road haulage or a scientist involved in coronavirus research the chances are that you will be able to travel as often as you want between Britain and France without any requirements to quarantine on return to Britain.

With city centres around the world deserted, many people are now seeking out the peace and scenery that comes with living away from the metropolis. In Italy, 'when in Rome, do as the Roman' has taken on a new meaning as many young people are forsaking Rome to experience la dolce vita in ancient hillside villages of cobblestones and forgotten castles. Here the horrors of the pandemic can be forgotten as the sun sets over Tuscan fields and there is still some chianti left in the glass.

In Britain not only are foreign holidays in doubt, but the opportunities to even imagine we are abroad reduce significantly, with the news that the future of the Café Rouge and Bella Italia restaurant chains are in doubt as their owner, the Casual Dining Group, announces it will appoint administrators, putting the future of more than 6,000 jobs at risk.

This further blow to the hospitality trade highlights how much the futures of young people have been put in peril by the lockdown and the economic downturn. As Chair of the National Youth Agency a few years ago I saw at first hand the uncertainties that young people faced in planning their careers when the country was gradually coming through the period of austerity, which had followed the banking crisis of the previous decade. But now young people face far greater anxiety from drastically reduced numbers of job offers from the worlds of business, the professions and the arts. And they also no longer have the fallback of temporary work cheerfully serving the public in the country's cafes, bars and restaurants. A report by the Resolution Foundation shows that 35 per cent of workers aged 18 to 24 are taking home less pay than they were at the beginning of the year.

Meanwhile, at the very youngest end of the age scale, the debate continues about whether primary schools should open at the start of June as the government had intended. Education experts say it is our youngest children who suffer the most when schooling transfers to remote learning from home, with those from poorer backgrounds likely to suffer disproportionately. The Institute of Fiscal Studies tells us that the children of the poorest fifth of families are receiving a third less education at home than more wealthy families. But teaching unions and some councils are concerned about the health risks of returning to school given the difficulties of imposing social distancing on very young children. The Labour led Liverpool council has already said its primary schools will not reopen on 1 June and other councils are preparing to do similarly.

With the weather remaining blissfully sunny, this is the week when crowds would flock to the Chelsea Flower Show. First staged in 1913, it has become an icon of the British early summer with thousands admiring the specially created show gardens and the profusion of plants in the Great Pavilion. With the Chelsea Flower Show cancelled for the first time since the Second World War the BBC comes to our rescue with the start of a week of programmes showing the highlights of recent years. Introduced by the soothingly cheerful voices of Monty Don and Joe Swift from their own gardens Don tells us, "we need gardens like never before," and Swift comments that a garden is "a complete sanctuary" from the coronavirus world. As if to celebrate, garden centres around the country have now finally reopened to satisfy Middle England's desires to acquire new items for their herbaceous borders.

DAY 64: TUESDAY 19 MAY: *246,406 confirmed cases 34,796 deaths*

Cambridge University has announced that all of its lectures in the next academic year starting this autumn will be online. What about punting on the Cam? Is that permissible? Presumably, as long as social distancing is with us, there will be no opportunity to woo sweet Ophelia whilst being gently transported along the river through Grantchester Meadow by a local punter. You know you are in Cambridge by the method of the punting. In Cambridge most punters stand on the till, the raised part at the end of the punt, and punt with the open end forward, while in Oxford they stand inside the boat and punt with the till forward. Students at Oxford and Cambridge frequently believe that theirs is the only correct style, to the extent that the till end is often known as the "Cambridge End" and the other as the "Oxford End".

With 11,000 UK coronavirus deaths in care homes, around a third of total virus deaths, the government continues to face criticism for having not given sufficient support to the care home sector, and for prioritising the needs of the NHS. Giving evidence to Parliament's Health and Social Care Committee, Professor Martin Green, the head of Care England, which represents independent social service providers, said that all people who were most at risk of dying from COVID-19 should have been prioritised from the beginning. This should have included care home residents. Professor Green also said there were still problems about PPE, and testing care home residents and staff for the virus. He also identified the risk that, with rising costs to deal with the virus, and the loss of large numbers of residents who have succumbed to COVID-19, some care homes could go out of business. No wonder, perhaps, that Quentin Letts, political sketch writer of The Times, observed that Matt Hancock, defending the government's approach in the House of Commons, suddenly looked older than his years, without his normal bounce and boyish appearance.

In our online regional NHS Board meeting today, colleagues based in Cambridge show graphs of our current experience of the coronavirus in Cambridgeshire and Peterborough. We seem to be past the top of our peak but not yet in a significant decline in terms of cases of infections and patients in hospital. But the good news, relatively speaking, is that hospital deaths in our region, which peaked at 14 on 23 April and have been around eight a day since then, have been less than we feared they might be in the early stages of the pandemic. We note with concern, however, that some residents in care homes in our area appear to have contracted the virus after testing negative when arriving at the care homes. It is possible, though, that the negative outcome of the test was incorrect or that they were just starting to be infected when they came into the homes.

Once again health news stories go hand in hand with other reports on the effects on the economy of the lockdown imposed to contain the spread of the virus. Today Chancellor Rishi Sunak conveys a very stark assessment of our economic prospects. Gone are the green shoots of hope for a speedy recovery from the downturn that the Bank of England had recently projected. Now Sunak was warning that, "it is not obvious there will be an immediate bounce back," and, "we are likely to face a severe recession, the likes of which we haven't seen, and, of course, this will have an impact on unemployment." The Chancellor's grim news is accompanied by a flurry of dramatic statistics: a record monthly increase of 850,000 in the number of people claiming unemployment benefit taking the total to over two million; and a further 10 million people receiving income support from the government whilst their work has been on hold, eight million employees who have been furloughed and a further two million receiving government support for the self-employed. This means 12 million people are relying on state benefits through lack of work, more than a third of the 33 million comprising the labour market before the coronacrisis.

One needs some good news on days like these. And there is something to cheer in the news that 100 year old Captain Tom Moore (recently promoted to Colonel) has been awarded a knighthood at the special request of the Prime Minister. Just over a month ago this unassuming Second World War veteran from Bedfordshire was unknown to the wider world. But, as news of his heroic efforts to push his walking frame a hundred times round his garden spread, donations to his NHS fundraising appeal flowed in and now stand at nearly £33 million. Arise Sir Tom, a job well done.

DAY 65: WEDNESDAY 20 MAY: *248,818 confirmed cases 35,341 deaths*

Who makes the decisions which have shaped the successes and failures of our response to the coronavirus pandemic? Sir Adrian Smith, the incoming President of the Royal Society, the world's oldest scientific academy founded in 1660, enters the debate. The government has repeatedly said it follows the science in making decisions. It says the science has informed their strategy on key issues such as social distancing, imposing the lockdown, deciding when to ease it and other matters such as whether we should wear face masks. Sir Adrian says ultimately it is politicians who make the decisions. His view is that scientific advice about the uncertainties of dealing with a new virus had been played down by the government which had wanted to present clear evidence for decisions and to appear decisive in making them.

Sir Adrian has a point. The more you don't know about a particular option the greater the chances that, whilst your chosen path may work well, it may also possibly produce bad outcomes because of relevant information you had not identified. Setting off for a weekend train journey without having checked whether there will be engineering work on the line, which will double the time of your journey, is an example of incomplete information adversely affecting outcomes. We have all, on occasion, done that so the happy excursion we were looking forward to becomes a lengthy tiring ordeal. Are there similarities there with our coronavirus experience?

This is why critics of the government highlight the lack of accurate data on who has had the virus. They see this as incomplete information which caused errors in government decision making, for example on whether the lockdown in March should have started earlier. These voices ask why we seem to have been so slow to implement a comprehensive test, track and trace system so that we know who has the virus and the people they have been in contact with. The government abandoned trying to trace those who had been in contact with people testing positive for the coronavirus on 12 March, when it became clear that the rate of infection was growing too fast to allow all people who might be spreading the virus to be located.

Now the Prime Minister has promised "a world beating" system staffed by 25,000 contact tracers to be available by 1 June. The app on your smartphone which will record details of other app using smartphone carriers that you come close to is still being trialled. But we are now told the app is not critical to the operation of the test, track and trace system as much of the tracing information will be drawn from discussions with those testing positive for the virus. If the new system works it should help to prevent a second virus spike. But did the failure to have an efficient system from the outset, as countries such as Germany had, play a major part in our death toll from the virus becoming the highest in Europe?

Looking back in this coronadiary I see that I have rarely mentioned President Trump. Perhaps that is my own bias of limiting references to a man who seems most of the time to be a parody of himself, a Spitting Image puppet at large in the real world. In recent days he has repeatedly told us he is taking an antimalarial drug to ward off the virus, despite medical experts saying there is no proven evidence of it protecting you from the virus. This, after he had lambasted the World Health Organisation as "a puppet of Beijing" and suggested that drinking disinfectant could be our saviour from the pandemic plague. Spitting Image would have nothing further to lampoon the US President with, he does it all himself.

But the reason for mentioning Trump is that he is overseeing a nation which has the world's highest death rate from coronavirus with 93,000 lives lost, well over a quarter of the world's total virus deaths which currently stand at 324,000. Added to which is the human misery of more than 38 million Americans now unemployed following the lockdown, more than the population of Canada and a level not experienced since the Great Depression of the early 1930s. Cars queue for miles to pick up parcels from food banks. Even Mercedes and Cadillacs are in the queues as families from the professional classes have suffered dramatic income losses when large US corporates slashed their workforces.

We shouldn't see this just as a failing of the Trump administration. The signs are everywhere as cutbacks in one business sector cause a domino effect on other sectors. Rolls-Royce, that most distinguished of brands, had warned that jobs were at risk as the contraction in the aviation sector slashed demand for its engines. Today it confirmed it will axe 9,000 jobs, around a fifth of its global workforce but mostly in the UK at Derby and other locations. We are doing this, "to protect the jobs we will have going forwards" is the management speak that provides Rolls-Royce leaders with the basis for their decision. And then how many of the businesses that Rolls-Royce normally relies on for parts will feel the pinch and how many of their staff will go home to tell their families that they have joined the growing army of the unemployed?

But still the beautiful sunny weather, which has been such a feature of this coronaspring, continues, almost mocking the human tragedies that have unfolded around the globe. In the still strong evening sunlight the elderly couple who live below me, who have been largely housebound in recent weeks, are persuaded out to sit in garden chairs on our lawn to feel the sun on their faces They suddenly look like happy teenagers enjoying a day out at Clacton beach.

DAY 66: THURSDAY 21 MAY: *248,293* confirmed cases 35,704 deaths*

A pack of four small hand sanitiser bottles arrived in the post. I had forgotten that I had ordered them almost two months ago when supermarkets and online suppliers had been run bare of all cleaning products and personal protection. But it felt reassuring to have them.

As the fine weather continues the papers carry front page photos of people once more enjoying parks and beaches, following the government's ruling that we can now travel to beauty spots although social distancing and not being with more than one person outside of your household should still apply. The pictures show how much people crave fresh air, pleasant green surroundings or the sound of waves crashing on the shore as an antidote to stressful times.

It isn't good news, though, on all outdoor locations. The National Trust will not open its historic houses and gardens until the end of August and faces a £200 million pound loss this year, director general Hilary McGrady tells Parliament. With nothing to visit many have cancelled their National Trust subscriptions, with cancellations running at four times the normal rate. "The longer you stay closed the harder it is for members to want to maintain their support," McGrady tells MPs, "and once that support declines it is incredibly hard to build up again." Even when allowed to open, the National Trust will have to introduce rigorous social distancing arrangements which will limit visitor numbers.

This then is the nub of the current dilemma. Businesses are faced with having to impose social distancing in a regulated way, and subject to inspection from health and safety officials. Any activities which people would normally enjoy in close proximity with each other, such as visiting, have to be changed so that only a very small proportion of those who would normally take part can now do so. The small socially distanced level of activity is often, then, not viable for the businesses to operate. As well as National Trust properties, restaurants, cafes, pubs, hotels, gyms, leisure centres, museums, theatres, cinemas and sporting venues are all

*a downwards revision to the previous day's figures

facing similar problems. Some business sectors, such as gyms and leisure centres, persuaded the government that they had workable solutions to enable an early re-opening. Other sectors are still trying to work out how they could make the government's regulations work. The pub sector is lobbying for the social distancing to be reduced from two metres to one metre as the only way, they say, to make pubs able to operate in the coronaworld.

My mind returns to the dire prognosis for the economy from Rishi Sunak on Tuesday. Two million now claiming unemployment benefit and ten million receiving the new income support arrangements from the government. With the economy plummeting many of the ten million on income support will be added to the unemployment figures if they do not have jobs to return to. The furlough scheme, where the government paid most of the wages of employees of businesses not needed during the lockdown, was an excellent idea. But it was supposed to be a temporary arrangement enabling businesses to retain loyal staff who would then return to the business when the lockdown ended. Now, because of the prolonged need for social distancing and the sharp economic downturn, the previous expectation that their jobs would be preserved will not be realised for large numbers of those who have been furloughed.

It feels to me as if there is a crisis looming of dramatically increasing unemployment figures if the government income support schemes come to a close, or if employers are not prepared to pay their proportion of the costs of these schemes as the government has asked for. Like a lighthouse beacon warning ships to stay clear of the rocks I now sense an urgent need for government and business organisations to highlight the dangers and help people avoid future financial ruin. Surely it would make sense for government and business organisations to identify areas where new jobs can be created in sectors where there will still be demand for goods and services in the coming months. Some positions could be split into two part-time roles to enable more people to return to work, both for their self-esteem and their future income. This planning must be started now so that new opportunities are there for at least a proportion of those who will lose their jobs with current employers.

In Italy, which for so long appeared to be devastated by the virus, life is gradually returning to more normal times. At last Italians can sit outdoors and enjoy their favourite coffee. For a price. It is not the price that they paid before the lockdown. In fashionable Milan the cost of an espresso has risen by 50 per cent from 1.3 euros to 2 euros. As Italians sit at their outdoor tables, perhaps they can ask for a little more froth on their cappuccino to offset their disappointment at the price rise.

DAY 67: FRIDAY 22 MAY: *250,908 confirmed cases 36,042 deaths*

The evidence is now fairly clear that the peak of the coronavirus epidemic we have been living through for the past two months is on the decline, certainly in London and the surrounding areas which bore the front of the initial storm. The total number of patients in hospital with COVID-19 has dropped below 10,000 for the first time since the start of the lockdown. Yesterday the main hospitals in London reported no COVID-19 fatalities in the previous 48 hours.

But whilst this feels like good news one cannot ignore that the virus is still spreading at faster rates in certain areas in northern England. And one certainly cannot forget that the total UK coronavirus death rate is the highest in Europe, and potentially even greater than the officially reported figure, now in excess of 36,000. The ONS says that the UK's "excess deaths", the extent to which deaths have been more than the seasonal average, have been 55,000 since the COVID-19 outbreak began. And this is only up to 8 May so the data is already two weeks out of date.

Sir Paul Nurse, who won the Nobel Prize for the physiology of medicine, says today that the country has been on the back foot tackling COVID-19, and that there needs to be a clearer publicly presented strategy for managing the virus outbreak. He says he would have much preferred the lockdown to have started weeks earlier.

The tension between the NHS and the largely privately managed care home sector continues. A Radio 4 File on Four investigation reports care home staff "reduced to tears" by what they claim were aggressive NHS hospital managers insisting that they accept into their care homes elderly patients the NHS wanted to discharge so that beds could be freed up for COVID-19 patients. But the care home staff say that many of these patients had not been tested for the coronavirus or had not been retested after having been earlier tested as positive. It seems that the spirit of a unified health and social care system which was behind the Health and Social Care Act of 2012 has been sorely tested during the virus outbreak.

One welcome piece of news for a significant proportion of those working in both the hospital and social care sectors is Boris Johnson's reversal of his previous opposition to abolishing the surcharge of £400 a year, which staff from outside the EU had been required to pay to use the NHS. The end of this surcharge is welcomed as a good common sense decision. The resulting loss in revenue to the government pales into insignificance, however, when compared to the overall cost to the government of trying to support the economy in these drastically constrained times. Treasury figures released today show that government borrowing for April, the extent to which its expenditure exceeded its revenue, was the highest on record, at £62 billion. This reflects low tax revenues because so many businesses are closed and much higher than normal government expenditure to support the millions of extra people now claiming benefits from the state, including the furlough scheme to pay the wages of staff whose employers have put their work on hold. The government is on track for total borrowings of £300 billion this year, equivalent to 15 per cent of the size of the economy.

More bleak news that retail sales declined by 18 per cent in April with clothing sales, despite an increase in online purchases, decimated by a drop of 50 per cent. The roll of well known companies shedding jobs continues. Italian restaurant chain Carluccio's is saved by the business operating Giraffe and Ed's Easy Diner, but at a cost of 1,000 jobs; the Specialist Leisure Group, owner of names like Breakaway Holidays and Shearings Holidays, formed in 1903, collapses leaving 2,500 out of work.

At least we have a bank holiday weekend to look forward to with a largely good weather forecast. Time to lie in the sun and pretend this all isn't happening.

DAY 68: SATURDAY 23 MAY: *254,195 confirmed cases 36.393 deaths*

As the Spring Bank holiday starts with a beautifully sunny morning, one person who has plenty of space and a nice view to look out on is Lucy Hutchings. She is the head of Hampton Palace, the home of Henry VIII and later Oliver Cromwell, which won't be welcoming its normal 20,000 visitors over this holiday weekend. Instead, with only a skeleton staff for company, she has time to explore at leisure the 1,300 rooms for which she has the keys and to walk in blissful solitude in the royal gardens.

The leader in The Times today questions Prime Minister Johnson's visibility during the coronacrisis and not just because of his period in hospital. The Times notes that since his televised address two weeks ago to announce the conditions for easing the lockdown Johnson has only made one statement to the House of Commons, which remarkably was his first since the crisis began; he has also not spoken at any of the Downing Street daily press conferences and has given no interviews. There are, of course, different types of leadership. Some leaders lead from the front, others have total faith in their teams to deliver what is needed. Reflecting on The Times leader I realise how much Johnson seems to have changed his style from his "this is how we are going to do it" approach on Brexit to his current approach of limiting his personal statements to key moments in the drama. Has Boris been become less sure footed since his spell in hospital or could he perhaps be uncertain of what really is the best way to get out of the crisis?

As if to compound the Prime Minister's problems, news breaks, following investigations by the Guardian and the Daily Mirror. that his chief adviser, the idiosyncratic and non-conformist Dominic Cummings, had seemingly broken the lockdown guidance by driving in March over 250 miles to Durham with his wife and four year old son, when his wife had developed coronavirus symptoms. Despite the government's very clear instruction to the public that those carrying the virus and their partners should self-isolate at home, Cummings and his wife made the journey north to arrange care for their four year old son fearing that both he and his wife would not be able to look after their child if he, too, became ill, as he subsequently did. According to reports they stayed in a separate part of the property owned by Dominic Cummings' parents, and his sister and niece left food outside for them. Cummings view, which Transport Minister Grant Shapps seeks to support at the daily Downing Street press conference, is that putting the care of the child first and driving to relatives was within the guidance, which, as we are now told, allowed leaving home whilst carrying the virus if it was a life-saving matter. One young mother tells ITV News at Ten that she was alone, very unwell with coronavirus symptoms, struggling to look after her child because she was certain the guidance was that you could not seek out other family members for assistance if you were at risk of infecting them.

So the human drama of working under pressure at the centre of the response to the coronavirus pandemic continues. We have already seen resignations from the Scottish Chief Medical Officer Catherine Calderwood for twice visiting her second home, and Professor Neil Ferguson, one of the government's main scientific advisers, for entertaining a married lover at his home, both in contravention of the lockdown guidance they so publicly endorsed. What now the future of Dominic Cummings?

DAY 69: SUNDAY 24 MAY: *257,154 confirmed cases 36.675 deaths*

I have not seen Dominic Cummings at work to be able to personally judge if he is good, bad or indifferent at his job as Boris Johnson's chief adviser. I am content though to accept reports that he has a very fast ability to analyse problems confronting the government and to identify solutions which others have not thought about. But I do know that I don't feel any particular affection for a man who has one of the country's most influential jobs but arrives in Downing Street wearing tracksuit bottoms and a casual shirt adrift at the waist. As my headmaster would have said, "I don't like the cut of his jib."

The Sunday press carries further allegations that Cummings breached the government imposed rules following the lockdown. The Observer reports a member of the public, having seen him on 12 April at Barnard Castle, a beauty spot 30 miles from where he was staying in Durham.

It is unclear whether Cummings was still self-isolating at this time but, in any event, with the lockdown at its height one was only supposed to leave home for shopping or exercise locally. The Observer also says that another source saw him in Durham for a second time in April after he had returned to work in London, a claim which Cummings denies.

If previous reports about his working style were correct, Dominic Cummings did not mind too much if he offended people who were in the Westminster bubble. That mindset works well when you believe the power you wield cannot be overturned. Cummings may now come to regret being unconcerned about his personal image if the tide of public opinion turns against him for his actions in Durham during lockdown.

Taking a break from the Cummings story I note that, as we continue to live in such dramatic and unusual times, the world is full of unexpected statistics. One consequence of the coronavirus outbreak and the subsequent lockdown is that crime is down by 25 per cent. It seems both criminals and those they would normally commit crimes against are much more likely to be staying within their respective homes and not coming into contact with each other. Even PC George Dixon, if he was still patrolling the streets of fictional Dock Green, would find less to report at the present time.

But not all crime has stopped and criminals are an adaptable breed. A much more disturbing statistic is benefit officials' estimate that as much as £1.5 billion may have been lost in recent weeks through benefit fraud. As the effects of lockdown hit home 1.5 million people applied for universal credit in the four weeks to 9 April, six times the normal level. My mental arithmetic spots a big problem here. If every one of the claimants had been acting fraudulently then each would have been taking away £1,000 to get to the total of £1.5 billion being misappropriated. So, on the assumption that most claims were honest and correct, some of the fraudulent claims must be worryingly large.

But the Dominic Cummings story dominates the news. After Transport Minister Grant Shapps, heroically and politely, tries to defend Cummings on the early morning Andrew Marr show (Marr: Did Dominic Cummings stop on his trip to Durham? Shapps: I don't have that level of detail) Boris Johnson emerges from his press conference exile to support his chief adviser at the afternoon Downing Street press conference.

Only yesterday The Times had questioned the Prime Minister's lack of visibility. Now he had made himself visible but to take on defending his most senior adviser on charges where most of the public, the Labour opposition party and the media have diametrically opposing views. It was a high risk strategy from Johnson to defend Cummings. Did he genuinely believe Cummings had done no wrong, or was the alternative of losing the adviser he most relied on worse than the task of defending him? He certainly conveyed no uncertainty on the matter "I think he has followed the instinct of every father and parent and I don't mark him down for that. I believe, that in every respect, he has acted reasonably and legally and with integrity." But Johnson's certainty on the issue opens the door for the media to ask Johnson whether he understands that many of the British public feel angry because they made so many sacrifices to stay at home if there was a risk of infection, as Johnson himself had instructed them to do. Now there appeared to be other rules for those in Downing Street. Johnson tries to appear empathetic "I get why people would feel confused and offended". But Johnson's words lack conviction when he has just pardoned his chief adviser for doing the opposite of what most of the public would have done in the same circumstances.

Labour leader Keir Starmer, who, with his probing legal mind is looking stronger day by day, is crystal clear in his criticism "This was a huge test for the Prime Minister and he failed that test. If I was Prime Minister, I would have sacked Cummings."

DAY 70: MONDAY 25 MAY: *259,559 confirmed cases 36.793 deaths*

The Dominic Cummings story floods out of the front pages (and the inside pages) of all the newspapers. Before reading the papers I try to consider what I feel about the story. At a humane level, it is possible to feel some sympathy with a situation whereby Cummings and his wife, who already had coronavirus symptoms, wanted to seek out family members to look after their four year old son, fearing that they, as parents, might both become ill with the virus.

What makes this such a difficult, and to the papers sensational, story are other issues arising from these unusual times we live in and the government restrictions we are all trying to live by to keep each other safe from this deadly virus. The first issue is that I doubt that hardly any members of the public would have been aware that making a 250 mile journey, to draw on the support of other family members, was, as Boris Johnson now maintains, both legal and within the guidance issued at the time of the lockdown. The message that people with virus symptoms, and their partners, should self-isolate at home was repeated so often that it will seem inconceivable to the wider public that any other options were available to self-isolating couples, even where the care of children was involved. Secondly, did Dominic Cummings and his wife consider other options for the care of their son nearer home? If no family members lived nearby were there friends in London who could have helped with the care of the Cummings' four year old in an emergency? Or could their local authority services have helped in any way? In other words, how essential was the 250 mile trip to Durham when non-essential travel was prohibited?

And the third issue, which is having such an impact on this story is that, because the public perception of Cummings, from what we have seen and heard about him, is that he walks through Whitehall with an air of arrogance, not at all afraid to upset others as he pursues the agendas he considers important, there is a "how have the mighty fallen" wish by much of the media and many of the public to see him receive his comeuppance. Retribution seems to many to be due to Cummings for acting in a way which, like his work persona, seems to have had no regard for the feelings of others, in this case the millions of British citizens who were making sacrifices to adhere to the mantra of "Stay at home, save lives, protect the NHS."

The Daily Mail, that great protector of Middle England, comes out fighting with headlines shouting "What planet are they on?" and a front page comment that Dominic Cummings has given every selfish persona licence to play fast and loose with public health. "Neither man," the comment opines on Johnson and Cummings, "has displayed a scintilla of contrition for this breach of trust. Do they think we are fools?" The Guardian front page headline, "No apology, no explanation: PM bets all on Cummings," highlights the risk that Boris Johnson has taken in backing the chief adviser he needs alongside him, but which is likely to turn public opinion against the Prime Minister. And not just public opinion. Professor Stephen Reicher, of St Andrews University tweeted: "I can say that in a few short minutes, Boris Johnson has trashed all the advice we have given on how to build trust and secure adherence to the measures necessary to control Covid-19. "Be open and honest, we said. Trashed. Respect the public, we said. Trashed. Ensure equity, so everyone is treated the same, we said. Trashed. Be consistent, we said. Trashed. Make clear 'we are all in it together'. Trashed."

With mounting criticism of Dominic Cummings for his apparent disregard for the spirit, if not the letter of, the Stay At Home regulations and of Boris Johnson for supporting his adviser, Downing Street arranged for Cummings to give an explanation of his actions. The stage was then set for one of the most unusual press conferences of recent times.

On a beautiful May Bank Holiday afternoon Dominic Cummings walked out into the Rose Garden of Downing Street and sat at a table in front of an invited audience of the media seated at socially distanced intervals on Downing Street chairs. Cummings was dressed, for him, quite smartly in a white, open-necked shirt and trousers. On a hot afternoon it felt as if waiters and waitresses in official attire should be quietly going round handing out glasses of Pimms and upmarket nibbles. Those with long memories may recall that Conservative Prime Minister John Major stepped into this Rose Garden in June 1995, to announce that he would take his opponents on by standing down as leader of the Conservative Party to allow a leadership election to take place. Major then won the election, and his opponents were vanquished. Now it was Cummings against the press. Who would come out as the victor?

Cummings read quietly from a prepared script. His usual brashness was replaced by a more quiet and considered approach, setting out an account of his travels from London to Durham after his wife had fallen ill with the coronavirus, and the thinking that had influenced his actions. He did not apologise but said that he tried to do the right thing and that "other reasonable people may disagree."

Dominic Cummings confirms that with his wife already suffering with the virus, he was concerned that he too might also become ill which could then mean the couple would not be able to look after their young son. With no-one he said to look to for childcare in London and also concerned about the levels of security at his home he decided to make the drive north to Durham. In Durham he stayed at a property on his parents' farm and close to his sister and nieces who could help with childcare if needed. Cummings did become ill with the virus for around a week but by then his wife had recovered so no assistance with the care of his son was needed. For a man who is usually concerned about the big issues today he was focussing on the detail, his compliance with the lockdown rules being based he said on the exemption from staying home "if a child's health was at risk."

On the trip to Barnard Castle, Cummings had an interesting excuse for the apparent breach of lockdown rules. He said that as his eyes had felt "a bit weird" he had decided to make the 30 mile drive to "test his eyes out," to make sure he was fit for the five hour return trip to London. He denied the Observer report that he had been sighted returning to Durham after he had resumed work in London.

The assembled media took it in turns to ask Dominic Cummings questions from a microphone placed in front of a chair in the sunshine of the Downing Street Rose Garden. It was all quite civil in a way as if Cummings was a visiting professor of politics giving an outdoor lecture. In this more polite and quiet style of explaining his actions, had Dominic Cummings done enough to save himself? There are still many, including Conservative MPs, who want to see him go. The next few days may be critical.

Defending his chief adviser is taking up a lot of the Prime Minister's time and energy. He was back at the Downing Street press conference for a second successive day to repeat his support for Cummings. But he did acknowledge the strength of public opinion on the matter. That many people felt Cummings knowledge of the details of the guidance had allowed him to travel long distances whilst most others would have followed the government's Stay at Home message: "Of course I do regret the confusion, the anger and pain," Johnson said.

There was other news that Boris Johnson wanted to get across. Almost secondary on a day dominated by the Cummings story, Johnson announced that from mid-June more shops would re-open, provided they have implemented appropriate safety measures.

The day ended with Robert Peston's observation on the possible fall-out from the Dominic Cummings story "Has he created a bad example about bending the rules? Will others be inclined to break the rules or not bother about making sure they keep to them?" Like Cummings' future, time will tell.

DAY 71: TUESDAY 26 MAY: *261,184 confirmed cases 36,914 deaths*

There is a mixed reaction to Dominic Cummings' performance in the Downing Street Rose Garden. 39 Tory MPs demand that Cummings should resign. Perhaps most surprisingly more than a dozen Church of England bishops have voiced criticism of Boris Johnson, saying that he is risking lives and jeopardising public trust in his leadership by refusing to sack Dominic Cummings. The Right Reverend Paul Bayes, the Bishop of Liverpool, contrasted Mr Cummings' action with the "many millions of people who have followed the government's advice and stayed at home, coping with difficulty. It's not good enough to treat the people of this country like sheep who can be fooled." Others question whether the Church of England can continue to work with the government on the response to the pandemic. But some feel that Cummings showed in his Rose Garden address a more sensitive side to his personality, as a husband and father trying to do the best for his family in a complex situation.

The continued very warm May weather shows two sides of the reaction to the social distancing. Many people are still concerned about sending their children back to primary schools, unsure whether social distancing can be upheld effectively with very young children. But with temperatures rising, and millions of people away from work, very large crowds head for the beach and parks now that we are allowed to spend as much socially distanced time outdoors as we want. James Kirkup of the Social Market Foundation think tank makes the point that the eight million people on the government's furlough scheme are effectively being paid to go the beach, but could make better use of their time learning new skills or volunteering to make a contribution to society and to increase their chances of getting future work if their current jobs are not continued.

At our regional NHS Board meeting with colleagues based in Cambridge we look again at the statistics of how our region has been affected by the coronavirus. We conclude that the figures show that we are on a slow downward trajectory. COVID-19 deaths have reduced to around 3 to 5 a day, this in our region of one million people living in the county of Cambridgeshire and Peterborough. In total we have suffered 416 coronavirus deaths (314 in hospitals. 86 in care homes and 16 in the community). We discuss the factors which have kept our overall deaths to a lower level than we had initially modelled. Our earlier fear was that, with London only 50 minutes away by train, the virus could spread easily to our region from the capital. This threat does not seem to have materialised. The Stay At Home message has kept travelling to a minimum and, in any event, many jobs for local people, particularly in medicine and at the university, are Cambridge based. Looking to the future, the hospitals in our region are now considering how to organise non-COVID-19 procedures to limit the fall in the number of patients who are being treated; this includes decisions on which treatments require full PPE, and which do not.

Although some have softened their feelings towards Dominic Cummings after his full explanation yesterday of his Durham excursion, those who would seek to criticise him continue to do so. There is still a strong proportion of the public who feel that, even if Cummings was within the letter of the rules, his actions were against their spirit, given the government had, on so many occasions, told us to stay at home if we were unwell. It felt uncomfortable that Matt Hancock, who, as Health and Social Care Secretary, had been one of the most vocal voices telling us to stay at home ("this is not a request, it is an instruction"), now confirmed that Dominic Cummings had acted in an acceptable manner by travelling to Durham. On Newsnight Emily Maitlis queries what Boris Johnson's "blind loyalty" to his chief adviser tells us about the workings of 10 Downing Street: "The public mood is fury, contempt and anguish. Dominic Cummings broke the rules, the country can see that and is shocked the government cannot."

DAY 72: WEDNESDAY 27 MAY: *265,227 confirmed cases 37,048 deaths*

Boris Johnson's emphasis in defending Dominic Cummings may help him keep the chief adviser he now relies on for the big pieces of government strategy. But he may struggle now to keep public opinion on his side. Many feel that public trust in the government has weakened; Richard Milet QC, in a letter to The Times, makes the point that the Dominic Cummings story has shown the public that they were unaware of the fine details of the regulations which then allowed the perception that there was "one rule for some, another for the drafters." The public have also seen growing dissension within the Conservative party with the number of MPs who have criticised Dominic Cummings rising to 60 and Douglas Ross, a junior Minster for Scotland, resigning. A new poll shows that the Conservative lead over Labour has been cut by nine points in just a week.

Boris Johnson tells Parliament's Liaison Committee in a video meeting that, whilst he is "deeply sorry for all the hurt and pain and anxiety" that had been generated, he will not be asking for a public inquiry into Cummings' actions, and now wishes to draw a line under the affair. Johnson sees the government's more important current agenda as being about taking further steps to ease the lockdown which will allow the public to start spending money again as shops reopen. All the signs are that it will be a gradual re-opening as shops put in place systems to maintain social distancing and to minimise coronavirus health risks; items of clothing for example, which have been touched but not bought by customers, will be quarantined before being put back on display.

Clothing chain Next says it will initially re-open 25 of its 100 shops; John Lewis says it will open its stores on a phased basis.

Sport is also about to return in the coming weeks with Premier League football and racing both due to restart behind closed doors next month. Tim Spector of Kings College, London reports that his analysis of coronavirus infections has identified "hotspots" which occurred after over 200,000 attended the Cheltenham racing Festival in March, and large crowds from Spain came to Liverpool to watch the Reds play Atletico Madrid. We won't be seeing large crowds at sporting events any time soon but we might hear them. Plans are being made to allow television viewers of football to select a crowd reaction to each incident which will be relayed through speakers in the empty grounds hosting the games.

The fear that the total of coronavirus deaths may be substantially higher than the daily reported figures is shown by the latest statistics from the ONS which show just over 45,000 virus related deaths, including suspected cases, based on death certificates. And this is based on the situation nearly two weeks ago, on 15 May.

The government today gives details of how the new test, track and trace system being launched today will work. Even though the much heralded app system is not ready to be launched, 25,000 trained telephone operators are standing by to telephone those who people testing positive for the coronavirus say they have had recent contact with. Health Minister Matt Hancock says that if we receive one of these calls it is our "civic duty" to self-isolate for 14 days whether or not we have tested positive for the virus. Boris Johnson says this will be a tougher lockdown for some in order to release Britain's 66 million population into a safer world.

As Italy continues to ease its lockdown, tourists are allowed back to the ancient ruins of Pompeii. Strange that some people wish to absorb what it was like to live through a Vesuvius created catastrophe of mass fatalities when this has been happening in the here and now courtesy of the coronavirus.

DAY 73: THURSDAY 28 MAY: *267,240 confirmed cases 37,460 deaths*

The government is reducing its alert level from 4, meaning transmission of the virus is high, to 3, meaning it is in general circulation but not currently at a high level. This is the basis on which it is beginning to ease the lockdown, particularly by allowing shops to open next month if safety measures are in place.

But how many people, who may now circulate more widely as the lockdown eases, are actually carrying the coronavirus? New figures from the ONS show that an average of seven out of ten people who tested positive for the virus had not displayed any symptoms in the previous week. If that really is a standard proportion then it raises serious concerns for containing the spread of the virus. It means that significant numbers of people who should be self-isolating at home, if they knew they had the virus, will be out and about, including inside shops, not realising they may be infecting others, some of whom may become unwell. The famous R number, about how fast the virus is spreading, is based on known cases. There must be the potential for the R number to be understated if there is a large number of people who, not displaying symptoms and therefore not seeking tests, don't know they are carrying the virus.

Only with widespread testing of the population, whether they think they have the symptoms or not, will the true picture emerge. Although the number of daily tests is increasing and anyone can now ask for a test, we are still a long way from having mass testing of the population. At yesterday's Parliament Liaison Committee Boris Johnson admitted that we had not been sufficiently prepared. "I think the brutal reality is that the country did not learn the lessons of Sars and Mers (previous viruses) and we didn't have a testing operation ready to go, on the scale that we needed." Yet officials had told Parliament in the past that the UK was the best prepared country in Europe for a pandemic. Did they really believe that?

Although the number of daily deaths from the coronavirus has dropped to levels which were experienced around the time the lockdown started, each day still brings tragedies to the family and friends of those who have died. Two Cardiff NHS colleagues, both originally from the Philippines, die on the same day. Dominga David, a 62 year old nurse and Allan Macalalad, a 44 year old theatre assistant.

Meanwhile, in America, the only country to have experienced more coronavirus deaths than Britain, the death toll passes 100,000, a greater loss than in any conflict since America's involvement in the Korean war.

As the clamour around the Dominic Cummings story of his lockdown trip to Durham begins to subside the BBC issues a public rebuke to Newsnight presenter Emily Maitlis for her strongly worded introduction to Newsnight on Tuesday, when she accused the Prime Minister for his "blind loyalty" to Cummings, who she said had "broken the rules" leaving the public with "fury, contempt and anguish." The top of the BBC deemed that this was not accurate reporting given that a proportion of the public were not experiencing those strong emotions. Also, whilst he may indeed have not followed the spirit of the Stay at Home instructions, Cummings apparently acted within the detail of the rules as the government has now explained them to us. Durham police said today that his subsequent short trip to Barnard Castle may have been a breach, but only a minor breach, of the rules. Maitlis, though, still has her supporters for her forthright views.

At the daily Downing Street press conference Prime Minister Johnson announces that the public, other than those who are shielding because of underlying health conditions, can now meet with people outside their own households in groups of up to six, provided this is outdoors and social distancing is observed. So grandparents can finally see newly born grandchildren for the first time, and couples can visit their parents; such normal interactions finally restored.

For the tenth week running the public stand outside their homes clapping and banging pots to applaud NHS and other frontline workers. But tonight is the last time. The originator of the idea, Anne Marie Plas, feels, with the pressure of caring for COVID-19 patients easing, it should now be concluded and does not want the weekly event to become politicised.

DAY 74: FRIDAY 29 MAY: *269,127 confirmed cases 37,837 deaths*

Every time the government announces more figures about their financial support to keep the economy afloat in the hope that there will eventually be some sort of recovery, the numbers get larger. Over 650,000 businesses, both large and small, have sought loans backed by the government totalling £27.5 billion. The number of people on income support from the government is now 11.0 million (8.5 million of employees on the furlough scheme and 2.5 million self-employed receiving income support), equivalent to a third of the total workforce and at a total expected cost of around £100 billion.

The concern remains that a significant proportion of those on the furlough scheme may not be needed by businesses experiencing lower levels of customers when they are allowed to re-open, As well as the lack of activity in the hospitality sector, some business experts estimate that, with the growth in online shopping since the lockdown began, as much as a third of non-food retail space could disappear from our high streets within six months.

The government also cannot continue making income support payments indefinitely at such a large cost. As the support is withdrawn so unemployment is likely to rise. The testing of the waters will arrive in the next couple of months. Chancellor Rishi Sunak announces today that as from August the amount of government support will start to reduce to be replaced (in the furlough scheme) by money that businesses will now be required to pay to their employees. But employees can work part-time and remain on the furlough scheme. The income support schemes will then end after October. So by then the amount of additional unemployment will be revealed as businesses lay off those members of staff they no longer require, to avoid making unnecessary salary payments.

This isn't the best of times to be young. The International Labour Organisation tells us that one in six young people worldwide have lost their jobs and those still in employment have had their hours cut by a quarter which partly reflects the large numbers of young people working in the hospitality sector. Many younger people finishing education will now find it much more difficult to find their first job. The young, already being referred to as the lockdown generation, will inevitably feel that their futures have been sacrificed to mainly protect the health of older people who were more at risk of becoming seriously ill from the virus.

The Bank of England admits that it will now be a longer and harder economic recovery than it had expected just three weeks ago. How could the combined minds of some of the country's most experienced economists working at the Bank of England have got that so wrong in early May, or does it reflect the high levels of uncertainty we now have to deal with in trying to predict the future?

Two pieces of information show some of the challenges there will be in introducing the test, track and trace project which the government is launching to encourage everyone who may have been in contact with a virus carrier to isolate at home. The new software which the army of contract tracers had been trained to use crashed on its first day in operation. And minutes released of the scientific advisory group SAGE show that the scientists believe that only half of those testing positive for the coronavirus do actually self-isolate.

In America, President Trump terminates America's relationship with the World Health Organisation which he continues to believe has been under China's control. Italians in the Lombardy region, which has suffered half of Italy's 33,000 deaths, many in makeshift field hospitals, rise up in protest against the Governor of Lombardy, Attilio Fontana. The Governor is given police protection as protestors berate him for not imposing a lockdown quickly enough and giving insufficient attention to care homes.

DAY 75: SATURDAY 30 MAY: *271,222 confirmed cases 38,161 deaths*

Hallelujah! To add to the many wonderful online musical offerings which have become available, Mark Strachan brings together a choir of 3,500 enthusiastic amateur singers for a performance of Handel's Messiah. For those whose summer would not be summer without the Proms, plans are in hand to create a special online Beethoven concert to mark the 250th anniversary of the great composer's birth with other concerts from the vast Proms archive.

Another baking hot day. May is drawing to a close as the sunniest and driest May since records began in 1929. Young people flock to parks to see friends, sunbathe, drink "cans" and play football, sometimes within social distancing rules, sometimes a little outside them. Michael Lucas aged 19 in Bushy Park, London tells The Times, "Being in quarantine is not good for my mental health because I can't have sex." His friend, Chloe Rowland, says, "We've been obeying the rules for the last ten weeks even though we're at the best years of our life. We should be going clubbing, making friends or meeting people at uni."

Still great uncertainty about the future of theatres and concert halls as re-opening with social distancing would reduce audiences to about a quarter of normal, This would not be viable for many venues and would also take away the essence of watching a performance being a shared experience for an audience. Oscar Wilde knew this when he said "I regard the theatre as the greatest of all art forms, the most immediate way in which a human being can share with another the sense of what it is to be a human being." Difficult to experience this if you are sitting in an almost empty auditorium. London's South Bank is the latest venue to sound the warning that without government support it fears it will go out of business. Theatre producer Sonia Friedman, who had to close down 18 productions because of the pandemic, including Tom Stoppard's much awaited new play, Leopoldstadt, says "British theatre is on the brink of total collapse, Without an urgent government rescue package 70 per cent of our performing arts companies will be out of business. It became clear the government had not noticed the extent of our problem and that we can't come back from social distancing."

The Downing Street press conference does not rest for the weekend. It is a seven days a week production. Today we are told by Deputy Chief Medical Adviser Professor Jonathan Van-Tam that, as we enter this period of easing lockdown, rather than being a sign that everything is becoming better, it is "a very dangerous moment." The scientists are unsure what the effect on the virus transmission rate will be of these further steps to come out of lockdown, schools reopening next week and many more shops in mid June; it is in effect a test to see what impact the easing of the restrictions will have on the numbers contracting the virus.

But there is good news for the 2.2 million people in the shielded category who have been at home for ten weeks without visitors, because their health conditions put them at risk of becoming seriously ill if they should become infected with the coronavirus. The welcome news is that they can now go out or, if living alone, arrange to meet with one person outdoors provided social distancing is maintained.

DAY 76: SUNDAY 31 MAY: *272,826 confirmed cases 38,376 deaths*

As the glorious weather continues estate agents report a significant upturn in the public's interest in moving home. Rightmove's online property site has just received six million visits in one day. Estate agents report substantial interest for properties in Cornwall, Devon and Hampshire as people seek a simpler life with plenty of fresh air to ward off the virus.

So finally, schools will open again tomorrow, or at least most primary schools will. So once more for some girls and boys that nervous, butterflies in the stomach feeling, and for most the happy expectation of being with friends again. Teachers have spent weeks creating classrooms and playgrounds which will encourage social distancing but are now ready to welcome the children back.

Bournemouth beach is one of many which is full to bursting point as thousands seek to make the most of the last day of what has been a record breaking May for sunny weather. There are some who are clearly socially distancing, but many others amongst the shorts and sandals crowds seem oblivious to the risks of being in close proximity to others.

For the first time since the coronavirus outbreak began it was not the main story on the BBC News at Ten, as riots spread across America to protest against police treatment of African Americans, prompted by the death of George Floyd whilst being detained by the police. But even here the coronavirus plays a part as many of those protesting are amongst the 30 million Americans now unemployed following the virus lockdown.

Boris Johnson had promised that 200,000 people a day would be tested for COVID-19 by the end of May. The government now falls back to an assertion that there is capacity to test 200,000 a day, although the actual number tested today was lower, around 115,000.

Brazil, where the government is said to be in disarray, is experiencing a surge in coronavirus deaths which now total 29,000 making Brazil the fourth worst in terms of virus deaths, having overtaken both France and Spain. But Brazil is a large country and we shouldn't be complacent about this news. Our rate of deaths per million people of 567 is over four times as high as Brazil's rate of 137 per million people.

Finally, on this sunny last day of May, where there was once Captain Tom, there is now Captain Tobias. Where 99 year old Captain Tom Moore walked with a frame around his garden to raise money for the NHS, now nine year old cerebral palsy sufferer Tobias Weller, also with the help of a walking frame, completes a remarkable marathon, 26.2 miles of slow painstaking effort, spread over 70 days, on the street outside his home. In so doing Tobias has raised more than £70,000 for Sheffield Children's Hospital and Paces, a centre for children with cerebral palsy.

DAY 77: MONDAY 1 JUNE: *274,762 confirmed cases 38,489 deaths*

A relaxing start to the new month. This is the day which sees a number of the further small steps that the government is taking to relax the lockdown restrictions. This is the day when we can now meet in socially distanced groups of six outdoors in England with slightly different arrangement in Scotland, Wales and Northern Ireland. Given the pictures of thousands of people who were crammed together on popular beaches at the weekend one wonders if the government's new rules for how we can meet up really are new freedoms. But, for those who have been following the government's regulations, they will be.

Around the country many sets of grandparents stood two metres away for a first glimpse of a new grandchild born during the lockdown. And those who have been shielding at home, because they were at a high risk of contracting the virus, took their first tentative steps outdoors after ten weeks isolating indoors. Coming out into the glint of the summer sunshine as if emerging into a new world. Buckingham Palace issued a picture of the 94 year old Queen riding out in the grounds of Windsor Castle, her first excursion outdoors since lockdown began. The picture was to show older people that there were small pleasures which could now be enjoyed again. And I am sure that the Queen would have been delighted that horse racing, the sport of Kings, returned today at Newcastle, albeit behind closed doors, where Zodiakos won the first race.

Most notably, today was the day when children returned to school, or at least perhaps half of them in the primary school age range did. Teachers welcomed them back with a temperature check to the forehead in the playground before guiding them into school buildings, where dots or tape on the floor showed the children how to keep at an appropriate distance from each other, before entering classrooms which contained smaller class sizes than usual and where only one child sat at each table. The first lesson was on social distancing and the importance of regular hand washing.

Cancer Research UK and Macmillan Cancer Support both highlight today the very large backlog which has accumulated in people not being seen for suspected cancers. Over two million people are not being examined quickly to confirm if treatment is needed. The delays have arisen either because hospital appointments are being deferred or missed, or because people have not seen their GP to seek a referral for examination. This is one of the additional human costs of the coronavirus pandemic which, if not addressed, could lead to additional deaths.

The government's much lauded new test, track and trace system, with 25,000 newly recruited staff trained to tell people to isolate if they had come into recent contact with someone who had tested positive for the virus, seems to have got off to a shaky start. A friend tells me that it has taken him several days to work through the complex logging in arrangements for the new staff, which involves accessing a number of different websites. And those who have managed to get past that stage say that they are waiting for the system to give them details of people they should speak to about the need to isolate. Matt Hancock, when challenged about this at today's Downing Street Press Conference, says that there is a low level of activity because the number of cases of people being infected with the virus is falling which is a good thing. But one surely would not go to the effort of training and paying 25,000 contact tracers if they were not going to do anything. In fact, there are still around 2,000 new cases a day, or almost 30,000 over the past two weeks, so there should be thousands of their contacts at risk of contracting the virus who need tracing. Also, to know whether it is safe to make further easing of the lockdown it must surely be a priority for large scale testing of the population to take place, and the contacts of those who test positive to be followed up. If Matt Hancock was returning to school today, I would only give him a beta minus for his answer.

Do you know one million people? The think tank Demos is keen to hear from you if you do as it launches its People's Commission on Life after COVID-19. This will take views from one million people about their hopes and concerns for life after the coronavirus pandemic.

I pop out to buy a birthday card and then have second thoughts about whether to post it. What is the current etiquette about whether to send birthday cards in the coronacrisis? To send with hand warmth all over it or not to send? I find helpful advice online from Royal Mail and the Greeting Cards Association who both encourage people to send cards saying that the coronavirus is unlikely to stay long on the surface of cards or envelopes.

The catalogue of people in the public eye being exposed for breaking the lockdown rules continues. Rosie Duffield MP, one of the Labour whips, resigns her post after the Mail on Sunday reports her for taking a walk with her lover in April before outdoor meetings with people from other households were allowed. And Prince Joachim of Belgium tests positive for COVID-19 after attending a party in Cordoba with his Spanish girlfriend. The question remains: are these breaches by well known people just representative of what a proportion of all people have been doing during the lockdown? Or does having privilege encourage behaviour which implies there is one rule for the public and another for those who lead us?

DAY 78: TUESDAY 2 JUNE: *276,332 confirmed cases 39,045 deaths*

Just how risky is it out there? Despite being told last Thursday that the government was reducing its alert level for the coronavirus pandemic from 4, meaning transmission of the virus is high, to 3 meaning it is in general circulation but not currently at a high level, it now transpires that the four Chief Medical Officers of the United Kingdom did not support this relaxation of the alert level, and it remains at 4. Did anyone tell that to the thousands of people flocking to the beach at the weekend? Would they have changed their plans if they had known?

Between 40 and 70 per cent of parents sent their children back to primary schools which re-opened yesterday, the remainder having concerns about whether it was safe to do so. But because of the need to have children spread out to observe social distancing, the proportion of children returning to schools may have been held down to a level optimal for schools to operate securely in the current corona environment. It is estimated that as many as three million primary school children may have had no face to face schooling in five months following the introduction of the lockdown at a critical stage of their development.

The government's plans to require those arriving in the UK to quarantine for 14 days has received strong opposition from the aviation sector, which has already announced large job losses as a result of the almost total lack of demand for flights, because of the virus risks associated with travelling abroad. Prime Minister Boris Johnson has recently accepted an invitation from Donald Trump to the next G7 summit in America where Trump is keen that world leaders should arrive in person as a demonstration that life is returning to normal. So potentially Boris may have to self-isolate for 14 days on his return. Even if there is some exemption he can claim from self-isolating, he may decide not to risk "one rule for the public, one for our leaders" after the recent Dominic Cummings trip to Durham affair. But, in response to the aviation industry concerns, the government is looking again at the idea of "air bridges" where travel would be allowed to and from countries with low rates of virus infection.

In our regional NHS Board meeting we are shown the results of a staff survey which was checking on the mental and physical wellbeing of our 250 staff who have been working remotely during the lockdown. Most seem to be enjoying working at home without the daily commute. 94 per cent say their level of "cheerfulness" is the same or better than usual though 66 per cent said that they were more concerned about the health of their family than previously. Staff seem to have adapted well to remote working with good levels of productivity. Our leadership team is considering what the best mix of remote and office based working will be when more normal times return.

My thoughts return to the plight of young people. They are more likely to be at risk of not finding a job or losing the one they had than more established workers. Around one in three of young people have lost their job since the lockdown began compared to one in six of the total working population. Being out of work brings a greater risk of being in debt. One in six young people have been increasing their level of debt compared with one in fourteen of the wider population.

I listen to an interesting webinar from the think tank, the Institute of Policy Research (IPPR) who have just published "Who wins, who pays" which looks at who are better off, and who are worse off, as a result of the coronavirus pandemic. Their argument is that the economic inequalities that previously existed between different groups of people will get worse as a result of the current economic downturn, despite the generous government income support packages and its various loan schemes. IPPR say that much of the financial support which the government has been giving to businesses and individuals will be paid over to banks and landlords, thus directing the government's money to sectors of society which, for the main part, are in good shape financially.

Although there is encouraging news that the most recent UK weekly coronavirus deaths total of 2,872 is the lowest for seven weeks there is also grim news from the ONS that excess deaths compared to more normal times are now running at over 60,000.

Finally, a message to Romeo and Juliet. The government has now made it a crime, not just a health risk, to stay overnight at someone else's home. You have been warned.

DAY 79: WEDNESDAY 3 JUNE: *277,985 confirmed cases 39,369 deaths*

As Mark Twain famously said, "There are lies, damn lies and statistics." Sir David Norgrove, Chairman of the UK Statistics Authority (UKSA), would presumably agree as he has just written to Health Minister Matt Hancock complaining about the government's statements about the number of people who have been tested for the coronavirus. Norgrove doesn't like the way that the government boosted the numbers by including large numbers of testing kits which had been sent out to the public without knowing how many of these were being used: "The aim seems to be to show the largest possible number of tests, even at the expense of understanding."

Keir Starmer, the Labour leader, who combines old fashioned civility with a probing legal mind, is beginning to lose his patience. Interviewed by the Guardian he is forthright. "I am putting the Prime Minister on notice that he has got to get a grip and restore public confidence in the government's handling of the epidemic. There is a growing concern the government is now winging it." He has a point. Boris Johnson made a big play about easing the lockdown, claiming that the scientific evidence supported lowering the virus alert level from four to a safer level of three. On that basis Johnson announced that schools and shops would re-open. But then the Chief Medical Officers of the UK all opposed reducing the alert level. So was the government right to go ahead with encouraging more people to interact in enclosed spaces if the alert level was unchanged? Or, as Starmer implies, is the government just making its mind up on key decisions, by following its own inclinations about how to balance protecting health with the desire for people to get back to work to stimulate the economy, and to reduce the public's reliance on the government's financial support?

At Prime Minister's Questions in Parliament Johnson gives a typically bullish endorsement of the government's achievements: "I am very proud of our record. We've protected the NHS, driven down death rates, there are far fewer hospital admissions." But is Johnson right to be so proud of the government's performance when, as well as the criticism over testing statistics, the ONS has just published data which suggests that the number of deaths from COVID-19 in the UK is over 50,000 based on the causes of death recorded by doctors, a higher number than the government's daily figures based on those who died after testing positive for the virus?

The Daily Telegraph breaks a story that the Prime Minister is going to "take back control" of the coronavirus crisis, with a shake up which will see the four groups overseeing the government's response chaired by the Ministers for foreign affairs, health, economy and business, and public services replaced by two committees: a strategy committee chaired by Johnson, and an operations committee chaired by Michael Gove. This mirrors the approach which was adopted for the final stages of Brexit. Some might ask what the Prime Minister has been doing if he is now, six months after the coronavirus first began its fateful journey around the world, "taking back control." Others may see this as a taking back control from his chief adviser, Dominic Cummings, who may have blotted his copybook after his controversial lockdown trip to Durham was revealed.

Parliament itself comes under scrutiny following Leader of the House Jacob Rees-Mogg's decision to require MPs to attend in person to vote, rather than use the online voting system that had been set up for them. Pictures show socially distancing MPs in a queue to vote stretching for over half a mile from inside the Palace of Westminster to outside in the gardens leading down to the Thames.

The concern that the virus risks are not receding as quickly as the government hoped they would is underlined by scientific adviser, Patrick Vallance, who says that the number of new people each day infected with the virus is coming down but only gradually. Vallance believes that around 8,000 people a day contract the virus, substantially higher than the 2,000 people a day who test positive for the virus. This highlights the need for the government's new test, track and trace scheme to be effective in its aim to contain the spread of the virus by identifying and isolating all those who have recently been in close proximity to someone known to have the virus. Initial information about how the new tracing system is working is not particularly encouraging. Only 40 per cent of those who have recently tested positive for the virus have input details of who they have been in contact with on to the tracing IT system; and only a third of those contacts have so far been spoken to and told to isolate. In other words, only just over 10 per cent of the people who need to be told to isolate to stop the spread of the virus have been contacted. The government says there is a huge amount of effort going into the tracing work so we will have to see if these figures improve in the coming days.

In Paris, cafes and restaurants have been allowed to reopen provided they serve customers outdoors. A first step in making Paris the centre of romantic encounters again. C'est magnifique!

DAY 80: THURSDAY 4 JUNE: *279,856 confirmed cases 39,728 deaths*

The weather has cooled after the remarkable long period of May sunshine. But in Waitrose local resident and television presenter, Richard Madeley, was sporting his permatan and his new beach blonde hairstyle. He looked as if he was ready to jet off to the sun but it is doubtful he will be doing that soon, given the requirement Boris Johnson is planning to introduce next week that those arriving back in the UK should quarantine for 14 days. This has been strongly opposed by the aviation and travel industries; a number of leading scientists have also said that it makes no sense to introduce a quarantine now when our rate of coronavirus infection is greater than most other countries. It would have made sense, the scientists say, to quarantine new arrivals in the early stages of the outbreak, when we could have shielded the UK from the virus coming in from countries which then had a higher rate of infection than we did. It seems that Boris Johnson and Dominic Cummings felt the public would be reassured by this move to quarantine new arrivals, even though this strategy had not been used earlier in the virus outbreak.

This is not the only issue where the Prime Minister has been looking to press ahead with responses to the current situation which would appear popular to the public, but at odds with the views of scientists, despite the government's oft repeated mantra that it "follows the science." Johnson had been keen to reduce social distancing from two metres to one, which was favoured by pubs and other businesses where imposing the two metres rule was likely to damage their trade; but his scientific advisers have opposed this change, as they had when Johnson wanted to reduce the alert level from four to three.

Some feel concerned that Johnson went ahead with saying that non-essential shops can re-open on 15 June when the alert level remained high at level 4; also, that this further relaxation of lockdown had come before there had been time to measure the effect on transmission of the virus from the 1 June change, allowing schools and workplaces to reopen and an increase in the number of people who can meet outdoors.

So we have a continuing tension between wanting to restore activity to our economy which had become almost dormant, and the risk that allowing more interaction between people, particularly inside buildings, may increase the spread of the coronavirus. We are not alone in having to consider this difficult balance. Sweden was one country which had sought to minimise restrictions on the public by keeping schools, bars and restaurants open with voluntary social distancing arrangements, rather than imposing a lockdown. But now, as their coronavirus deaths climb to 4,500, state epidemiologist Dr Anders Tegnell feels that the country should have pursued a middle road between their business as usual approach, and a full lockdown.

I listen to two talks today which show the impact on businesses of our own lockdown. At a webinar run by business advisers SchoolforCEOs, an online poll shows that 26 per cent of those participating are seriously concerned that their business is struggling to cope with the effects of the economic downturn. And a presentation by food sector expert Peter Backman reveals the dramatic effect that the lockdown is having on the landscape of the eating out sector. Many restaurants, which were already operating on small profit margins, will no longer be viable as the need for social distancing will reduce the number of customers they can cater for. Even those who can continue are likely to find that some customers stay away, concerned about the health risks and the idea of waiters and waitresses in masks. Inevitably many of the jobs of the two million employed in the sector will be at risk, although take away food outlets and home delivery businesses may find demand increases as the public moves away from eating in restaurants.

Another challenge to Prime Minister Johnson's statement yesterday on the government's coronavirus performance, "I am very proud of our record." Stephen Reicher of St Andrew's University clearly has a different view of the government saying, "It is so patently out of touch with reality that it lowers trust and undermines government's influence."

Each day brings stories of human kindness or something to soften the harsh realities of a world in crisis. In Barcelona, a patient in a critical care bed is wheeled out by five medical staff in protective clothing on to the promenade to look out at the beach and the sea. Nearer home, in Peterborough, Suzanne Vaughan is joyously reunited with her two daughters Bella aged nine, and Hetty aged seven, whom she had not seen for nine weeks as she worked 50 hour weeks as an operating department practitioner at Kings Lynn Hospital.

Someone, somewhere, always does well out of a crisis. Eric Yuan, founder of video conference platform Zoom, finds his 20 per cent shareholding is now worth 10.8 billion dollars as daily worldwide users of Zoom have increased from 10 million before the pandemic to 300 million today. But even Yuan cannot sleep easy as Zoom faces increasing competition from Microsoft, Facebook and Google all looking to create a bigger presence in the video conferencing market place.

5 EMERGING INTO A NEW NORMAL

Days 81 to 100: 5 June to 24 June

DAY 81: FRIDAY 5 JUNE: *281,661 confirmed cases 39,904 deaths*

My friend, who a few days ago was still struggling through a complex logging in and training process to become one of the government's 25,000 new contact tracers, is still not at the stage where he can start work. He tells me that he is waiting to access what will be the fifth different website he has to deal with as part of his application and he is still only part way through the training. His difficulties are reflected in a webinar comment to tracing staff by Chief Operating Officer Tony Prestedge, who says that the tracing system at present is "imperfect" and will not be fully operational until September or October. The much lauded app to enable smartphone users testing positive for the virus to trigger follow-up calls to other app users they have been in close contact with, part of what Boris Johnson called "a world-beating system", is not ready to be used. In trials the public are yet to feel comfortable with using the technology.

There are increasing feelings that some of the government's current actions should have been in place at a much earlier stage of our response to the coronavirus pandemic. Should plans to quarantine new arrivals in the country, boosting the number of people who can be tested for the virus each day, and introducing the system to trace and isolate the contacts of those who test positive for the virus all have been there from the outset? A report by Public Health England and the Universities of Manchester and Cambridge on 12 February, which has just been made public, recommended a ten fold increase in the test and trace capacity. But this does not seem to have been followed up; the government then found in early March that there were too many new cases of the virus to contact everyone who might be at risk, and concentrated testing on hospitals and subsequently, care homes.

Transport Minister Grant Shapps, who previously said the evidence for wearing face masks on public transport was inconclusive, now instructs us that face masks are to be worn on public transport to provide some reassurance to those now returning to offices or businesses they had vacated when the lockdown commenced.

The protests in America about the death of African American George Floyd whilst being detained by a white police officer is now gaining momentum as an international movement, Black Lives Matter. Protests in sympathy with African Americans, and highlighting institutional racism in other countries, are now planned in Britain and around the world at a time when large gatherings had been banned because of the risks of spreading the coronavirus.

At the Downing Street press conference today Health Minister Matt Hancock has the sorry task of announcing that UK deaths from the COVID-19, based on those who had tested positive for the virus, have passed 40,000. He is pressed by BBC Health correspondent Hugh Pym for his reaction given that the government's scientific adviser Patrick Vallance had said at the outset of the outbreak that 20,000 deaths "would be a good outcome." A sombre Hancock says it is "a time of sorrow for us all. Each one is an impact on a family which will never be the same again." He says "I will redouble my efforts to fight this virus." Sadly, a different doubling has already occurred if we are at twice the level of deaths that was defined as "a good outcome." It seems impossible not to conclude from these figures, and our position as second only to America in coronavirus deaths, that the government's response to the pandemic has overall been poor, notwithstanding the huge efforts made by the NHS, care home staff and other front line workers to look after the population in these dangerous times.

DAY 82: SATURDAY 6 JUNE: *283,311 confirmed cases 40,261 deaths*

I have become used to making some attempt to cut my own hair. But those yearning for a long awaited return to a hairdresser will have to wait a little longer. Hairdressers will not reopen before 4 July at the earliest. This prompts leader of the House of Commons Jacob-Rees Mogg to rather improbably describe himself as "a long haired lover from Liverpool."

The government is planning to allow supermarkets and other large shops to open all day on Sunday as part of the plans to re-stimulate the economy. This is, however opposed by Mark Spencer. I was initially surprised that Marks & Spencer would be against increasing their opening hours but it turns out that Mark Spencer is the Conservative Party Chief Whip. He is concerned that more conservative Conservatives will be against extending shopping hours on the day of rest.

The Times carries a remarkable story which highlights how desperately the government had to seek new avenues for procuring PPE at the height of the coronavirus outbreak. The government entered into many contracts with companies it did not normally do business with but which had access to PPE supplies. As part of this, PestFix, a small pest control company with only 16 employees, was awarded a staggeringly large contract worth £108 million, on the basis that it had told government officials it had contacts with PPE suppliers.

In Brazil, President Bolsonaro is taking a gamble. As Brazil's death rate from the virus is increasing daily and now totals 34,000 (the third highest behind America and Britain) Bolsonaro announces that he is keen to ease the lockdown saying, "Brazil cannot go on like this. The collateral impact of the lockdown will be far greater than those people who unfortunately lose their lives." The spectre of mass unemployment looms over all countries which are having prolonged lockdowns.

Black Lives Matter protests are becoming large scale around the world. Here thousands attend rallies in London, Manchester, Leicester and Sheffield. The cause that they are protesting about, the end of racism within organisations which impact on our daily lives, is heartfelt. But as a largely peaceful demonstration in central London turns to violence against police in Whitehall, one senses an air of pent up emotion is being released against those who wield authority in these dark times we are living through. Home Secretary Pritti Patel asked people not to demonstrate because of the risk of the coronavirus spreading amongst large crowds saying, "We must put public health first."

Those who need respite from all these anxious times will, from 15 June, be able to seek individual moments of private prayer in places of worship but the shared experience of a service with a congregation will not be restarting for the time being. Presumably a socially distanced confession could, however, be arranged if required.

DAY 83: SUNDAY 7 JUNE: *284,868 confirmed cases 40,465 deaths*

John Edmunds, an epidemiologist of the London School of Hygiene and Tropical Medicine, tells Andrew Marr that "lockdown should have happened earlier." He says "I think it would have been hard to do it. I think the data we were dealing with in the early part of March and our situational awareness was really quite poor. And so I think it would have been very hard to pull the trigger at that point, but I wish we had, I wish we had gone into lockdown earlier. I think that has cost us a lot of lives unfortunately,"

Health Minister Matt Hancock is interviewed on the same show by Marr. Asked whether he felt the government should have acted earlier he says "Taking into account everything we knew my view is that we made the right decisions at the right time guided by the Chief Medical Officer and the Chief Scientific Officer." Is this a coded answer which means that there was insufficient information in early March on which to instruct the country to begin a lockdown? That an absence of information which might have informed a decision to lockdown earlier than 23 March then makes the decision to lockdown on 23 March the right decision? Does Hancock in his heart really believe that 23 March was the optimal date to lockdown when, inevitably, the more the virus had already spread by then the greater the number of deaths that would ensue?

On the subject of testing, Hancock acknowledged that only now, on 7 June, had testing kits been delivered to all care homes and admitted that this didn't mean that all residents and their carers had now been tested. This does seem a weakness in the speed of arranging testing of a substantial group of people who were most at risk of contracting the virus with the added risk that carers might spread the virus into the wider community. New analysis, which suggests that care home residents are on course to account for more than half of deaths caused directly or indirectly by the coronavirus, reinforces this view.

Whilst the government plans to allow supermarkets and other large shops to open all day on Sundays spare a thought for our "nation of shopkeepers", a phrase attributed to Napoleon though nobody knows if he really did say that. More than six in ten High Street shops urgently need more cash to prevent closure whilst only one in five expect to survive the pandemic, says the Independent Retailers Association. It is not just High Street shops whose future is in peril but dentists also. They have been allowed to reopen but face very high expenditure for the protective clothing they will need to wear whilst examining our fillings, which could add £30 to the cost of treating each patient.

For the second day running large crowds demonstrate in UK cities against racism in the Black Lives Matter campaign which started in America. Some of the protesting has a violent overtone. There has been daubing of the statue of Winston Churchill in Parliament Square and the toppling in Bristol of a statue of Edward Colston, an eighteenth century philanthropist who had endowed schools, hospitals, almshouses and churches in Bristol, but made his money from the trade in African slaves. When asked why the large crowds of protestors are not having greater regard for the pandemic and the need for social distancing one female protestor says, "There are two pandemics and we have to address the pandemic of racism."

The day ends with some good news. Deaths from the coronavirus in the past twenty four hours were 77, the lowest since the lockdown commenced on 23 March.

DAY 84: MONDAY 8 JUNE: *286,194 confirmed cases 40,542 deaths*

It feels as if we are entering a period of peace but without knowing whether the peace will be prolonged or if another war is about to flare up around us. Today brings the news that, whilst there were 55 more reported deaths yesterday of people testing positive for the coronavirus, and this may be an understatement because there is sometimes a lag in reporting weekend deaths, this daily figure is the lowest since 20 March, three days before the lockdown began. The number of new coronavirus cases is also at its lowest level since lockdown.

Matt Hancock sounds like Shakespeare's Henry V rallying the troops at Agincourt when he says, "Coronavirus is in retreat across the land." If it stays this way those of us who have survived will all be grateful. We should not, though, be too self-congratulatory given tens of thousands of families have lost loved ones before this welcome period of relative calm. The big unknown of course is whether the coronavirus will continue its retreat, or whether it will see the opening of non-essential shops next week, and the government's plans to allow pubs and restaurants to serve outdoor food and drink later this month, as opportunities to mount a new offensive against the British public.

In the meantime, the government is seeking to wage war against the virus on other fronts. Today its new rules requiring most people entering the UK to spend 14 days in quarantine came into force. The phrase continually used by Prime Minister Boris Johnson, Health Minister Matt Hancock and other Ministers has been that the government's strategy in fighting the virus is "following the science." Yet on this important new policy the scientific group advising government (SAGE) was not consulted.

A number of scientists continue to argue that there was a stronger case for imposing quarantine arrangements in the early stages of the virus outbreak to limit the spread of the virus by people arriving from China, and other countries where the virus had taken a hold. The government chose not to do this saying it would not help significantly given the virus was already freely spreading within Britain. But imposing quarantine arrangements, or stringent testing of new arrivals into Britain in the very early stages, would surely have limited the number of people carrying the virus who were then in a position to infect others. New Zealand, which totally closed its borders on 19 March (as Australia also did the next day), has now declared itself coronavirus free after 17 successive days with no new infections identified, and a total of only 22 deaths from the coronavirus since the outbreak began.

Sensing that the British public may not relish having to quarantine on returning to the UK from overseas holidays, Prime Minister Johnson has asked officials to look at how "air corridors" could be set up with countries with low infection rates, where going into quarantine on return to the UK would not be necessary.

A report by consultants Laing Buisson estimates that by the end of June more than half of all coronavirus related deaths will have occurred in care homes with care home deaths from the virus in excess of 30,000. Today Matt Hancock announces a task force to tackle infection rates in care homes. He pledges that care homes will have the support, the training and the resources they need. Should this particular stable door not have been bolted two months ago? Is there not a similarity with the introduction now of the quarantine rules for returning to the UK, an idea with some merit, but which would have been far more effective if it had been in place as the coronavirus first began to spread in Britain.

In NW England, where increasing cases of the virus are causing concern, many primary schools have not reopened as they have in other parts of the country. Where pupils have returned to the classroom a number of head teachers have said that jackets and ties should not be worn because of the difficulty of cleaning them regularly. How many schoolchildren of previous generations longed to cast off their jackets and ties as the thermometer soared during the summer term.

DAY 85: TUESDAY 9 JUNE: *287,399 confirmed cases 40,597 deaths*

A good new initiative called Internship UK will give young people the opportunity to experience online internships during these difficult times.

The young people will be able to talk to an organisation's staff and take part in discussions and exercises to learn more about the nature of their work. Young people need to be shown where job opportunities may be available for them as many had job offers and internships withdrawn when the lockdown put a brake on business activity. Those young people who find, in the coming months, that their furloughed jobs in the hospitality and retail sectors are not continued because of the downturn, need to be given the chance to retrain for sectors which can employ them. The recently announced new government apprenticeship scheme may help with this.

Our online regional NHS Board meeting today spends time focussing on the future. We decide to launch a project to encourage the million people living in our region of Cambridgeshire and Peterborough to address obesity. This makes sense from a general health perspective given that obesity is often the trigger for diabetes. But dealing with obesity will also help people avoid falling into the category of those who are at a higher risk of developing serious illness if they become infected with the coronavirus. We also discuss the extra demand for mental health services in these troubling times. GPs are already seeing an increase in the number of people displaying symptoms of anxiety, and some of these will need access to counselling and other services in due course. Today NHS Confederation, which represents NHS organisations, says that by the end of the year almost 10 million people may be waiting for hospital procedures because infection control and dealing with COVID-19 patients will reduce patient throughput; to improve our understanding of this issue we discuss our work to estimate the demand for different hospital services, and the capacity we will have to meet this demand.

The way in which so many people have responded to the coronacrisis with acts of kindness and charity has been one of the truly uplifting aspects of these recent weeks. Some acts have been small ones: collecting shopping and leaving it outside the door of an elderly person who is isolating, or those who have taken the time to telephone a friend or family member they had lost touch with. And there has been an increase in charitable giving which rose by 41 per cent in April. But there is a paradox here. Whilst donations to the NHS and food banks have surged other charities have experienced a substantial fall in donations, as fundraising events, both big events like the London Marathon and smaller local events, have been cancelled. New data shows that giving to charities not linked to the NHS has dropped by 50 per cent with the top 50 charities faring particularly badly, recording a 93 per cent drop in income. New ways need to be found to reactivate the public's previous generosity to these charities. Pro Bono Economic estimates that as many as one in six charities may run out of funds to continue their work by the end of the year.

The government has had to backtrack on its aim that all children of primary school age would return to school before the autumn. Arranging classrooms in a way which allows social distancing has meant that a smaller number of children can be accommodated. Because those schools which have reopened were phasing the return of pupils and some parents were choosing not to send their children back to school the difficulties in coping with previous pupil numbers did not initially materialise. But the government now accepts that time is needed to rethink how schools will be able to take back all their students into a safe environment for learning.

George Smiley would have been quietly amused. Sir Andrew Parker, the recently retired head of MI5, reveals that after he attended a meeting on the pandemic with government Ministers and their advisers in early February, he immediately implemented MI5's pandemic emergency plan which included the bulk buying of hand sanitiser. Smiley might have preferred gloves.

DAY 86: WEDNESDAY 10 JUNE: *289,140 confirmed cases 40,883 deaths*

Do you have a toothache? I hope not. Only a third of dentists are opening in England after the government allowed them to, and those that are may only be able to see around a quarter of the number of usual patients because of the need to continually clean their treatment rooms. Dentists are also asking for access to government stocks of PPE. But definitely try not to get toothache in Cardiff or Swansea; dentists in Wales are not reopening until January 2021.

My friend e-mails to say he is still waiting to complete the logging in stage to the government's new contact tracing system two weeks after signing on as one of the government's new team of 25,000 contact tracers. Scientists tell the House of Lords that as few as 15 per cent of those who have tested positive with the coronavirus are isolating properly; if this is correct, it wastes all the effort of running a test, track and trace system as the virus will still be passed on if people who are, or may be, infected, don't stop coming into contact with other people.

Professor Neil Ferguson of University College, London, whose modelling early in the coronavirus outbreak told the government that it risked as many as 500,000 deaths if it did not impose a lockdown, now says that if the lockdown had been imposed a week earlier than it was, on 23 March, half of COVID-19 deaths could have been avoided. "Government scientists did not realise how many people were already infected in early March," says Ferguson. Disturbing disclosures showing how critical the timing of the lockdown was as the virus began to spread widely.

Two days after Matt Hancock announced the formation of a taskforce to address infection rates in care homes new figures show that in the week to 29 May deaths in care homes were still running at high levels, 49 per cent above average for the time of year. The tensions in running care homes under pressure is shown by new data from the charity Compassion in Care; they say they have had reports from staff members of 23 care homes where information about residents testing positive for the coronavirus was withheld by managers from staff and families for fear of alarming them, or giving the care home a bad name.

Two more reports highlight the serious impact on business activity as a result of closing shops in the lockdown. The OECD says that Britain's economy could shrink by 11 per cent this year (or more if there is a second wave of the pandemic); this would place us as the worst affected prosperous nation, and significantly more affected than the USA and Germany where economic activity is forecast to reduce by 7 per cent. The World Bank predicts a worldwide contraction in economic activity of 5 per cent and the deepest global recession in decades. On 7 May the new Bank of England governor, Andrew Bailey, suggested that the British economy could recover by the end of 2020 if easing lockdown proved successful. A lot depends on the events of the next few months; to what extent will consumer demand return to stimulate business activity, and can we avoid another wave of virus infections and a further lockdown period?

Boris Johnson, at the Downing Street press conference, at least had some good news. Bubbles. From Saturday, those living on their own, or single parents with children, can form a "support bubble" by going to live with another household. As the Prime Minister explains, this is to alleviate loneliness and to allow many people on their own to live with loved ones; this may enable a parent on their own, for example, to live with a married son or daughter or a single mother taking her children to live with her parents. It also permits a flourishing of new coronavirus romances and living together arrangements when, in recent weeks, new lovers visiting each other had become illegal. Oh, and zoos can reopen. Folksinger Julie Felix, who died in April, is doubtless reprising in the great folk club in the sky her most well known song "We're going to the zoo, zoo, zoo, how about you, you, you?"

DAY 87: THURSDAY 11 JUNE: *290,143 confirmed cases 41,128 deaths*

Following the Prime Minister's announcement yesterday that single people can form a "bubble" with another household, could we soon be seeing bubbles forming all over the place rather like those little soap tubes we used to have as children where you would blow through a ring and see a succession of newly formed bubbles float away through the air? There is certainly a great potential for new bubbles as 6.6 million people live on their own and 1.5 million are single parents who are also allowed to "bubble" with another household under these new arrangements. There does not seem to be any requirement under these new rules for people to register that they are moving into a "bubble" so we may never know how many new bubbles Boris Johnson has created with his Prime Ministerial soap tube.

Whilst Johnson continues to avoid responding on whether the government has made mistakes, saying it would be "premature" to come to any judgements on the government's performance, Chief Medical Officer Chris Whitty was open in yesterday's press conference, acknowledging that his greatest regret is the slow increase in testing in the early stages of our coronavirus outbreak. One got a sense of the difficulties Ministers faced in making decisions in Whitty's comment that "We were unable to work out exactly where we were and we were trying to see our way through the fog." It may therefore be "Whitty's fog" that contributed to the view that Professor Ferguson expressed yesterday that, had we entered a lockdown a week earlier, half of the coronavirus deaths could have been avoided.

Much later than some would say it should have started, the government's new test and trace system is finally swinging into action. There were mixed results from its first full week of operations. Of the just over 8,000 new cases of positive test results tracers reached around two-thirds to get details of who they had been in contact with; but around 2,700 could not be reached. Those testing positive who were contacted provided details of 32,000 people they had been in contact with, and we are told that 85 per cent of these are now self-isolating. As usual Health Minister Matt Hancock is schoolboy bullish about the scheme "It has made a huge impact. I am confident it will be world class." He would have to say this, wouldn't he, given that Prime Minister Johnson had previously said it would be "world beating."

Her Majesty Zooms. It's official. Pictures are released of The Queen taking part in her first ever official public video call. A group of people with caring responsibilities were invited to a Zoom conference call with Her Majesty and Princess Anne. Introduced by a senior courtier with the words "Her Majesty the Queen is ready to join the call" the Queen asked the group questions about how they coped and told them "I am very impressed by what you have achieved already. I am very glad to have been able to join you today."

DAY 88: FRIDAY 12 JUNE: *291,409 confirmed cases 41,279 deaths*

Although Boris Johnson said two days ago that it would be premature to come to any judgements on the government's performance in managing the coronacrisis, The National Audit Office (NAO) has published the first independent report into the preparations for the pandemic. The report particularly highlighted the difficulties facing care homes, which the NAO attributed to the "problematic" relationship between social care and the NHS, which had never been fully integrated despite successive attempts which included renaming the government authority as the Department of Health and Social Care.

The NAO report noted that 25,000 patients had been discharged to care homes at the height of the pandemic, but not all of these had been tested for COVID-19 before discharge, with priority being given to patients with symptoms. The NAO also underlined the problems with PPE, noting that central government stocks had only met 20 per cent of the gowns needed for a reasonable worst case scenario, 33 per cent of eye protection and 50 per cent of aprons. Care homes had been less well supplied with no more than 15 per cent of their PPE coming from government stocks. Meg Hillier, the doughty Labour MP who chairs Parliament's Public Accounts Committee, said "front line workers had been "badly let down by the government's failure to prepare properly" and that "care home residents were an afterthought." It does seem remarkable in the cold light of day that, for a government that had been supposedly regularly practising for a possible pandemic and claimed to be "very well prepared," these failings should have occurred when the real situation arrived.

Back in the here and now the sharp drop in the number of people presenting themselves for possible cancer treatment continues to concern the medical profession. In April the number of referrals by GPs sending patients to hospital for cancer symptoms to be investigated was 80,000, sixty per cent lower than the just under 200,000 in April 2019. It appears many people were concerned about contracting the virus from GPs or hospitals, or they did not want to overburden the NHS. Either way it means that cancers may have been developing undetected making the patient more at risk if the cancer is not treated early. And for those who did need treatment the NHS goal of starting treatment within two months was only achieved in 74 per cent of cases (compared with a target of 85 per cent), a reflection of the reduced capacity in hospitals whilst COVID-19 was the central focus and strict infection control throughout a hospital had to be maintained.

The tension between health and wealth continues. The government's desperate wish to restart the economy to avoid high unemployment and a permanent slump in business activity, weighed against not wanting increased social contact to produce another wave of coronavirus infections. The seriousness of the economic decline produced by the lockdown was brought into stark reality by new figures today. In April the output of the economy collapsed by a staggering 20 per cent, three times higher than the drop following the 2008 banking crisis. But hardly surprising with non-essential shops, restaurants, pubs, hotels, visitor attractions, gyms, theatres and cinemas all closed. Prime Minister Johnson says "we will bounce back" but to what extent can such a dramatic loss of business activity be recovered?

The government is hearing the cries of pubs, theatres and many shops that the two metre social distancing rule severely restricts the customers they can accommodate, making many of them potentially unviable. The government would like to relax the two metre rule if they can feel fairly confident that this will not lead to a surge of new virus cases. The scientific group SAGE advising the government says that at two metres there is a 3 per cent chance of catching the virus from someone who transmits it through the air, and at one metre's distance the risk increases to 13 per cent. But they note that ultimately it is a political decision on the trade-off between the benefits to the economy of reducing the distancing rule, and the possible increase in infections this may bring.

Caution versus common sense seems to have caused an awful muddle in the advice for boarding aircraft during the pandemic. New advice from the Department for Transport says that those arriving at airports are "strongly encouraged" to check hand luggage into the hold. Michael

O'Leary, Chief Executive of Ryanair, says that, given up to eight people may typically handle luggage between check-in and luggage collection, "anyone with an IQ above that of a plant will realise that checking in bags is a far riskier proposition in a COVID world than you bringing your own carry-on luggage." You pays your money . . .

DAY 89: SATURDAY 13 JUNE: *292,950 confirmed cases 41,481 deaths*

On the day that "support bubbles" can release people from the torment of living on their own Lucy Gibson makes a 200 mile trip by two trains and a taxi from her home in Watford to visit her sister and children in Stockport. The three children run to greet her, just one sign of normal life returning to a wider family network which will have been repeated in hundreds of homes across the country.

Lucy Gibson is not the only person with cause for celebration today. A sunny day marks the Queen's official 94th birthday. Instead of the usual Trooping of the Colour ceremony, the Queen sits on a dais in the grounds of Windsor Castle watching a carefully executed socially distanced musical march past by Welsh Guardsmen and the Band of the Household Division. And celebration in New Zealand, which so carefully avoided the worst effects of the coronavirus and is now virus free, as rugby returns, not behind closed doors, but in front of a packed cheering crowd. When will we see that again at Twickenham?

In The Times, columnist Matthew Parris is in a combatant mood. Have we, he asks, sold ourselves into a world where the economy has been devastated though lockdown by believing scientific forecasts of the doom that the coronavirus would deliver if those of us who are fit and well continued to go about our normal lives? Parris understands that steps such as social distancing and lockdown will have suppressed the virus but he queries how much benefit was derived from particular lockdown measures. He also believes that the model produced by Professor Ferguson of Imperial College, London, which predicted that as many as 500,000 might die if the virus was left to just spread across the community, may have been over-cautious; Parris points to Imperial's previous advice on foot and mouth disease which led to the slaughter of six million animals, most of them uninfected. It is reasonable for Parris to pose these questions. Unfortunately, we will never know for certain the answers as, in making its particular decisions on the lockdown, the government determined that the alternatives were not pursued.

Television news shows disturbing scenes of aggressive violence against police in central London by mob crowds supposedly seeking to protect statues threatened by those who support the Black Lives Matter campaign which has gained momentum over the past week, following the death of George Floyd in America whilst detained by the police. A significant number of the hard line mob attacking police were from football supporter groups. Have the weeks of government restrictions, including the cancellation of sporting events, given rise to pent up frustrations which are now being released when a suitable cause emerges?

DAY 90: SUNDAY 14 JUNE: *294,375 confirmed cases 41,662 deaths*

Boris Johnson appeared in public today for the first time since the lockdown almost three months ago. He was going shopping. Or more accurately, he was going to the shops, to the Westfield shopping centre in East London, to rally the public to return to shopping when non-essential shops reopen tomorrow. The message he wants to get across is "shop with confidence." But will the public rush back to the shops when faced with social distancing and strict infection control arrangements over the handling of clothing, books and other items? Many people will have the cash that could be spent because shops, restaurants and pubs have been closed for so long; but will they be prepared to venture out to spend it, particularly when they could buy what they need online and avoid the restrictions of visiting a real shop? Chancellor Rishi Sunak appeals to our "animal instincts" to shop (have you seen kangaroos or koala bears shopping?) and hints at a possible reduction in VAT to encourage shoppers. Back at the Westfield shopping centre Johnson orders a cup of coffee from a man working behind a Perspex screen.

The requirement to keep two metres apart for social distancing is seen by many retailers and also restaurants as restricting the number of customers they can deal with and also deterring some potential customers from turning up, so that re-opening may ultimately prove to be unviable. So the Prime Minister announces a review of the two metre rule and other possible alternatives, with the aim of completing the review before pubs and restaurants are due to re-open on 4 July. Many of the public are cautious about relaxing the two metre rule but Johnson also has the voice of shop, restaurant and pub owners in his ear about easing the rule. He also makes the point that with infection rates now down to only one in 1,700 the chances of people coming into contact with someone who has the coronavirus has significantly reduced in recent times. France now operates a one metre rule but with the requirement to wear face masks in public places.

But just when we thought things were getting easier concerning news from China of a second wave of infections, or a possible new virus, as 64 new deaths are recorded, the majority linked to a food market in Beijing. The government's new arrangements to quarantine travellers arriving in the UK, criticised as being too late to have much effect, would suddenly appear very prescient if there is a new wave of infections in China.

Many of those who like to put out the clothes they will wear the next day before they go to sleep will also put out tonight a face mask. Tomorrow they are compulsory on public transport and 3,000 extra police and transport officers will check they are being worn.

DAY 91: MONDAY 15 JUNE: *295,889 confirmed cases 41,698 deaths*

They were queuing at 7.30am in Birmingham on the day that shops (or non-essential shops to be precise) reopened. For those who had been yearning for three months for that sense of anticipation of a good shopping trip, thinking of what they wanted to buy, prepared to be lured by an unexpected bargain, the day they had waited for had finally arrived. Retail therapy had returned. Around the country (but not those in Scotland and Wales, who will have to wait a little longer) shoppers patiently queued two metres apart, the queues snaking down streets or around car parks. A Nike store in central London was a rare example of an undisciplined first day of the sales rush to gain access to the store. One female shopper told BBC News "I am really excited, it's a bit of normality, a shopping spree is different than going online."

The numbers of people who had come out shopping looked like it was almost normal although retail experts said it was about a third down on this time last year. The careful arrangements retailers had put in place inside the shops, where many staff were protected by masks and screens at serving points, customers were distanced from each other and goods which had been touched and not bought were withdrawn from sale to be cleaned, worked well. But despite the great efforts made by both customers and shops to re-establish the culture of shopping, many retailers were still concerned by the loss of trade which was inevitable from adhering to the two metre distancing. Peter Cowgill, Chief Executive of JD Sports, says that ultimately the two metre rule is not viable for business. So we await the review of the distancing rules which Boris Johnson announced yesterday.

One topic not mentioned in this diary to date, but which can make its first appearance here is: BREXIT. Prime Minister Johnson returns to BREXIT discussions with European colleagues to try to advance discussions on a trade deal as not completing one by the deadline of 31 January 2021 would add more woe to our devastated economy. One imagines Johnson is also a little envious of President Macron who has been able to tell France the coronacrisis is over with schools open and restaurants now able to return to serving customers indoors. Somehow Macron makes it sound so typically French when he says "We are going to rediscover the pleasure of being together, of going back to work fully but also of entertaining and cultivating ourselves."

Whilst French students returned *en masse* to school England took a further small step to reopening schools with secondary schools taking back 25 per cent of their full complement of pupils on any given day; this will mean most students will receive a day a week of face to face tuition. This on a day when a study by University College London shows that two million children, one in five of all schoolchildren, have been doing less than an hour of school work a day or none at all during lockdown. Even the average is only two and a half hours a day.

On this day, when non-essential shops re-opened, more pupils returned to school and face masks became compulsory on public transport, we await to see whether these changes can take place without any significant increase in the coronavirus infection rate. Possible glimmers of hope for a better summer ahead: Majorca today welcomed 200 Germans arriving in Palma to test its plans to open up again as a tourist destination. And some scientists in Italy and America, countries which have suffered significantly from the pandemic, now perceive that the virus is possibly not as strong in its ability to cause serious illness as it was at the outset of the outbreak. Time will tell whether we are over the worst.

DAY 92: TUESDAY 16 JUNE: *296,857 confirmed cases 41,736 deaths*

A day of biblical proportions as finally medicine finds a way of easing some of the effects of the coronavirus. A test on 6,000 COVID-19 patients by the epidemiology department of Oxford University finds that a widely available steroid tablet, Dexamethasone, which costs just 50 pence a day, can significantly ease the condition of COVID-19 patients who are receiving ventilator or oxygen support in hospital. Testing found that the steroid reduced deaths of those on ventilators by a third and those on oxygen by a fifth. It helps patients by stopping the immune system from over reacting to the coronavirus which weakens patients and can precipitate death. Prime Minister Johnson says he is delighted by this breakthrough by British medicine which will be a success story worldwide, given Dexamethasone's general availability.

As had been expected bad news on the job front. Benefit claimants (those unemployed or on low incomes) have increased to 2.8 million, the highest for 27 years. This may only be the tip of the iceberg as businesses are due to be making decisions this week on how many of their furloughed staff they can afford to keep on; they must give their staff notice of any proposed redundancies in August when businesses must start contributing to the costs of the furlough scheme. British Airways, which had announced it was going to cut 12,000 jobs because of the slump in the aviation sector, was branded "a national disgrace" by Parliament's Transport Committee but later on the company said that no final decisions had been taken and it would meet with employees to discuss the way forward.

At a time when many families are struggling with financial worries as a result of the lockdown Manchester United footballer Marcus Rashford has prompted a government U-turn to help families on low incomes. Rashford, United's 22 year old star striker, spoke about his own experience as a child from a disadvantaged background when urging Boris Johnson to reverse his decision not to extend the free school meals system into the summer holidays. Today Rashford's plea was acted upon as Johnson reversed his stance; now 1.3 million free school meals will be enjoyed by those most in need of them.

On BBC this evening a tense three part series portraying the public health response to the infamous novichok poisonings in Salisbury in 2018 reached its finale. Filmed before the coronavirus pandemic there were chilling similarities, the need to quickly track down anyone who may have come into contact with the poison and the need to communicate with an anxious public whether there were risks to their safety. Salisbury eventually came through the scare and we must hope that we do too.

And even in a lockdown Royal Ascot, that most familiar event of a Great British summer, still goes ahead albeit with no crowds of cheering spectators. But many of those who would normally have been at Ascot upheld its traditions by dressing up at home, morning suits for the men, summer frocks and fascinator hats for the women. And much loved jockey, Frankie Dettori, does his trademark flying dismount when winning on Frankly Darling.

DAY 93: WEDNESDAY 17 JUNE: *298,136 confirmed cases 41,969 deaths*

After yesterday's news that those claiming benefits for being unemployed or on low income had increased to 2.8 million, the country awaits to see what will happen to the 9.1 million people who are on the government's furlough scheme (that is being paid by the government whilst having had their work put on hold by their employer). Also, a further 2.6 million self-employed people are receiving government support because their income has reduced or has stopped completely. It seems likely that a significant proportion of this total of 11.7 million people (more than a third of the nation's workforce) could become unemployed in the coming weeks. Businesses, now required to start paying towards the furlough scheme, may start to shed staff and some of the self-employed may declare themselves as unemployed if work opportunities do not materialise.

It appears a particularly difficult time for young people with news that graduate job openings are down a disturbing 77 per cent, from nearly 15,000 to just over 3,000. And for those lucky enough to get job offers, salaries are lower than before the pandemic. For those who can't find a job in the field they had hoped for, previous opportunities to "temp" in hospitality or retail, whilst looking for jobs in their preferred occupation, are now going to be few and far between. The ONS said that unemployment had doubled for young people aged 18 to 24 between March and May, with young people four times more likely to be unemployed than people of other ages. Prince Charles, who set up the Prince's Trust in 1976 to help young people's job prospects, warned today that the problems faced by young people and a lack of support were "potentially devastating," and called for action to "prevent this crisis from defining the prospects of a generation."

Today alarm bells were also sounded over the threat to the livelihoods of thousands of self-employed actors, musicians and others in the performing arts. A hundred leading figures in the performing arts sector sign a letter calling on the government to take urgent action to prevent the closure of the sector. Theatre and other types of performance are facing ruin because the two metre distancing rule makes them unviable as so few people can attend the performance. Leading theatre impresario, Sir Cameron Mackintosh, has been forced to cancel his top shows until 2021, no Les Miserables, Phantom of the Opera, Hamilton, or Mary Poppins. Mackintosh says it was "heartbreaking" to take this decision but he had no alternative because of the lack of a government response to repeated requests by the performing arts sector to address the issue. Andrew Lloyd Webber says he was advised by government officials that musicals could go ahead "provided there wasn't any singing."

Boris Johnson can take some comfort from knowing that other world leaders also face the slings and arrows of outrageous fortune in their efforts to respond to the coronavirus pandemic. President Macron of France only a few days ago was celebrating the return of normal life to his country as schools, shops and restaurants all opened. Now the President is faced with criticism by the French National Assembly for the way that France responded to the pandemic, with protests from doctors and nurses calling for a massive increase in healthcare funding. In the National Assembly an inquiry into the handling of the outbreak told Jerome Salomon, France's general director of health, that France had been reactive rather than proactive in addressing the pandemic and had carried out far fewer tests than Germany in the opening weeks of the crisis. Prime Minister Johnson can use those questions as a dry run for possible challenges he may face in any future public inquiry.

Hats off to Her Majesty The Queen. On Day two of Royal Ascot, but without the crowds and The Queen in person, her two year old horse, Tactical, won the Windsor Castle Stakes. The Queen was watching at Windsor on the royal box rather than being in the royal box at the race course but was said to be "delighted" by this, her first Royal Ascot winner since 2016. And a small piece of late sports news: Football returned. Manchester City beat Arsenal 3-0.

DAY 94: THURSDAY 18 JUNE: *299,251 confirmed cases 42,153 deaths*

"World-beating" Boris Johnson called it. The app which would quickly tell other app users if someone they had been near to had tested positive for the virus. Now, not world-beating, but in chaos. Two possible apps, one being developed by Apple for the government and another being developed by Apple and Google jointly, are both found to have defects which means they cannot be made available for the public to use. Health

Secretary Matt Hancock has a plan. The government will now try to take the best of both systems to see if together this can make a third app system that will work. Health Minister Lord Bethell tells Parliament's science and technology committee that an app which the public can use may not be available until the end of the year. So contact tracing manually, which relies on people testing positive making available details of people they have been in contact with, will continue. Meanwhile accounting firms KPMG and Deloitte are both developing their own apps to test the health of their staff.

The government is also coming under pressure for its perceived lack of a clear plan to support young people and to make sure they are all able to return to school. More than 1,000 paediatricians sign a letter calling for a national recovery programme for young people to avoid "scarring the life chances of millions of children." A leader in The Times is critical of Education Secretary Gavin Williamson for not having come forward to set out how the government will get all children back to school.

On the health front more reassuring news. The figures now show that the effect of the virus is waning rapidly as virus deaths over the last seven days are down to 144 compared with 933 a week ago. This seems to justify the government's re-opening of non-essential shops and greater freedom of movement. Can the figures remain low now that people are moving about and interacting with each other much more is the question which the next few weeks will answer. In our NHS discussions in Cambridge we return to the subject of understanding how much capacity we have for non-COVID hospital work, in a world where wards and operating theatres have to be subject to infection control and regular cleaning, which may reduce how many patients can be seen each week. Whilst this assessment is still under way patients with the most urgent medical conditions are being booked in for treatment, and we agree that the public should be given clear information on how long they may have to wait for less urgent procedures.

For those hoping that the government will allow hotels to re-open next month so that a late summer holiday in this country may still be possible, Cornwall has a warning for the public to think twice about a trip to Newquay or Padstow this summer. "You are going to find lots of places aren't open, lots of places you will need to queue, and please don't be surprised if there are some tensions." Underlying this message may be local fears of thousands of us from the metropolis, wishing to holiday at home to avoid quarantine requirements, bringing the virus with us to "the Cornish Riviera" rather than our sunhats and golf clubs.

Today updates about the coronavirus took second place to the sad news that Forces Sweetheart Dame Vera Lynn had died at the grand age of 103. The wonderful thing about the longevity of her career was that her songs were still being mentioned and sung in recent weeks as the virus and lockdown returned us to the communal spirit of the Second World War years. At the start of the pandemic The Queen ended her broadcast to the nation echoing the words of Vera Lynn's most famous song by telling the country "We will meet again"; and only a few weeks ago in socially distanced VE Day celebrations up and down the land, people drew strength in the midst of the coronacrisis by joining together to sing Vera Lynn's wartime songs. As we say goodbye to one of the country's most enduring entertainers, we hope there will once more be blue birds over the white cliffs of Dover.

DAY 95: FRIDAY 19 JUNE: *300,469 confirmed cases 42,288 deaths*

It was Boris Johnson's birthday today. He was 56. He celebrated by visiting Bovington Primary Academy in Hemel Hempstead where he practised social distancing with the children and stood in line waiting to wash his hands before entering the building. Later in the day Education Secretary Gavin Williamson announces (following the criticism of a lack of a government plan) that all schoolchildren will return to school in September. Financial support of £1 billion is given by the government to help with the extra costs of making schools a safe environment, with funds also going to the families of vulnerable children to pay for top-up tuition to help alleviate their loss of learning time whilst schools were closed.

But many people would not want Boris Johnson to celebrate too much on his special day. A survey for The Times CEO Forum found that 80 per cent of businesses felt that Ministers had not done a good job of dealing with the coronavirus, whilst nearly 60 per cent believe the recession will last for at least 18 months. With a 20 per cent contraction in the economy expected in the quarter to the end of June the Bank of England warns that unemployment may rise in the coming months more than it previously forecast; the Bank plans to pump a further £100 billion of new money into the economy by buying up Treasury gilts held by investment funds.

Much more welcome news is that the first wave of the coronavirus outbreak does seem to be truly over as the number of deaths from all causes returns to normal levels. And now the alert level is finally reduced from 4 indicating a high rate of transmission of the virus to 3 meaning the virus is in the community but not transmitting at a high rate. The one in 1,700 people who now have the virus compares with four times this number in early May. But as Oxford professor Neil Smith makes clear, we shouldn't be complacent as the improvement in the figure "is not permanent deliverance, the virus is still here and can spread." Evidence of how the virus can come back at short notice can be seen in Germany, which generally has controlled the virus much better than many countries, where 6,000 staff working in a large abattoir are quarantined after around 1,000 workers there test positive for the virus. Some scientists believe the virus may be more easily transmitted between people in cold conditions such as those found in the abattoir.

More figures for those who like large numbers. Government borrowings (that is the amount government expenditure exceeds income) was at a record monthly high of £55 billion in May as we head for an annual deficit of £300 billion, a level which normally would never be countenanced. Little wonder then at how keen the Prime Minister is that the economy should be seen to be reviving from its recent lockdown collapse. "We are moving to a world which is less apprehensive" Johnson says. We all very much hope we are.

DAY 96: SATURDAY 20 JUNE: *301,815 confirmed cases 42,461 deaths*

Y Viva Espana! Spain will allow British tourists to take holidays in one of our favourite holiday destinations without the need to quarantine when arriving in Spain. This is a one way benefit as those returning to the UK still have to quarantine on arrival for 14 days. It is, though, possible that this requirement will be relaxed to create a no quarantine "air corridor" between England and Spain in both directions. Majorca will also be open again to British tourists but no boat trips and no nightclubs. These rules, which have been imposed by local officials to reduce coronavirus risks, may make Majorca more attractive once again to older visitors if some of the alcohol fuelled revelry of the younger generation is contained by the absence of nightlife.

But Brazil remains off limits for long haul trips as it wrestles with a serious spreading of the virus. As many as 54,000 new infections a day are being recorded. A total of a million people have tested positive for COVID-19 with 49,000 deaths. Particularly serious are the large numbers of deaths within indigenous tribal communities. "We are facing extermination" reports one tribe as the virus sweeps through tribes killing leaders, elders and traditional tribal natural healers, leaving irreparable damage to tribal history and medicine. The Munduruku people alone have lost 10 *sábios*, or wise ones. "We always say they are living libraries," said Alessandra Munduruku, a tribal leader. "It's been very painful." President Bolsonaro continues to attract widespread criticism for his laissez faire attitude to the virus, scorning wearing a mask and encouraging people to go out to restaurants as deaths rise. "Yes, it's Bolsonaro's fault," said Thais Couto, a 32-year-old lung surgeon in Sao Paulo, who like many doctors around the nation is exhausted and overwhelmed as Brazil sees roughly 1,200 deaths per day or one a minute. "From the beginning, he hasn't taken this seriously, laughing about the disease and saying it's just a flu and not a big deal."

And where are we now in Britain in respect of the coronavirus? We seem to be over the first wave but know the virus is still amongst us and could reignite in certain locations if transmission rates rise as the lockdown restrictions are eased. The government is desperate to get the economy going again to prevent large scale unemployment as businesses have to choose between starting to pay some of the wages of the nine million staff on the furlough scheme as it unwinds, or laying staff off. But overall there is a growing feeling that, both in the early days when a lockdown was held off whilst the virus was spreading with deadly consequences, and in more recent times when the schools reopening was delayed, the government has been too often "muddling through." It has not demonstrated a totally confident and effective strategy for balancing protecting health and rebuilding people's livelihoods and education prospects.

DAY 97: SUNDAY 21 JUNE: *303,110 confirmed cases 42,589 deaths*

The enigma that is the COVID-19 coronavirus continues. Germany, a country which has been a role model with its early large scale testing programme and a death count of under 9,000, which means that its deaths in relation to population size is only a sixth of the British rate, is suddenly faced by a rapidly developing new wave of the virus. The German R number, the number of people which someone infected with the virus will in turn infect, is 2.9 which indicates a virus spreading quite freely in the community. The previously reported outbreak in a large abattoir is a factor but German health officials say new cases are being experienced in nursing homes, hospitals, institutions for housing asylum seekers and refugees, delivery companies, harvest workers, religious events and family gatherings. A long list which will add to the concerns of those who believe the UK government's relaxation of the lockdown to open up shops, and before long the hospitality sector, may be the lull before the storm of a second wave of COVID-19, as people return to interacting with each other.

If there should be a second wave of the virus in Britain will doctors and nurses be ready to deal with it, having learned lessons from the first wave? Or will many be mentally and physically drained by their valiant work during the first wave and unable to give their all a second time?

A survey by the British Medical Association finds that 30 per cent of their members are "not very confident" at the prospect of dealing well with a second coronavirus wave, with a further 19 per cent "not at all confident." Behind their fears is a concern that the NHS may become swamped by a second wave because hospitals will be trying to juggle treating COVID-19 patients from the first wave, new COVID patients from a second wave and restoring normal health services to deal with the significant patient backlogs which developed during the first wave.

The concerns that we have not gone about dealing with the pandemic in a particularly well organised manner, giving rise to questions about the timing of decisions on key health responses, is borne out in a new exercise by Oxford University. This shows Britain languishing in position 155 out of 179 nations scored for how well they had followed key World Health Organisation targets for controlling infection.

For Britain's economy to recover there is a need for new jobs to be created where there will be demand for goods and services so that work opportunities will be available to those who become unemployed, particularly in hospitality and retail, where large job losses are expected. The Local Government Association appears to have a good solution. It has announced it will encourage 100,000 "homes for heroes", rented accommodation for NHS and other frontline workers who need to be near their place of work, and to also house those who have lost their relatives to the virus. This has echoes of the large 500,000 new homes programme which was launched in 1919 by Prime Minister David Lloyd George to provide good quality homes for those returning from World War One.

It is estimated that there could be a kitten boom of over 80,000 extra kittens as a result of vets not exercising birth control procedures on male cats during the lockdown. But this could create much needed new jobs in cat food production.

DAY 98: MONDAY 22 JUNE: *304,331 confirmed cases 42,632 deaths*

Can you come up with other ideas to create new jobs? The government would like to hear from you. With the prospect of unemployment increasing sharply as the furlough scheme unwinds, the government would like to finds job opportunities for those needing a new occupation. Ministers have been asked to identify bold new projects to kick start the economy and provide further jobs. So, what other parts of the country could benefit from a new high speed rail link may be the next question. The government is also considering giving an education allowance which those seeking work can use to invest in retraining in new skills, to make them more marketable in the sectors where job opportunities will exist.

Whilst Britain may be coming to the end of the first wave of deaths from the coronavirus no-one should assume this will definitely be the end of the virus. The World Health Organisation reports that there were 183,000 new cases of COVID-19 across the world yesterday which is the biggest one day increase in coronavirus infections since the pandemic began. America and Brazil continue to be particularly affected And as we saw yesterday, cases of the virus have been increasing in Germany, which had previously had a low rate of infection. We expect to hear from the government tomorrow that there will be further easing of the lockdown arrangements. But will we then experience an upturn in the number of virus infections?

University College London, that haven of epidemic modellers, now predicts a threat of a second wave of the coronavirus in the UK early next year. The concern is whether this could overwhelm the NHS if it occurs in winter, with hospitals already busy with non-COVID patients.

We cannot be complacent. Here in Britain "excess deaths", that is the increase in the number of deaths compared with normal levels since the virus reached our shores, is approaching a sobering 65,000. Most of the excess deaths are likely to relate, directly or indirectly, to COVID-19. Whenever these current statistics are mentioned, thoughts return to the words of the government's Chief Scientific Adviser, Sir Patrick Vallance who told Parliament on 17 March that limiting deaths to 20,000 would be "a good outcome." We did not achieve that.

My friend, after three and a half long frustrating weeks, finally completes what has been an incredibly complicated process of training, and logging into the government's test, track and trace system which is supposed to ensure that all those at risk of carrying the virus are asked to self-isolate to prevent the virus from spreading more widely. There are apparently multiple computer systems which have to be accessed which has made it so difficult for enthusiastic volunteers like my friend to get started in this important work. Having finally struggled through the induction programme my friend is now told to wait until mid-July for a first day when he can now start contact tracing. The impression increases that this system which was supposed to be "world beating" is a long way from operating at maximum efficiency.

In the afternoon I go to my local Evans Bike Shop in Chalk Farm to get a puncture fixed, only to find that it is now completely empty. It is not clear if this closure is a casualty of the lockdown economic slump (which seems unlikely as bicycles were supposed to be a growth area as people shun public transport) or the victim of a reorganisation by Sports Direct, the new owner of Evans Bike Shops. Luckily, I find a helpful small bicycle shop in nearby England's Lane called Impressed, where I am as my flat tyre is repaired.

On the way home at tea time I see a socially distanced queue of parents waiting to collect their young offspring from a primary school in Hampstead. A teacher releases the children one by one into the care of their mothers and fathers, one mother patiently waiting holding on to two pink scooters. The excitement of running out of school to recount the stories of the school day has thankfully returned.

DAY 99: TUESDAY 23 JUNE: *305,289 confirmed cases 42,647 deaths*

As we near the end of the hundred days of our coronadiary Prime Minister Boris Johnson tells us "Our long national hibernation is coming to an end and life is returning to our streets and to our shops. The bustle is starting to come back." Johnson announces that as from 4 July restaurants, pubs, hotels, guest houses, cinemas, museums and many other attractions, including model villages, can reopen provided they follow government safety guidelines. The Prime Minister makes one major concession to make this easier for businesses by replacing the two metre social distancing rule with a new one metre plus guideline. This means that we may come within one metre of other people provided that other protections are in place, such as a screen or wearing a mask.

So we can eat again in our favourite restaurant or visit our local pub but the experience will be very different to what we were used to. There will be no standing at the bar as drinks and food will now be pre-ordered and brought to your table which, in many establishments, is likely to be kept apart from other tables by screens. We can also go on holiday in this country; hotels and guest houses are expecting to see an upturn of bookings from families not wanting to risk going abroad this summer. The overall package of openings is more than many expected and includes hairdressers though small talk with the client is to be discouraged, which may remove half the benefit of a visit to the hairdresser for many. But surprisingly, given their potential health benefits, there is no re-opening of gyms and swimming pools; and there are to be no audience attended performances in theatres and music venues. The performing arts sector continues to feel neglected with still no financial support despite many well known voices continuing to say that the majority of venues are close to total financial collapse.

But overall, it is a bold statement from the Prime Minister. It also allows people from two households to meet indoors provided they socially distance. Even Labour leader Keir Starmer acknowledges that, through this new package of easing restrictions, Johnson "has done the right thing." But it comes with strings attached. The Prime Minister urges us to be cautious in the way we use these new freedoms and is clear that if coronavirus infections start to rise again then either local or national lockdown measures will be reimposed. Chief Medical Officer Chris Whitty underlines the caution saying "This is absolutely not risk free. We're in this for the long haul. I will be surprised and delighted if we are not in this current situation through the winter and into next spring."

To reinforce the view that we are at least returning to some version of a more normal way of life Johnson announces that the daily Downing Street press briefings, which have become a fixed feature of teatime television, will now stop. The briefings, or Hancock's Half Hour as vintage radio buffs dubbed them, have made unexpected household names of Whitty, Chief Scientific Adviser Sir Patrick Vallance and their deputies. Jonathan Van-Tam, Whitty's deputy, has been a particularly articulate understudy. Some people will suffer withdrawal symptoms at their sudden departure from our screens.

DAY 100: WEDNESDAY 24 JUNE: *306,210 confirmed cases 42,927 deaths*

The final day of our coronadiary brings a beautiful hot sunny day, the same lovely weather that carried on regardless for much of the period we were instructed to stay at home, except for limited time, outdoors. But now Boris Johnson has encouraged us to come out of hibernation and to take opportunities to visit hotels, leisure attractions, pubs and restaurants. As the coronadiary approaches its end is this the long awaited return to normal ways of living which we so suddenly abandoned in March, or are we standing on a dangerous precipice with the virus waiting for us below?

Once the worst of the coronavirus outbreak had passed there began a tension which still remains. On the one hand, the desire for businesses to reopen and the public to become customers again, to avoid even more damage to our ravaged economy, where only generous government support packages have prevented mass unemployment. And on the other hand, the wish to avoid another surge in the spread of the virus which would put people's health and the NHS at risk, and prompt a resumption of the lockdown restrictions.

The only way to find a balance between these two potentially conflicting aims is to reduce the spread of the virus by continued social distancing (now reduced to one metre if other measures such as masks or screens are in place). But scientists remain concerned. Britain's new confirmed cases of coronavirus are still running at one thousand a day, a rate higher than other European countries, and the promised "world-beating" test, track and trace system is far from fully effective. This creates a mix of risks which could tip us over that precipice into a second wave of COVID-19 infections. Looking down at the sea from the safety of a clifftop can be beautiful but one step too far can be fatal.

Prime Minister Boris Johnson has said "We are indebted to our scientific colleagues for their advice but it is our responsibility to choose." He meant it was ultimately the government's choice to decide how much of the economy should be reopened. But as individuals we also have a choice on how much risk we take on through our interactions with each other. Many will be cautious about going out again to enjoy pubs, restaurants and leisure activities; but others will not see the hidden risks of these new freedoms which is evidenced, on this hottest day of the summer so far, by pictures of thousands flocking again to packed beaches around our coastline. As the scales of the coronavirus stand in judgement above us will our behaviour in the coming days cause them to tilt towards the spread of the virus continuing to decrease, or will they tilt in the other direction bringing another surge in virus infections?

Our regional NHS Board in Cambridge continues to talk about the ongoing work to assess the capacity of hospitals in our region to deal with non-COVID health procedures, at a time when theatres, wards and patient assessment areas have to be regularly deep cleaned to minimise the risk of the virus infecting staff or patients. Nationally the percentage of those waiting more than six weeks for a diagnostic appointment has risen from just under three per cent in February to a concerning 56 per cent, whilst Cancer Research UK and other health charities highlight a significant reduction in donations to fund their medical research because of the economic downturn. The search for a vaccine which will release us from the threat of the virus continues with British efforts led by Oxford University and University College London. Their team hopes to produce a vaccine where two million doses will fit inside a one litre water bottle.

As the hundred days that changed our lives draw to a close just under twelve million people, over a third of Britain's workforce, are receiving financial support from the government but for many, whether they will continue to be working in the coming months is very uncertain.

The weather into the evening is warm and sunny as it was on the day this coronadiary began. Since then, 42,892 people have died in the UK from the coronavirus we know as COVID-19.

SUBSEQUENTLY . . .

We did, for the remainder of summer 2020, move back into a world which seemed more familiar. There was prolonged warm weather during which large crowds gathered on beaches. Social distancing rules were still in force, but people took holidays whilst hotel receptionists sat behind glass as they greeted us. Captain Sir Tom Moore was knighted by the Queen on a sunlit Windsor Castle lawn to much public acclaim following his remarkable NHS fundraising as he became a centurion. Businesses came out of hibernation and began to plan for the future. Friends and families returned to restaurants encouraged by the Chancellor's Eat Out to Help Out scheme where the government paid part of the bill. We were unsure what the winter months would bring but for the time being the worst of the virus seemed to be behind us. The sunshine brought warmth and optimism.

But as soon as we entered September virus cases started to rise again fuelled by a new surge of cases across Europe. The government was caught between wanting to avoid another wave of COVID-19 putting renewed strain on hospitals, and wanting to press ahead with opening up the economy. The possibility of a short "circuit breaker" was considered but not pursed. Instead the government introduced a system of tiers where the extent of the restrictions in a particular area depended on how seriously the virus was spreading. But, as cases continued to rise, the government was forced into a second national lockdown during November.

As the virus returned in the autumn so the devastating effects of the first wave became apparent. A Parliament report lambasted the failure to stop the virus running through care homes as "reckless and appalling," NHS waiting lists were at record highs following the focus on COVID patients, there was controversy over how school exam grades would be awarded after exams were cancelled and, despite the government avoiding mass unemployment by extending its furlough scheme, many High Street businesses failed or contracted, Debenhams and Top Shop went under, Pizza Express closed over 70 restaurants.

Boris Johnson tried to rally the nation saying we would "rebuild together" and promising us we could look forward to being with family again at Christmas during a five day relaxation of the rules for meeting indoors. Late November brought both a lifeline and new fears. To world wide applause the Pfizer/Biontech vaccine flew through its tests and was approved, closely followed by the British Oxford University/AstraZeneca vaccine. On 8 December a smiling 90 year old Margaret Keenan in Coventry became the first to be vaccinated. But, just as the government was moving the country back to a tiered system of restrictions, a new strain of the virus, originating in Kent, was found to be transmitting 70 per cent more rapidly and new cases and hospitalisations soared. The government cancelled our Christmas plans and began a race to give the vaccine to those most at risk as COVID-19 once more rampaged across the land. UK COVID deaths, which had reached 50,000 on 11 November, took only just over two months to double to a deeply disturbing 100,000 by 26 January, at which point the country was back where it had been in March 2020 in a full national lockdown with Britain's death rate from COVID-19 the highest in Europe.

PART 2

AND THREE SKILLS GOVERNMENT HAD BEEN TOLD TO IMPROVE

WE STOOD ON OUR DOORSTEPS

We stood on our doorsteps to clap for the NHS. It was a spontaneous and emotional expression of gratitude. For the outstanding efforts which NHS staff had made to care for the thousands of people who had been in hospital with COVID-19. Many desperately ill. Some who would not survive.

We clapped for the acts of kindness, nurses holding the hands of patients unable to be visited by family, doctors phoning relatives to provide updates. We clapped for the doctors and nurses who had put their own health at risk through daily contact with COVID-19 patients and had borne the mental stress of dealing with so many critical decisions where lives were on a knife edge. And we clapped for all the others involved in the delivery of care: GPs donning PPE to continue seeing patients in their surgeries, NHS staff driving ambulances or working behind the scenes to plan and manage medical care and those looking after the residents of care homes.

When we recall the images from that time of hospitals working at full stretch with large numbers of patients wearing oxygen masks we naturally think of the human side of medicine, the commitment to always do the best for the patient. But to deliver good medicine in such pressurised conditions also requires high quality management skills which would be needed in any well run organisation; skills which were essential to bringing order and good decision making to the unprecedented challenge which NHS staff faced in providing the extent of care needed to deal with COVID-19.

To respond effectively, in the way they did, those who worked on the front line in hospitals needed:

- Core management skills (effective project planning, making good use of data, risk management);
- The medical and personal skills which doctors and nurses acquire through their training and ongoing experience of looking after patients;
- Further knowledge of the particular characteristics of COVID-19 which the doctors and nurses acquired through caring for patients during the first wave of the virus.

All three of these elements had to be working well to produce the standard of care we applauded from our doorsteps. The first of the three elements, core management skills, does not sound particularly exciting. They were not the skills of doctors and nurses which we were thinking about as we saw images of doctors and nurses dressed in full PPE. But the ability to make effective and efficient plans, having the right data and interpreting it appropriately and managing risks are essential skills which doctors and nurses are using on a daily basis. Not just doctors and nurses, hospitals will have scores of support staff who are also using these skills to ensure the efficient overall running of their hospitals.

Table 1 sets out examples of how these core management skills (effective project planning, making good use of data, risk management) were used in the NHS during the COVID pandemic:

TABLE 1: Examples of the use of core management skills in the NHS during the COVID pandemic

Core Management Skills	Examples of the use of them
Effective project planning	• hospitals will have put into operation major incident plans for responding to sudden events creating a large influx of patients • daily plans for bed utilisation, including those in intensive care • a plan of medical care for each patient
Making good use of data	• taking regular readings of medical data such as oxygen levels to plan patient care • estimating how long patients are likely to stay in hospital to assist plans for how beds will be used • analysing waiting lists for non-COVID conditions to identify those who should be given priority for treatment
Risk management	• major incident plans identifying risks which need to be managed with prepared strategies for dealing with them • introducing enhanced cleaning procedures to minimise the risk of non-COVID patients catching the virus in hospital • assessing the risks that COVID patients face as a result of underlying health conditions

There are many other aspects of managing a hospital which will draw on these core management skills. But you can begin to see how important effective project planning, making good use of data and risk management are to running an efficient and safe hospital.

NEXT SLIDE PLEASE

Government was dealing not just with the health challenges faced by the NHS, but also with many other complex issues arising from the pandemic. All of this taking place in a fast moving and, at times, seemingly unpredictable environment. Measures to combat COVID impacted on the economy . . . schools . . . care homes . . . owners of hospitality businesses . . . the travel industry . . . the arts sector. Every part of our lives was affected in some way by the COVID pandemic, thus creating an ever mounting list of difficult issues for the government to address.

The previous section identified three areas of skills those working in NHS hospitals needed to respond to the pandemic. The skills needed by the government in responding to the COVID-19 pandemic also had three elements:

- Core management skills (effective project planning, making good use of data, risk management);
- Ability to use the machinery of government effectively (collaboration between different parts of government, gaining the support of Parliament, communicating with the public);
- Further knowledge of the particular characteristics of COVID-19 which the NHS and scientists gained during the first wave of the virus.

You can see that two of the elements are the same as the skills needed by those working during the pandemic in NHS hospitals: core management skills (effective project planning, making good use of data and the management of risk) as well as the ability to adapt plans in the light of learning more about the COVID-19 virus. It is the second element, the specialist skills, which differ: the NHS bringing medical skills and the government bringing its experience of working with multiple areas of activity and its ability to engage with Parliament and the public.

The Downing Street press conferences, held daily during the peaks of the pandemic and at other times, to make important announcements, enabled the government to update us on how they were managing the pandemic. "Next slide please" became a familiar refrain as the latest data about the spread of the virus and the number of COVID hospital cases was displayed.

If you were to devise your own slide to assess the outcome of the government's actions to combat COVID-19, what information would you include and what conclusions might you come to?

You could construct a scale to measure outcomes

You would probably want to find a way of comparing the outcome of the pandemic with initial expectations. At the outset of the coronavirus outbreak the government's Chief Scientific Adviser Sir Patrick Vallance, who appeared regularly at the daily press conferences, told the Health Select Committee in Parliament that "20,000 deaths would be a good outcome." At the time even an outcome with that number of deaths from this new unknown virus seemed a harrowing prospect, so it was clear "a good outcome" was a relative measure.

Using that benchmark for what the Chief Scientific Officer thought would, relatively speaking, represent success one might at the time have constructed a scale to compare the subsequent actual outcome with this initial view of what "good" might look like. Table 2 sets out how such a scale might have looked.

TABLE 2: A possible scale for measuring the effectiveness of the government's response to the coronavirus pandemic

Good outcomes	
Level 1	Virus suppressed very quickly with few deaths. Any further outbreaks are also suppressed quickly.
Level 2	Virus spreads widely but deaths are limited to the "good" outcome of no more than 20,000.
Moderate outcomes	
Level 3	Virus spreads widely and deaths are higher than the "good" outcome but within 50% more than that outcome (ie no more than 30,000 deaths)
Level 4	Virus spreads widely and deaths are considerably higher than the "good" outcome at 50-100% more than that outcome (ie 30,000-40,000 deaths)
Poor outcomes	
Level 5	Virus spreads widely and deaths are more than double the "good" outcome (ie over 40,000 deaths), but the NHS is not overwhelmed
Level 6	Virus spreads widely and deaths are more than double the "good" outcome and the NHS is over-whelmed.

Even in the early stages of the COVID pandemic when "the first hundred days" of the coronadiary ended in June 2020 we were already at Level 5 on the above scale with over 42,000 COVID deaths. That was according to the official government statistics, reported at that time, based on those who had tested positive for the virus within 28 days of death. The true number of COVID deaths was very likely higher; excess deaths (that is the difference between actual deaths from any cause and normal experience) were then at around 65,000 since the start of the pandemic.

At the time of writing, in March 2021 on the anniversary of the first lockdown, the official number of deaths has reached 126,000 with excess deaths running slightly above the official government figures.

We also know we have the highest COVID death rate in Europe (around 25 per cent higher than Italy which has the next highest number of COVID deaths) and the fifth highest number of deaths in the world after the USA, Brazil, Mexico and India. Perhaps of most concern, the UK has the highest rate of COVID deaths per head of population for any country in the world with a population of over 20 million. Our rate is around 1,850 COVID deaths per million people, 13 per cent higher than Italy, the country with the next highest rate.

Only the third national lockdown in January 2021, the start of the vaccination programme and the exceptional efforts of the NHS to manage the care of COVID patients prevented the NHS being overwhelmed (which would have put us at Level 6 on the scale in Table 2). But we came very close to that worst of all outcomes.

It is clear we have achieved relatively poor results compared with both the Chief Scientific Officer's initial view of "a good outcome" and also compared with the experience of other countries. The government cannot claim a success in its management of the COVID pandemic in the UK and many will be highly concerned about the loss of life we have experienced.

There is a lasting impression that this was not a government machine working at maximum effectiveness during its COVID response. This creates two questions: why was the machinery of government not firing on all cylinders from the outset of the pandemic? and what could have been done differently?

There may have been alternative strategies
for managing the pandemic

We only know for certain the outcome that we experienced as a result of the actual government decisions which were taken during the pandemic.

We do not know for certain how alternative government decisions would have played out in terms of the numbers of people catching the virus, needing hospital treatment or dying from COVID. But now that the passage of time has given us a clearer perspective on the events of 2020 one can see alternative strategies which might have been more effective in managing the pandemic. These potentially better strategies include:

1. A better ready to use plan for dealing with a pandemic involving respiratory illness;

2. A faster reaction to the threat that, in a world of international travel, the initial virus outbreak in China might spread to the UK;

3. More rigorous border controls and testing of arrivals in the UK (there was no border closure and less than 300 people were quarantined out of 18 million arrivals in the UK in the first three months of 2020);

4. An earlier first lockdown when it became apparent that testing and tracing was not going to contain the spread of the virus;

5. Greater use of mass testing to identify who was carrying the virus (including those not displaying symptoms) so that they, and their contacts, could be required to isolate to minimise virus spread;

6. Greater stocks of ready to use PPE with a logistical plan for making these quickly available to hospitals, care homes and GP surgeries;

7. Clearer arrangements for sourcing more quickly an adequate supply of ventilators for COVID hospital patients (there were delays as government sought 26,000 additional ventilators from various industry suppliers);

8. Being more alert to the risks of discharging elderly people from hospitals where COVID had been present, into care homes (over 25,000 patients were discharged into care homes as hospitals sought to free up beds);

9. Earlier data on the spread of the virus within care homes (initially only data relating to hospitals was reported);

10. A short "circuit breaker" lockdown in autumn 2020 when it became apparent that the number of virus infections was beginning to rise again.

As noted above, we cannot be certain how these alternative strategies would have worked out as they were not applied in real time as the COVID pandemic progressed. But these alternative strategies have common characteristics of a faster more rigorous approach to containing the virus which suggests they had the potential to limit the adverse outcomes of the pandemic.

We may have thought the government was repeatedly outwitted by a COVID virus it had never had to deal with before. But many of the apparent shortcomings in the government's approach to managing the COVID pandemic arose through not applying core management skills which would be relevant to managing many other government projects or business situations. The same management skills which helped the NHS to deal with the extreme demands of patient care during the pandemic.

Table 3 shows how each of the ten alternative strategies for responding to the COVID pandemic required the better application of the core management skills of effective project planning, making good use of data and managing risk.

The analysis in Table 3 shows that:

- all ten strategies which may well have led to better outcomes required managing risks more effectively; and
- each of the strategies would have also required a better approach to one or both of project planning and making good use of data.

There is no doubt that Ministers and civil servants faced significant challenges in trying to develop at pace strategies to combat the spread of the potentially highly dangerous new virus. But the analysis in Table 3 suggests that a greater focus, at all stages of the pandemic, in these three core management skills: effective project planning, making good use of data and risk management would have led to alternative actions which almost certainly would have produced better outcomes and ultimately less loss of life.

TABLE 3: How more effective alternative strategies depended on better use of core management skills

Alternative strategy	Project planning	Good use of data	Managing risk
1 A better ready to use plan for dealing with a pandemic involving respiratory illness	x		x
2 A faster reaction to the threat that, in a world of international travel, the initial virus outbreak in China might spread to the UK	x		x
3 More rigorous border controls and testing of arrivals in the UK (there was no border closure and less than 300 people were quarantined out of 18 million arrivals in the UK in the first three months of 2020)	x		x
4 An earlier first lockdown when it became apparent that testing and tracing was not going to contain the spread of the virus		x	x
5 Greater use of mass testing to identify who was carrying the virus (including those not displaying symptoms) so that they and their contacts could be required to isolate to minimise virus spread	x	x	x

Alternative strategy	Project planning	Good use of data	Managing risk
6 Greater stocks of ready to use PPE with a logistical plan for making these quickly available to hospitals, care homes and GP surgeries	x	x	x
7 Clearer arrangements for sourcing more quickly an adequate supply of ventilators for COVID hospital patients (there were delays as government sought 26,000 additional ventilators from various industry suppliers)	x		x
8 Being more alert to the risks of discharging elderly people from hospitals where COVID had been present, into care homes (over 25,000 patients were discharged into care homes as hospitals sought to free up beds)	x		x
9 Earlier data on the spread of the virus within care homes (initially only data relating to hospitals was reported)	x	x	x
10 A short "circuit breaker" lockdown in autumn 2020 when it became apparent that the number of virus infections was beginning to rise again		x	x

Patients being treated in hospital for COVID-19 relied on doctors to use these core disciplines of planning, data, risks. The patients' lives depended on these disciplines being applied to the highest standards. Yet the analysis set out above suggests that the same disciplines of attending to planning, data, risks were much less successfully applied by the government in its high level response to the pandemic.

LIFE IS FOR LEARNING . . . OR SHOULD BE

Life is for learning, full of absorbing new information and interacting with the world around us. Our interactions with the world may be based on the knowledge we have acquired or may involve exploration, testing or using "trial and error" to identify which actions work well, and those which do not produce desired outcomes.

Sometimes our actions lead to success; sometimes situations don't go our way. When we sense we have made mistakes or not been able to deal well with a situation we have a choice: to adjust our approach or to stay with previous methods creating the risk that we will fail again when the same situation returns.

When we are young we may be reprimanded for some misdemeanour. Do we adjust our behaviour, or do we risk the further anger of parents or teachers? Entrepreneurs starting out in business often find that their first business venture fails. Do they learn from this first mistake and go on to success, or do they oversee a string of business failures? If we fail in personal relationships, do we take time to understand why, or do we repeat our unhappy experiences? It is human to make mistakes. The greatest tragedy is to fail to learn from mistakes and to repeat them over and over again.

The work of government is subject to such close scrutiny that there are many opportunities to learn from previous experience. There is scrutiny from Parliament and the work of its committees. There is the

Public Accounts Committee, known as the PAC, which holds government to account for its spending of public funds, and committees such as the Health and Social Care Select Committee looking at particular areas of government activity. The government's auditor, the National Audit Office (NAO), produces around 50 reports a year on various areas of government expenditure. The Institute for Government also produces many reports on the way that government goes about its work, as do a number of external "think tanks." Then there is the continuous scrutiny and analysis from the mainstream media, the ongoing commentary about government affairs on social media and other views expressed through letters to MPs and ultimately at the ballot box.

Yet, despite scores of reports from the NAO, Parliament committees and other organisations such as "think tanks", all making recommendations on how government should learn from previous errors to achieve better outcomes in the future, government has a history of repeating its mistakes. Labour MP Margaret Hodge spent five years scrutinising government projects as the Chair of the PAC. In her 2016 book *Called to Account* she wrote **"All too often government seemed institutionally incapable of learning from its past mistakes . . . the same things seemed to go wrong time and time again.** This was, in part, because the cycle of politics, coupled with the career structure within the Civil Service, created no institutional memory and a very short-term approach . . . **The Civil Service continues to lack the appropriate skills and experience required for modern government."**

Fast forward five years to January 2021 and Margaret Hodge's successor as Chair of the PAC Meg Hillier said in a report on major government projects **"Skills and leadership remain a persistent problem in delivering major projects."** Still the focus on the need for better skills to deliver government projects and the sense that previous warnings had not been fully addressed.

So, dare we consider whether some of the apparent shortcomings in the government's approach to the COVID-19 pandemic were as a result of repeating previous mistakes which had been brought to their attention?

THREE SKILLS GOVERNMENT HAD BEEN TOLD TO IMPROVE

We have seen that, to deal with the exceptional demands of the pandemic, NHS staff needed a range of skills which fell into three categories. They needed their medical and personal skills, the ability to learn about COVID-19 as they treated the first wave of COVID patients and also the ability to use three core management skills to resolve the multiple complex situations they faced on a daily basis.

The three important core management skills were:

- effective project planning;
- making good use of data; and
- risk management

So what had government been told about these three core management skills and how did that relate to the COVID experience?

EFFECTIVE PROJECT PLANNING

What government had been told

The National Audit Office, which reports on the way that government uses its resources, said in its 2016 report *Delivering Major Projects in Government* **"The track record of delivering government projects has** been poor." The NAO went on to say, "We and the Public Accounts Committee identified a number of recurring issues across departments that were contributing to poor performance." **One of those issues was "poor early planning."**

In a subsequent 2017 report on *Capability in the Civil Service* the NAO surveyed government departments and found that **many did not think they were strong enough on skills including project delivery and project planning.**

The Institute for Government also referred to these issues in its 2017 report *Professionalising Whitehall.* Noting the large scale risks inherent in many government projects the Institute said **"it is critical for the civil service to have the project management skills to deliver projects"** and noted that where projects had not performed well **"departments either lacked the specialist skills they needed or failed to make effective use of what they did have."**

When taking projects forwards there is a repeated tendency for government to believe it has set in place appropriate plans only to fall short in practice. This was highlighted by a NAO report in 2018 on the government's approach to planning and spending which said, **"Optimism bias remains a problem in major projects."**

The COVID experience

In the beginning . . .

The COVID virus arrived in the UK at the end of January 2020 as the World Health Organisation announced that the virus spread was now a pandemic. In the weeks that followed the government faced a series of major decisions, as it sought to respond to a rapidly spreading virus of which it initially had relatively little knowledge. As we look back to that critical moment in time the NAO "recurring issue" of "poor early planning" rings ominously true. It was not clear, in the early stages of the pandemic, that the government was rolling out a programme of measures to combat the virus which it had formulated in advance, tested and had confidence in. This despite the threats posed by a pandemic being high on the government's risk register of issues which could have a devastating effect on the life of the nation.

Uncertainty seems to have dominated in those early weeks which would determine the course of the virus and thousands of lives. Uncertainty on:

- how our borders would be managed as the virus began to travel around the world;
- the number of people who had been infected by the virus, which hampered decisions on when to lockdown ;
- the plans for making PPE available to all those with caring roles during the pandemic; and
- the way in which a sufficient supply of ventilators to deal with a respiratory illness pandemic would be produced.

This level of uncertainty on such key aspects of the pandemic response all point to an absence of a clear prepared plan for dealing with a serious, rapidly spreading virus.

Some issues did not appear to be on the government's radar even when the pandemic arrived in the UK. It seems astonishing now that it was only in June 2020 that Health and Social Care Secretary Matt Hancock announced a review of the arrangements relating to care homes during the pandemic. This despite over 25,000 patients being discharged into care homes from hospitals where the virus had been present, as the hospitals sought to free up beds, as the peak of the first wave of COVID patients arrived. Care homes housed thousands of vulnerable men and women who were amongst those most at risk of becoming seriously ill with COVID-19. It soon became abundantly clear that care home residents in their thousands were becoming ill, and in many cases dying, from the virus.

The first few weeks after the COVID-19 virus arrived in the UK were critical in terms of the government response. Get on top of the virus quickly and you have a chance of keeping its threat level within reasonable bounds; let it get out of hand and you are into a cycle of imposing stringent restrictions to bring down the high level of infections and having to re-impose the restrictions when easing them drives the infection level up again.

That there were so many uncertainties and blind spots in how the government responded to the arrival of COVID-19 indicates a lack of adequate preparation for a pandemic of this nature. Individual hospitals are geared up for dealing with a major incident in their locality. But the government appeared a long way short of being ready to deal with the major incident of a UK wide pandemic.

Sadly, this appears yet more evidence of the recurring issue of poor early planning in government projects which the NAO and PAC had repeatedly flagged.

Reproduced with permission of Peter Brookes and News UK, publishers of The Times

Everything will be alright . . .

Health and Social Care Secretary Matt Hancock may have believed his statement to the House of Commons in January 2020 that "the UK is well prepared for these types of outbreaks," but was it borne out by the evidence? Looking at the extent of the uncertainty on how to respond effectively to the virus it feels impossible to avoid the conclusion that the statement that we were "well prepared" was another example of the "optimism bias" within government which the NAO had drawn attention to in 2018.

The optimism over the country's preparations for a pandemic are particularly concerning given the findings of the Public Health England report on the 2016 exercise, Cygnus, which sought to simulate how the UK would respond to a flu-like pandemic. This report which, under pressure, was finally made available once the COVID pandemic had taken hold in the UK, had concluded that our capability was "not sufficient to cope." It is unclear what steps the government had taken to address the issues raised by the report.

Optimism bias was to evidence itself repeatedly in the subsequent months from the initial belief that the virus could be contained without a lockdown to the Prime Minister's promise of a "world-beating" test and trace system (a system which the PAC later concluded had not made a measurable difference to the pandemic) and through to the government's plans for family members to be with each other over Christmas which had to be abandoned.

Steering the best course . . .

Boris Johnson said on a number of occasions that as Prime Minister he took full responsibility for the decisions which the government made during the pandemic. As issues discussed within government departments and Cabinet committees arose and were brought to the PM's attention in Cabinet meetings and other briefings, Johnson took on the role of being the government's ultimate project manager. His role involved resolving differing views on possible courses of action, and making strategic decisions on what he perceived to be the best ways of combating the effects of COVID-19 as it rampaged its way across the country. But were we placing too much dependence on Prime Minister Johnson as project manager in chief? Particularly when he, himself, was badly affected by COVID-19 in late March and April 2020 just at the time when the virus was on its first virulent wave across the country.

In shipping no captain will put to sea without a chief officer on board, also sometimes known as a chief mate or first mate. The chief officer's role is to control the ship's operations, its equipment and crew with the overall aim of ensuring the safety and security of the ship. It is not apparent that the government had someone in their team playing that chief officer role. Was Johnson therefore overburdened with the responsibility of being both captain and chief officer of HMS The United Kingdom during the greatest storm to hit our nation since the Second World War?

Let us return to the words of the NAO and the Institute for Government set out at start of this section. Both had placed emphasis on the importance of high quality project management skills to deliver complex government projects. Boris Johnson has many talents but is he a skilled, experienced project manager? The coronavirus pandemic arrival in the UK created one of the most intensely complex, multi-dimensional, fast moving, high risk projects that the government could have been faced with. If ever a project needed the most skilled project manager available, overseeing operations, it was surely the response to COVID-19.

Was one of the country's best project managers in charge of the response to COVID-19 project? Boris Johnson had been a journalist, an author, a user of words before rising to become an MP, Mayor of London and ultimately Prime Minister on the back of persuasive oratory, a populist image and the ability to network with those in power. It is true that Johnson has a "can do" attitude which is useful in driving projects along. And as Prime Minister he has clear sight of all the workings of government. But, in terms of his core skills, he does not come from a background of assessing the costs and benefits of different options, identifying and managing risks and plotting the most efficient route through the multiple strands of activity needed to deliver a complex project. To what extent could that have led to sub-optimal responses to the virus as the pressure mounted on Johnson to make huge decisions on behalf of the nation as the government sought to deal with the COVID-19 threat?

It does seem surprising that one of the country's finest project managers (from either the private or public sectors) was not brought in to take control of co-ordinating the plans across government for responding to COVID-19, making sure that risks were assessed and managed and providing advice which would help the Prime Minister make the big decisions. It was a complex high risk project which demanded outstanding project management skills. The captain needed the best possible chief officer at his side.

Sir John Armitt, who chaired the Olympic Delivery Authority, which built the venues and facilities for the 2012 London Olympic Games, is an example of someone who has successfully overseen large complex projects for the government. Within the ranks of the private sector there will be others who have steered large projects to the finishing line managing multiple risks along the way. A project to combat a life threatening pandemic deserved to have the best possible project manager at its helm.

With an expert project manager on board, Ministers of government departments would have still worked with their civil servants to deploy their specialist knowledge to best effect, scientists would have still advised on the health risks the country was facing and the Prime Minister would still have taken the final decisions. But with an outstanding project manager at the helm the Prime Minister would have had an additional expert, whose advice he could draw on before signing off the strategy for each stage of managing the pandemic, a person who would then work with Ministers to ensure the strategy was being enacted to best effect.

Given the various uncertainties surrounding the pandemic, for example the extent to which the virus might return during the winter months as restrictions were eased in summer 2020, an expert project manager would also have been assessing how different winter scenarios could be managed, a technique known as scenario planning. An expert project manager would have been a welcome sight at the Downing Street press conferences to provide reassurance on how plans were being formulated and co-ordinated across government. It would have also provided someone who could have worked with Ministers to keep the momentum of decision making moving along in those critical weeks in late March and April 2020 when the Prime Minister was out of action fighting his own battles against COVID-19.

Putting the theory into practice . . .

Following the earlier concerns about the need for better project management the government had been taking action in recent years by establishing the Civil Service Project Delivery Profession and a Major Projects Leadership Academy both aiming to train public officials in the skills needed to manage large government projects. Yet we have seen that there were clear shortcomings in the preparations for a pandemic reaching the UK and in the government's early response to the spread of the virus. The pandemic should have been an opportunity to put what is learned in the classroom into action.

SUMMARY: *How addressing project planning skills the government had been told to improve could have helped the COVID response*

We would have had a thought through pandemic plan ready to put into action when COVID-19 arrived in this country. The government's communications with the public would have been realistic rather than over-optimistic. We would have had one of the country's best project managers helping the Prime Minister and the government to plan, co-ordinate and execute the government's response to the pandemic.

MAKING GOOD USE OF DATA

What government had been told

The National Audit Office 2016 report on *Delivering Major Projects in Government* highlighted that amongst a number of recurring problems was **a lack of clear, consistent data with which to measure performance.** The NAO returned to the theme of data in a report published in June 2019 on *Challenges in using data across government* where they identified "three substantive issues": **"data is not always seen as a priority; the quality of data is not well understood; there is a culture of tolerating and working around poor quality data."**

These shortcomings in the quality of data for decision making had also been highlighted by the Institute for Government in its 2018 report *Gaps in government data* which noted that whilst more government data is available then ever before problems remained in the way that the data was used. **"Some relate to the way that data is published – often late, or in a form that is hard to use or to compare. Others are outright failures on the part of government to record or publish data which would be of immense value to many people dealing with government."**

Yet another report in 2018, by the Reform think tank, came to similar conclusions saying " **Government has not yet created a clear data infrastructure, which would allow data to be shared across multiple public services, meaning efforts on the ground have not always delivered results."**

The COVID experience

> *The right data, interpreted well, should*
> *bring the right decisions . . .*

The NAO's three substantive issues, including that "data is not always seen as a priority", and the Institute for Government's warning that government data is often published late, or in a form that is hard to use or compare, now seem alarmingly relevant when one thinks about:

- the lack of reliable data in early March 2020 as to how many people in the UK were carrying the virus and infecting others. It is inevitable that this was a major factor in the first lockdown being imposed later than it would have been if good data on the extent of virus infections had been available. Chief Scientific Adviser Sir Patrick Vallance has described the absence of reliable data on infections in the early stages of the COVID-19 pandemic as his greatest regret; Chief Medical Officer Chris Whitty said, "We were unable to work out exactly where we were and we were trying to see our way through the fog."

- the information reported on virus cases and deaths from COVID-19 was initially based on hospital data and did not include the experience in care homes, despite the vulnerability of care home residents to catching the virus. This seems a blind spot which the government took far too long to recognise.

- incomplete information about the extent of PPE which each location required, and how this compared with available stocks of PPE. If data on the adequacy of PPE stocks had been available the shortage of PPE stocks would have been apparent. Steps could then have been taken to build up stocks to avoid the critical delays in delivering it to hospitals, GPs and care homes where it was needed.

Let's work out what information we need . . .

Anyone who has planned their summer holiday in Cornwall will think about the information they need to make the journey and the holiday experience a success: the route if travelling by car, information about any expected traffic congestion, how long the journey is likely to take, the location of service stations for a mid-journey break, whether the hotel has onsite parking, what the weather forecast is for the duration of the holiday, attractions which can be visited if the weather turns cool. The same is true of any project: identifying the information you need in advance makes for a smoother, less fraught experience later on.

In a well run project, for example when a pharmaceutical company plans a trial of a new drug, a "data plan" will be drawn up at the outset identifying:

- the types of data which will be critical to making appropriate decisions;
- how much of the required data is readily available;
- what new data needs to be collected; and
- the method for collecting new data and the timescales involved.

Preparations for a pandemic should have identified how much relevant data was already available and how other data would be collected once a pandemic started. For example, identifying in advance how many people over the age of 70 lived with families, on their own or in care homes would have been helpful in terms of planning how to protect elderly people during a pandemic. Once the virus arrived it was essential that there was a ready to use test and trace system to measure the extent of virus infections in different regions and to inform decisions on whether a lockdown was a necessary.

Given the gaps in key information which arose once government was endeavouring to contain the COVID virus in spring 2020, it is difficult to see how the data needed for dealing with a pandemic had been properly thought through in exercises aimed at anticipating how the government would respond to the arrival of a new and dangerous virus. Did the government prepare a "data plan" to identify the key data it would need to manage its response to a pandemic arriving in the UK?

Closing the stable door . . .

It is noteworthy that in December 2020, nine months after the COVID virus was spreading widely within the UK, the government launched a new National Data Strategy for how it would put data at the centre of decision making going forwards. If implemented well, this new data strategy will be useful for future government activity. But the establishment of a National Data Strategy had been in the government's pipeline for some years as a proposed response to the critical external reports on the government's use of data published between 2016 and 2019. Unfortunately, the new data strategy arrived too late to make a positive impact on the government's response to COVID-19.

SUMMARY: How addressing data skills the government had been told to improve could have helped the COVID response

Steps would have been taken in advance to draw up a data plan of key data that would be needed to manage a pandemic, and to identify how much of this data was available or needed to be collected. An effective test and trace system would have provided more accurate early data on the extent to which the virus was spreading when it first arrived in the UK to inform lockdown decisions. Better data would have helped other important activities such as the roll out of PPE to those who needed it and the protection of residents in care homes.

RISK MANAGEMENT

What government had been told

The National Audit Office 2016 report on *Delivering Major Projects in Government* said: **"There are still concerns and shortages of skills in specific areas such as risk management."**

In 2017 Parliament's Public Administration and Constitutional Affairs Committee reported concern that government had not addressed the Committee's earlier recommendation that **"government needs to set out how it will better educate civil servants at all levels to think about systemic risk, risk management, uncertainty and future challenges."**

Meg Hillier, as Chair of the Public Accounts Committee, voiced similar concerns in 2018 saying: **"Too often we see not enough long term thinking about the risks and consequences of decisions."**

This issue had been recognised within government, HM Treasury Permanent Secretary Nick Macpherson writing in 2015: **"I want to see an even more professional approach to risk management. If we can make it integral to all our work we will be better placed to be innovate and deliver better results for the public."**

The COVID experience

"We are taking all necessary steps to minimise the risk . . ."

Health and Social Care Secretary Matt Hancock said in February 2020 as the first cases of coronavirus in the UK were identified: "We are taking all necessary measures to minimise the risk to the public." An understandable statement for a Health and Social Care Secretary to want to make and Hancock presumably believed what he was saying. But was it really born out by the evidence?

Good project managers take the following steps to address possible risks to the successful completion of their projects. They:

- identify at the outset all foreseeable possible risks;
- assess the probability of those risks materialising and the impact they could then have on the project;
- summarise the risks and make this information available to all meetings where the future of the project is discussed;
- mitigate the risks, that is to say take steps to reduce the probability that those risks will occur and the impact they could have; and
- develop contingency plans for how the project will be put back on course if the adverse events do occur.

Let us look again at Table 3 which set out alternative strategies that might have produced better outcomes during the pandemic and consider the role that managing risks would have played in adopting these strategies.

TABLE 3: How more effective alternative strategies depended on better use of core management skills

Alternative strategy	Project planning	Good use of data	Managing risk
1 A better ready to use plan for dealing with a pandemic involving respiratory illness	x		x
2 A faster reaction to the threat that, in a world of international travel, the initial virus outbreak in China might spread to the UK	x		x
3 More rigorous border controls and testing of arrivals in the UK (there was no border closure and less than 300 people were quarantined out of 18 million arrivals in the UK in the first three months of 2020)	x		x
4 An earlier first lockdown when it became apparent that testing and tracing was not going to contain the spread of the virus		x	x
5 Greater use of mass testing to identify who was carrying the virus (including those not displaying symptoms) so that they and their contacts could be required to isolate to minimise virus spread	x	x	x
6 Greater stocks of ready to use PPE with a logistical plan for making these quickly available to hospitals, care homes and GP surgeries	x	x	x

Alternative strategy	Project planning	Good use of data	Managing risk
7 Clearer arrangements for sourcing more quickly an adequate supply of ventilators for COVID hospital patients (there were delays as government sought 26,000 additional ventilators from various industry suppliers)	x		x
8 Being more alert to the risks of discharging elderly people from hospitals where COVID had been present into care homes (over 25,000 patients were dischargedl into care homes as hospitals sought to free up beds)	x		x
9 Earlier data on the spread of the virus within care homes (initially only data relating to hospitals was reported)	x	x	x
10 A short "circuit breaker" lockdown in autumn 2020 when it became apparent that the number of virus infections was beginning to rise again		x	x

We can see from Table 3 that all ten of the alternative strategies which might well have produced better outcomes during the pandemic involved a closer attention to the management of risk.

Most organisations have a risk register which sets out the main risks they face and this is regularly discussed by the Board and senior management. The government itself has a risk register and the threat of a pandemic was high on that list. But we were never shown a risk register of all the risks which the government had identified and was seeking to manage in its response to the pandemic. It is not clear whether such a document existed.

We knew the risks that the pandemic
posed to our health . . .

The risks COVID-19 posed to the NHS and our health as individuals were clearly addressed by the government and communicated to the public. Downing Street press conferences underlined the significant risks the country faced, including the possibility that the NHS would be overwhelmed if the public did not adhere to social distancing and lockdown restrictions. The press conferences included the views of the government's medical and scientific advisers, who explained the risks that modelling suggested could arise if we, the public, did not act for the greater good by giving up personal liberties. The government had a scale to measure the threat level that the pandemic posed to indicate how serious the risks posed by the virus were at any point in time. All of this was important and valuable. It gave a high level view of the risk environment in which the government was working to respond to the impact of COVID-19 on the NHS and the public.

But what about other risks? . . .

Despite the extensive information on the health risks that the virus posed all ten of the alternative strategies which were likely to have better addressed the threat of the pandemic involved taking a more rigorous approach to risk management. So where was the government lacking in its assessment and management of risk?

Here is an example of a concise statement of risks, setting out the nature of the risks, the adverse effects those risks may have with numbers to give an indication of the quantification of the risk:

Flooding and coastal erosion put lives, livelihoods and people's well-being at risk. The Environment Agency estimates that 5.2 million homes and businesses in England are at risk of flooding and that around 700 properties are vulnerable to coastal erosion over the next 20 years. In addition, more than two thirds of properties in England are served by infrastructure sites and networks that are at risk from flooding.

Despite the extensive information on the risks to the NHS and public health which COVID-19 posed, there were many other important areas where a clear concise assessment of risk, as in the example above, seemed to be lacking. How much clearer the risks the government faced in responding to the pandemic would have been if we had seen quantified statements of this clarity about the risks relating to:

- border controls: what were the risks to COVID infections spreading for different levels of border restrictions or testing of new arrivals in the UK? We now know that the early border restrictions imposed by New Zealand contributed to their success in keeping COVID deaths to just over twenty.
- care home residents: what were the risks to them of being exposed to COVID-19 as the NHS discharged into care homes large numbers of patients from hospitals, where COVID had existed, to free up beds?
- PPE shortages: what was the likely impact of PPE shortages on "front line" workers?
- the Test and Trace system: what change would there be in the level of infections, hospitalisations and COVID deaths as a result of the Test and Trace system working a long way short of maximum effectiveness?

And we should not forget that as infection levels rose, creating dangers for both the public and the NHS, so the impact on the economy worsened as more stringent restrictions on business and personal activities were introduced. As a result, by early 2021, unemployment had risen to 1.7 million with a further 4.7 million kept on the books of businesses through the government's generous furlough scheme. Debenhams, Top Shop and some John Lewis stores were amongst the familiar names disappearing from our High Streets whilst the government bill for state support during the COVID pandemic has rocketed to just over £400 billion, inevitably raising the prospect of higher taxes or government cutbacks to pay for this in the coming years.

Those inside government and the Bank of England will have been monitoring very closely these economic impacts of the response to the pandemic. But for the rest of us there has been little information to help us understand how the government balanced the need to address the health risks posed by the COVID pandemic with the desire to limit the adverse consequences for the economy from imposing restrictions to deal with the health risks.

How an expert project manager could have
improved risk management . . .

In the earlier section on project planning we saw that there was a strong case for bringing on board an outstanding project manager to work with Ministers, and to provide assurance to the Prime Minister that the different strands of the response to the pandemic were being co-ordinated with maximum efficiency. An outstanding project manager would have supplemented the work of the medical experts and scientists by drawing up a list of all risks which needed to be managed and would have discussed with Ministers and the Prime Minister how those risks should be addressed. It seems unlikely that there would have been the ten areas shown in Table 3, all where risks could have been better managed, had someone with strong project management skills been addressing those risks.

SUMMARY: *How addressing risk management skills government had been told to improve could have helped the COVID response*

A more detailed analysis of the risks that a pandemic posed would have enabled the government to have better plans in place to deal with COVID-19 once it spread outside Wuhan, China where it originated. An outstanding project manager, working with Ministers and the Prime Minister, would have closely monitored the risks and co-ordinated strategies for managing those risks to reduce their adverse consequences. It is then likely that most or all of the better strategies for managing risks set out in Table 3 would have been identified at an earlier stage, thus reducing the impact which the spread of the COVID virus had on the health of the nation, the NHS, the care home sector and the economy.

WHY LESSONS HAD NOT BEEN LEARNED

It may seem surprising that the previous strong advice to government that significant improvements were needed to core management skills such as how to plan projects effectively, make better use of data and manage risks had not been actioned sufficiently to prevent those same shortcomings adversely impacting the government's response to COVID-19. The warnings were set out very clearly.

Meg Hillier, in her annual report in 2017, as Chair of the Public Accounts Committee, said "The Committee spends a lot of time scrutinising individual departments. **This helps us see cross-cutting issues about how Government works—a lack of key data to measure performance, concerns about skills in the civil service, poor project management . . . We see a depressingly regular return to the same old problems.**"

Her predecessor as Chair of the PAC, Margaret Hodge, had an even more damning conclusion in her 2016 book, *Held to Account,* when she wrote **"The Civil Service continues to lack the appropriate skills and experience required for modern government."**

But in early 2021 Meg Hillier was still referring to the same concerns about **"government's perennial inability to manage and deliver projects."**

So how could these important lessons not have been learned when they had been clearly set out in earlier reports on government activity?

When reports highlighting areas the government needs to address are published they are usually scrutinised by central government (the Treasury and Cabinet Office) and by spending departments (such as the Department of Health and Social Care or the Department for Transport) when the report relates to their specific areas of government spending. The intention behind this initial scrutiny is for lessons to be learned but actually putting this into practice is frequently more difficult and less successful.

A first step in trying to disseminate lessons to avoid further mistakes is usually guidance to staff issued by senior officials in central government or spending departments. That is useful to a degree but, if further mistakes are to be avoided, other officials must:

- know about the guidance;
- read it; and
- then reflect on what it is saying sufficiently that they remember the guidance and implement it in their future work.

As someone who has run many training courses for government officials, I am all too often amazed to find that officials, even those who have been working in government for many years, do not know about some of the potentially very useful guidance issued by central government to help them plan and deliver large government projects. Or sometimes officials say they know that certain guidance exists but they have not made the time to fully absorb its content. How can the guidance lead to changed behaviour which avoids repeating previous mistakes, if people do not know about it or only have a superficial awareness of its content?

Here are some reasons why the lessons that could bring about improved performance in government are not fully absorbed:

- too often the new guidance joins the thousands of pages of other central government instructions which have been carefully compiled but are not being regularly consulted;
- insufficient steps are taken to embed the guidance in the consciousness of public officials through quality training which brings the points in the guidance alive in a way which will be remembered;
- government officials, being the busy people they are, may rush from one project to the next without pausing to find out whether there

are new approaches which could help them to eliminate previous mistakes; and

- many Ministers and civil servants do not stay in particular posts or departments for a long time, and others arrive to take their places, all of which quickly reduces the institutional memory of previous mistakes and what needs to be done to avoid them recurring

When Margaret Hodge wrote, **"All too often government seemed institutionally incapable of learning from its past mistakes . . . the same things seemed to go wrong time and time again,"** we can see that this unsatisfactory outcome was influenced by the factors set out above.

One further thought: when issues about training arise, we normally think about training in the context of the civil servants whose role it is to follow up the ideas of Ministers, to research what the impact would be of new policies, to brief Ministers and to then implement the public service projects that Ministers instruct them to take forwards. But who trains the Ministers? They came from a diverse range of backgrounds before entering Parliament (Table 4).

TABLE 4: Ministers' careers before entering Parliament

Boris Johnson	journalist, political columnist, editor
Michael Gove	journalist, television current affairs
Rishi Sunak	investment banker, hedge fund manager
Matt Hancock	economist at Bank of England specialising in housing
Pritti Patel	press officer, public and corporate relations
Dominic Raab	lawyer, diplomat
Gavin Williamson	fireplace manufacturer, MD of pottery firm

Note: Matt Hancock and Dominic Raab began their careers in Parliament before becoming MPs as Chief of Staffs to Ministers (Hancock for George Osborne as Shadow Chancellor, and Dominic Raab for David Davis and Dominic Grieve)

So those who were leading our country in the greatest national emergency since the Second World War initially arrived in the corridors and debating chamber of Westminster with their hotchpotch of career and life experiences, some perhaps more relevant to their current roles than others. They then acquired more knowledge about how government carries out its business by their experience as an MP, serving on Parliamentary committees and in their eventual roles as Ministers. There is, however, no requirement for all those who serve us as Ministers to have a common level of expertise in the core management skills we have been examining: effective project planning, good use of data and risk management.

Classically, Ministers rely on civil servants to use these skills when carrying out the actions that Ministers require. But in the frenetic urgency and complexity of dealing with a pandemic raging across the country didn't we need Ministers, as people in charge of running the country, who had been trained to focus on the vital role that effective project planning, good use of data and risk management play in making government decisions at a time of crisis? It is about having the right mindset, when working under pressure, to always be thinking about these core elements: planning, data, risks. These needed to be at the front of Ministers' minds even when, or perhaps we should say particularly when, seeking to protect the public from a virus as serious as COVID-19.

Because of the fast moving nature of the COVID-19 pandemic Ministers themselves were having to make potentially life or death decisions on an often daily basis rather than being able to wait in a more leisurely, ordered manner for their civil servants to do all the ground work to come up with proposals which the Ministers could then review and sign off. Under this intense pressure it seems inevitable that Ministers, themselves not trained to a common standard in project planning, making good use of data and risk management, were more likely to make errors in their decisions than if they did have a consistent level of expertise in these core skills. The ten critical areas which could have been handled differently in dealing with the COVID-19 pandemic were, as we saw previously in Table 3, related to these three issues we have continued to return to: planning. data, risks.

So, despite the scrutiny of previous government activity by auditors, Parliamentary committees and the media identifying lessons which were supposed to stop the same mistakes happening again, there have been too many factors which have prevented a real improvement in the skills which Ministers and their officials bring to government business.

When the COVID-19 pandemic arrived in the UK in early 2020 no-one realised that the government failure to fully address the shortcomings which had been highlighted in project planning, the use of data and risk management was going to have such an impact on the events that followed.

WHAT NEXT?

There will in due course be a public inquiry into the government's handling of the COVID-19 pandemic. There will be more books and more television documentaries which will also analyse what happened and what could have been done differently.

We will hear the phrase "Lessons will be learned" as we always do following events which give rise to large scale loss of life. There have been too many factors which have restricted government's ability to make big improvements in its ways of working from previous recommendations for change. We need to ensure that the lessons which emerge from the COVID-19 pandemic really do become embedded in new approaches to dealing with complex situations faced by government.

There are signs that government and the Civil Service is beginning to focus on the skills which are needed for government to operate effectively in today's complex fast moving world. The launch in December 2020 of the National Data Strategy for making better use of data within government was followed in January 2021 by Better Training, Knowledge and Networks which envisages a new approach to the training of the nation's 450,000 government officials. The training will cover areas such as project management, analysing evidence, data handling and interpretation and commercial skills, together with the attributes needed to be an effective manager or leader. This will build on other recent developments such as the establishment of the Civil Service Project Delivery Profession and the Major Projects Leadership Academy.

These are welcome new initiatives which will improve the skills those working in government use in decision making. This will help to equip public officials for the challenges they will face in the post COVID world. But we have seen in the analysis presented in this book that the government had been told for several years that it needed to make improvements in the skills it used in the three key areas of planning, data, risks. If the government had responded with greater urgency to the warnings it had received the skills initiatives now being implemented in 2021 could have been available earlier to improve the government's response to the COVID pandemic. That in turn could have reduced the adverse outcomes we experienced.

It seems clear that Ministers also need a common standard of management skills when taking on their responsibilities for leading the country. In normal times, appropriate skills in project planning, the use of data and risk management would help Ministers to direct the work of their civil servants to better effect. And in times of national emergency, such as responding to a pandemic, having these core skills, sharpened and ready to use, would increase the chances of Ministers making good decisions when working under intense pressure and with less time available for the preparation of briefing from their civil servants.

The Institute for Government, in looking down at the activity they observe in Parliament, once memorably opined, "The skills needed to win elections are very different from those required to be an effective Minister." We must hope that those who become Ministers in future can find time to sit in a lecture room, even for a week or two, to absorb a common set of skills which will enhance their decision making in complex situations and to reflect on how they will use those skills in their work.

We have been focussing on three core management skills which go to the heart of dealing with the many complex projects which government undertakes; skills which were essential if the response to the COVID-19 pandemic was to be successful. They can be summed up in three words:

- Planning
- Data
- Risks

Ministers and civil servants need to have these three words at the front of their minds . . . continuously. Whatever the issues they are dealing with.

Every time Ministers and civil servants switch on their laptops, tablets or smartphones these three words should flash up to remind them to focus on these words in all their work. Government apps for these three topics should be available, civil service coffee cups should have these three words emblazoned on them, wall charts for planning, data and risks should be in every Ministerial and government department office to allow people to list what they need to focus on under each of these three essential areas.

Here, in conclusion, are six particular recommendations I would draw from the analysis set out in this book:

PLANNING

1. For any possible future national threat, which would need to be addressed urgently if it materialises, there needs to be a well thought through plan showing how different possible scenarios would be managed.
2. The government needs to have a list of the most skilled project managers from both the public and private sectors so that it can draw in the best possible project managers to help co-ordinate complex fast moving government projects.

DATA

1. All expected future projects, including those that might arise in national emergencies, need to have a "data plan" showing what data will be needed to manage the project effectively, how much of that data is already available and how the remaining data will be collected.
2. Data that will be relevant to managing a national emergency needs to be updated on a regular basis.

RISKS

1. Serious consideration needs to be given to the risks that can prevent effective decision making in government. These risks include whether both public officials and Ministers have at their disposal skills which are relevant for managing complex projects, whether they have been trained to put these skills into action when working under pressure and whether major projects have the right mix of people in leadership positions.

2. Each major project needs to have its own risk register setting out the main risks which could cause adverse outcomes or delays in completing the project successfully. Ministers in particular need to be realistic about the level of risk in the projects they are engaged with and should avoid optimism bias in communications with the public.

"Fail to prepare and be prepared to fail" is the oft quoted warning attributed to US President Benjamin Franklin. Let us make sure we prepare well all those who work in government to enable them to deal with confidence with any further national threats. Our futures depend on that.

APPENDIX

Covid-19 Timeline up to 23 March 2021

Adapted from information provided by the British Foreign Policy Group

21 December 2019

The first cluster of patients with 'pneumonia of an unknown cause' identified in Wuhan, China.

31 December

Chinese authorities confirm to the World Health Organisation they are treating dozens of cases of pneumonia of an unknown cause.

11 January 2020

Chinese state media reported the first known death from an illness caused by the virus. It was a 61-year old man who was a regular customer of the market in Wuhan where the virus is believed to have originated.

20 January

The World Health Organisation reports the first confirmed cases outside mainland China have occurred in Japan, South Korea and Thailand.

21 January

The first confirmed case of the virus in the US in Washington State, where a man in his 30s developed symptoms after returning from a trip to Wuhan.

22 January

Public Health England announces it is moving the risk level to the British public from 'very low' to 'low'.

23 January

Chinese authorities suspend travel in and out of Wuhan (population over 11 million). It is estimated approximately 100,000 people had taken journeys from Wuhan Train Station in recent weeks.

17 people worldwide are believed to have died from the virus.

29 January

A plane evacuating Britons from Wuhan arrives at RAF Brize Norton. Passengers go into a 14 day quarantine at a specialist hospital on Merseyside.

30 January

The World Health Organisation declares a global health emergency amid thousands of new cases in China.

31 January

The UK's first individuals to test positive for the coronavirus are confirmed after two Chinese nationals from the same family staying at a hotel in York fall ill.

The US suspends entry into the country by any foreign nationals who had travelled to China in the past 14 days, excluding family members of US citizens or permanent residents.

Over 250 people worldwide, mainly in China, are believed to have died from the virus.

1 February

Spain confirms its first case of the coronavirus in the Canary Islands.

4 February

The UK directs its citizens to leave China if possible.

5 February

A cruise ship in Japan quarantines 3,600 people after a two-week trip to Southeast Asia. 218 people onboard the ship tested positive for the virus.

7 February

The Chinese doctor Dr. Li Wenliang, who tried to ring early alarms that a cluster of infections could spin out of control, dies after contracting the virus. He was reprimanded by authorities in early January and was forced to sign a statement denouncing his warning as an unfounded and illegal rumour.

11 February

The disease is named 'Covid-19', an acronym that stands for coronavirus disease 2019. Over 1,000 people in China have died from COVID-19.

14 February

France announces the first coronavirus death in Europe – an 80-year-old Chinese tourist.

23 February

Italy sees a major surge in coronavirus cases – up to 150. Officials locked down around 50,000 people in 10 towns in Lombardy after a cluster of cases suddenly emerged in Codogno, southeast of Milan.

26 February

Brazilian health officials report their first COVID-19 case as a 61-year-old Sao Paulo man, returning from Italy, tested positive for the virus.

28 February

The first British victim of COVID-19 dies on board the Diamond Princess.

UK authorities confirm the first case of the illness to be passed on inside the country.

The worst week for the global stock markets since the 2008 financial crash.

The World Health Organisation raises the coronavirus alert to the highest level.

29 February

The US records its first COVID-19 death and bans travel to Italy, South Korea and Iran where the virus is spreading.

3 March

UK government publishes a Coronavirus (COVID-19) Action Plan. The plan at this stage is to try to contain and monitor the virus. The Plan says "The UK is well prepared for disease outbreaks. Our plans have been regularly tested and updated to ensure they are fit for purpose." The Plan also says "The UK maintains strategic stockpiles of the most important medicines and protective equipment for healthcare staff who may come into contact with patients with the virus. These stocks are monitored daily with additional stock being ordered where necessary."

4 March

Cases of Covid-19 surge in the UK, as officials announce the biggest one-day increase so far as 34 cases bring the total to 87

Italy announces it is shutting schools and universities.

5 March

The first UK death from the coronavirus is announced. A woman in her 70s, with underlying health conditions, dies from COVID-19 at Royal Berkshire NHS hospital.

6 March

Chief Medical Officer Chris Whitty confirms the UK has changed its response to the coronavirus outbreak from contain to delay.

9 March

London Stock Market suffers largest fall since banking crisis of 2008.

10 March

Cheltenham Races Festival commences, attracting around 200,000 spectators in total from all over the UK during its four days. This event was subsequently seen as being an opportunity for the coronavirus to spread amongst large numbers of people.

Nadine Dorries, a junior health minister, becomes the first MP to test positive for coronavirus.

6 people in the UK have now died of the illness, with 373 testing positive

11 March

The World Health Organisation declares the COVID-19 virus a pandemic.

Stock markets plunge.

The US blocks travel from European countries other than the UK for 30 days.

Chancellor Rishi Sunak announces a £12 billion package of emergency support to help the UK cope with the expected onslaught from the coronavirus.

Liverpool host Atletico Madrid in the Champions League. The 52,000 crowd includes 3,000 fans from Madrid which was then already in partial lockdown due to the virus. This event was subsequently seen as an opportunity for the coronavirus to spread.

13 March

The US declares a national emergency and makes $50 billion in federal funds available to tackle the coronavirus.

A host of UK sporting events announce their postponement including the London Marathon. Premier League fixtures are suspended.

16 March

Boris Johnson begins daily press briefings, urging everybody in the UK to work from home and avoid pubs and restaurants to give the NHS time to cope with the pandemic.

The UK's death toll rises to 55, with 1,543 confirmed cases, though it is believed 10,000 people have already been infected.

Latin America imposes restrictions on their citizens to slow the spread of the virus. But Brazilian President Jair Bolsonaro encourages mass demonstrations by his supporters against his opponents in congress, urging greater virus controls.

17 March

Chief Scientific Adviser Sir Patrick Vallance tells Parliament's Health Select Committee that keeping coronavirus deaths to under 20,000 would be "a good outcome."

Rishi Sunak unleashes the biggest package of emergency state support for business since the 2008 financial crash, unveiling £330 billion-worth of government-backed loans and more than £20 billion in tax cuts and grants for companies threatened with collapse.

France imposes a nationwide lockdown, prohibiting all gatherings and only allowing people to go out for fresh air. France had more than 6,500 infections with more than 140 deaths

The EU bars most travellers from outside the bloc for 30 days.

18 March

The UK government announces most schools across England will be shut down until further notice. Wales and Scotland announce they will also close schools.

19 March

Boris Johnson says that the next 12 weeks could "turn the tide" of the pandemic.

20 March

The UK government orders all pubs, restaurants, gyms and other social venues across the country to close.

Chancellor Sunak announces the furlough scheme whereby government will pay up to 80 per cent of wages for workers at risk of otherwise being laid off

For the first time, China, where the COVID-19 originated reports zero local infections, raising the prospect that the circulation of the virus within China has been contained.

23 March

Prime Minister Boris Johnson, in a televised address to the nation, imposes a lockdown saying that Britons should only go outside to buy food, to exercise once a day, or to go to work if they absolutely cannot work from home. Citizens will face police fines for failure to comply with these new measures.

Worldwide figures stand at more than 270,000 cases and 11,000 deaths.

25 March

Prince Charles tests positive for COVID-19.

In the US, a $2 trillion coronavirus rescue package intended to assist businesses and millions of Americans amid the halt in the US economy, is agreed.

Indian Prime Minister Narendra Modi announced a 21-day lockdown of the country's 1.3 billion residents. India has only recorded 536 cases of COVID-19 so far.

Brazilian President Jair Bolsonaro rails against coronavirus measures being taken in his country, as local officials take preparedness into their own hands.

26 March

Britons across the UK clap, cheer, and ring bells at 8pm to thank NHS workers and other carers for their service in tackling the pandemic.

Chancellor Rishi Sunak unveils a package of measures to help self-employed workers during the economic downturn, giving those earning less than £50,000 a taxable grant equal to 80 percent of their average profits.

27 March

PM Boris Johnson and Health Secretary Matt Hancock test positive for COVID-19.

28 March

French President Emmanuel Macron issues a plea for European solidarity to fight the coronavirus crisis, saying 'I don't want a selfish and divided Europe'

UK Chief Medical Officer, Chris Whitty, announces he is self-isolating after experiencing symptoms of the coronavirus

30 March

Foreign Secretary Dominic Raab announces the government is to spend £75 million on charter flights and airline tickets to repatriate up to

300,000 Britons stranded abroad as countries have closed their borders to limit the spread of the coronavirus.

31 March

Spain joins the US and Italy in surpassing China's coronavirus case total, reporting 85,195 cases and 8,189 deaths.

2 April

The number of worldwide coronavirus cases passes one million.

5 April

Prime Minister Boris Johnson is admitted to St Thomas' hospital for testing after his coronavirus symptoms persist.

Scotland's Chief Medical Officer Catherine Calderwood resigns from her post after she is pictured visiting her second home, despite urging Scots to stay at home and avoid all but essential travel.

6 April

Boris Johnson is admitted to an Intensive Care Unit as his coronavirus symptoms worsen.

7 April

The airline industry cuts 90% of its flights in Europe.

9 April

The UK records its highest daily death toll at 938 deaths recorded in 24 hours.

China releases new measures to try to prevent asymptomatic 'silent carriers' from causing a second wave of infections.

Pope Francis holds a mass on Holy Thursday with no public participation.

10 April

Number of confirmed deaths worldwide passes 100,000.

12 April

Virtual services take place to commemorate Easter Sunday, including the Archbishop of Canterbury leading a service from his kitchen.

14 April

Prime Minister Boris Johnson discharged from hospital having recovered from COVID-19.

15 April

Confirmed COVID-19 infections globally passes 2 million.

US President Donald Trump cuts World Health Organisation funding, claiming the organisation has turned a blind eye to China's role in the early stages of the crisis. Americans who have lost their jobs during the COVID-19 crisis exceed 20 million.

17 April

Hospitals in Japan on the brink of collapse due to new wave of infections.

NHS bosses to ask doctors and nurses to work without some PPE as supplies begin to run out.

19 April

99 year old British war veteran Captain Tom Moore raises more than £30 million for walking 100 laps of his garden.

20 April

Brazilian President Jair Bolsonaro joins anti-lockdown protesters.

21 April

The UN warns that the world is at risk of widespread famines of 'biblical proportions' caused by the COVID-19 pandemic.

22 April

UK human COVID-19 vaccine trials start.

24 April

The UK will host a 'global vaccines summit' on 4 June to encourage nations to come together to support the development of a global COVID-19 vaccine.

At least 150 doctors have died in Italy from COVID-19

25 April

US confirmed death toll from COVID-19 passes 50,000.

Worldwide COVID-19 deaths reach 200,000.

27 April

Prime Minister Boris Johnson returns to work after recovering from COVID-19.

France, Italy and Spain all prepare to ease lockdown restrictions.

27 April

US reaches 1 million COVID-19 cases.

29 April

US GDP falls 4.8 per cent in worst economic decline since 2008.

The International Labour Organisation reports that nearly half of the global workforce risk losing their livelihoods due to the COVID-19 pandemic.

30 April

Boris Johnson says that the UK is 'past the peak' of COVID-19.

1 May

UK now providing 100,000 COVID-19 tests a day.

US president Donald Trump claims there is evidence that COVID-19 originated in a Chinese laboratory.

4 May

Global COVID-19 death toll passes 250,000. Cases in Brazil rising sharply.

5 May

Virgin Atlantic to cut 3,150 jobs and plans to quit Gatwick Airport.

Professor Neil Ferguson resigns from the government's scientific advisory group SAGE after breaking lockdown rules by entertaining a female friend.

7 May

The Bank of England reports that the UK economy is set to shrink by 14 per cent in 2020.

Analysis from the Office of National Statistics has shown that black men and women are nearly twice as likely to die from COVID-19 as their white counterparts.

10 May

Confirmed COVID-19 cases worldwide pass 4 million.

Boris Johnson announces plans for the easing of lockdown, which includes allowing unlimited exercise and going back to work if you cannot work from home.

People flying into the UK will be made to quarantine for 14 days.

14 May

World Health Organization Emergencies Director Mike Ryan warns that COVID-19 may 'never go away.'

COVID-19 worldwide death toll passes 300,000.

20 May

Cambridge University announces lectures will be held online in the next academic year.

21 May

COVID-19 cases worldwide pass 5 million.

23 May

Prime Minister Boris Johnson defends senior advisor Dominic Cummings' decision to travel to Durham during March, despite widespread criticism of Cummings' actions.

25 May

UK schools to begin phased reopening beginning from 1 June, and non-essential retailers may reopen from 15 June.

Dominic Cummings defends his lockdown breaking actions in the Downing Street Rose Garden.

27 May

US COVID-19 death toll passes 100,000.

England to launch 'test and trace' system aimed at replacing lockdown restrictions.

Hospitals in New Zealand report no COVID-19 patients, with only 21 non-hospitalised cases in the country.

29 May

Further easing of lockdown restrictions in England with groups of up to six people allowed to meet from 1 June whilst maintaining strict social distancing rules.

Premier League football set to return from 17 June to complete the 2019/20 season.

30 May

The US withdraws from the World Health Organisation after President Trump's criticism of the organisation's response to the pandemic.

31 May

Global COVID-19 cases surpass 6 million.

COVID-19 cases in Brazil pass 500,000, the next highest after the USA.

5 June

UK COVID-19 death toll passes 40,000.

UK makes masks compulsory on public transport starting 15 June.

7 June

Global COVID-19 deaths pass 400,000.

8 June

Health Secretary Matt Hancock announces task force to draw up safety plans for residents and staff in care homes.

9 June

Global COVID-19 cases reach 7 million.

All COVID-19 restrictions in New Zealand, except overseas travel, have been relaxed. No new infections have been reported in the country for two weeks.

11 June

US reaches 2 million confirmed COVID-19 cases.

14 June

Worldwide COVID-19 death count passes 300,000 as cases reach 8 million.

16 June

A drug trial finds that a cheap and widely available drug, dexamethasone, could significantly reduce deaths among critically ill coronavirus patients.

17 June

English Premier League football returns behind closed doors.

18 June

Bank of England announces a £100 billion stimulus package to aid UK economic recovery.

19 June

UK Chief Medical Officers suggest that the threat level should be lowered.

Brazil passes 1 million coronavirus cases.

The World Health Organisation warns of 'new and dangerous phase' of coronavirus as pandemic hits 150,000 cases in a day – the highest since the start of the pandemic.

20 June

Spain announces that British visitors will be allowed to enter the country without quarantining.

Australian state of Victoria reimposes strict restrictions over fears of a second spike.

21 June

Survey by the British Medical Association finds that a large proportion of doctors are not confident in their ability to cope with a second wave.

22 June

Number of confirmed coronavirus cases worldwide hits 9 million.

UK government announces that those who are shielding can meet groups of up to six outdoors and form a "support bubble" with one other household from 6 July.

23 June

Coronavirus reproduction rate continues to soar in Germany after lower rates than other European countries in early stages of the pandemic.

Government announces that England's pubs, restaurants and hotels will reopen on the 4 July.

UN report estimates that in the long term over 100 million children could be pushed into poverty in South Asia due to the knock-on effects of coronavirus.

24 June

Volunteers in the UK, Brazil and South Africa begin to receive injections of vaccine developed by Oxford University.

The International Monetary Fund estimates that the world economy will take a 12 trillion dollars hit from the pandemic.

UK health officials warn of risk of second wave.

25 June

'Major incident' declared in England after thousands flock to the coast as lockdown eases and temperatures soar.

Thousands flock to the streets of Liverpool, despite coronavirus warnings, to celebrate Liverpool winning the Premier League.

26 June

In response to the crowds which had gathered the previous day, Boris Johnson calls for people to stop 'taking too many liberties' with social distancing or face restrictions being reimposed.

UK government changes quarantine regulations to allow people to holiday in places such as Spain and Greece.

28 June

Confirmed coronavirus cases reach 10 million as death toll passes 500,000.

UK scientists warn of second wave if people do not act "sensibly" over the summer months.

29 June

Lockdown reimposed on Leicester after surge in local infections.

1 July

UK businesses cut 11,000 jobs in 2 days.

Brazil death toll passes 60,000.

4 July

Pubs, restaurants, barbers and places of worship reopen in the UK in what is dubbed 'Super Saturday'.

President Trump uses his 4 July speech to celebrate America's impending 'victory' over the virus.

5 July

UK Government announces £1.57 billion in support for UK arts industry.

8 July

Chancellor Rishi Sunak unveils further £30 billion support to prevent mass unemployment including giving businesses a £1,000 bonus for every member of staff they keep on, cutting VAT on food, accommodation and attractions to 5 per cent and providing 50 per cent discounts for the public to eat out in August in a scheme called "Eat Out to Help Out."

In Brazil President Bolsonaro, who has played down the seriousness of the coronavirus pandemic and has often appeared in public without a mask, tests positive for COVID-19.

Coronavirus cases in the US hit 3 million.

9 July

John Lewis announces plans to close eight stores putting 1,300 jobs at risk.

10 July

UK rejects offer to join the EU's coronavirus vaccine programme and plans to arrange its own contracts with future vaccine suppliers.

11 July

US President, Donald Trump, appears in public wearing a face mask for the first time.

13 July

Beauticians, spas and tanning salons reopen in the UK.

Wearing face masks in shops to become compulsory in the UK from the 24 July.

UN report suggests 130 million may go hungry because of the coronavirus.

16 July

Spain reports steepest daily rise in cases for two months.

Brazil passes 2 million virus cases as India reaches one million.

20 July

Major breakthrough in the search for a vaccine, as vaccine from the University of Oxford found to provide immunity.

22 July

Global cases pass 15 million.

US agrees to pay Pfizer $2 billion to receive 100 million doses of a Covid-19 vaccine by December.

24 July

Cases in Europe, including France, Spain and Germany, rise sharply.

25 July

UK Government advises against all but essential travel to Spain and reimposes 14 day self-isolation for those returning from Spain.

SAGE professor admits the UK will never know the true scale of how many died from the coronavirus due to a lack of testing in the early stages of the pandemic.

27 July

Warnings issued that the UK economy's recovery from Covid-19 could take 18 months longer than initially predicted.

29 July

US coronavirus deaths pass 150,000 as Twitter restricts Donald Trump Junior's twitter account for spreading misinformation about Covid-19.

France sees its highest daily increase in cases in over a month.

30 July

UK imposes local lockdown on a number of areas in the North of England.

Data reveals that the US economy shrank by 32.9 per cent between April and June.

France rules out a second national lockdown despite a surge in cases in Europe.

31 July

UK reverses decision to ease lockdown further by postponing the reopening of casinos and bowling alleys for at least two weeks.

1 August

Thousands protest in Berlin against coronavirus restrictions.

Health experts warn that the UK may need to choose between keeping pubs or schools open in order to limit infection rates.

2 August

Australian state of Victoria calls a 'state of disaster' as cases continue to soar.

3 August

UK's 'Eat out to help out' initiative begins, offering 50 per cent off food in participating restaurants, up to the value of £10, every Monday to Wednesday in August in a bid to save the restaurant industry.

HSBC accelerates plans to cut 35,000 jobs globally and DW Sports enters administration putting 1700 jobs at risk.

5 August

Facebook and Twitter remove social media content from Donald Trump which claimed that children are 'almost immune' to coronavirus.

France and Spain record highest increase in cases since June.

6 August

50 million masks bought for the NHS will not be used due to safety concerns.

7 August

Total number of confirmed coronavirus cases passes one million in Africa, although the true scale of the outbreak in the area is unknown.

India becomes the third country to reach 2 million cases.

8 August

Face coverings must now be worn in museums, cinemas and places of worship in England and Scotland.

9 August

US passes 5 million confirmed cases.

Brazil hits 100,000 confirmed deaths.

Nearly 1,800 companies in the UK plan to cut 20 or more jobs.

10 August

Large decrease in coronavirus deaths in the UK since peak of the pandemic confirmed by the Office for National Statistics.

11 August

The number of employed people in the UK fell by 730,000 between March and July.

12 August

UK economy shrank by 20.4 per cent between April and June, the biggest slump on record.

13 August

A study by Imperial College London suggests 3.4 million people in England have had coronavirus, 10 times higher than official figures.

UK announces France and the Netherlands will be added to the two-week quarantine list from the 15th, causing chaos for holidaymakers.

14 August

Lockdowns in the North West of England extended

15 August

UK recommenced the easing of lockdown with indoor play centres, indoor performances and wedding receptions given the go ahead.

16 August

UK Government plans to scrap Public Health England (PHE) and replace it with a specialist pandemic unit.

17 August

A-Level and GCSE Students in England given their teacher assessed grades after outcry over results given by algorithm following school shutdowns.

18 August

Figures show depression among British adults has doubled during the pandemic.

20 August

First Minister of Scotland Nicola Sturgeon announces that Scotland will remain in phase three of its lockdown easing whilst the country manages flare ups of the virus.

22 August

Global Covid-19 death toll reaches 800,000 as cases surpass 23 million.

23 August

US President Donald Trump announces emergency authorisation for a new blood plasma treatment for Covid patients, despite inconclusive evidence on effectiveness.

27 August

The World Health Organization announces that an international team of experts will visit Wuhan in China to study the origins of Covid-19.

29 August

Far-right extremists attempt to storm the German parliament after a day of protests over Germany's coronavirus restrictions.

Thousands of Israelis protest in Jerusalem calling for the Prime Minister's resignation over his handling of the pandemic.

30 August

Globally the number of confirmed COVID-19 cases passes 25 million.

31 August

US passes 6 million confirmed cases. Russia reaches 1 million confirmed cases.

India's President 2012-2017, Pranab Mukherjee, dies from the coronavirus.

2 September

Victoria state in Australia extends its state of emergency for another six months.

4 September

Virgin Atlantic announces a further 1,150 job cuts.

Italy's former PM, Silvio Berlusconi admitted to hospital after contracting coronavirus.

7 September

India overtakes Brazil to become country with the second highest number of coronavirus infections.

8 September

Spending watchdog, the National Audit Office, declares that the UK's coronavirus bill has so far cost the UK Government £210 billion.

9 September

Government bans gatherings of more than 6 people over fears about a second wave.

Reports suggest Government is pinning hopes on "Operation Moonshot," a £100 billion mass testing programme, to avoid a second lockdown.

10 September

Global coronavirus death toll passes 900,000.

15 September

UNICEF reports that half the world's children are not at school due to COVID.

In the UK the Office of National Statistics says the first UK COVID-19 death, previously thought to have been in early March, may have been preceded by an earlier COVID-19 death in January.

16 September

India passes 5 million coronavirus cases.

17 September

World Health Organisation warns of "alarming rates of transmission" across Europe.

18 September

Coronavirus cases hit 30 million worldwide.

21 September

The scientific advisory group SAGE recommends a short circuit breaker lockdown.

Pubs in England to shut at 10pm to halt rise in cases.

Fears over second UK lockdown wipe £50bn off the FTSE 100.

156 countries agree to a Covid vaccine allocation deal to ensure equitable access.

22 September

US coronavirus death toll passes 200,000.

UK records highest daily tally of cases since May as new measures are introduced including encouraging working from home.

23 September

France tightens coronavirus measures and introduces new "danger zones" map.

600 students at Glasgow University told to self-isolate after outbreak.

24 September

Study finds that coronavirus is continuing to mutate.

25 September

Rio de Janeiro's carnival postponed for the first time in 100 years.

26 September

Anti-lockdown protestors clash with police in London.

28 September

Lockdown tightened in North-East England as cases continue to surge. Wales also announces local lockdowns.

29 September

Global death toll passes one million

World Bank announces $12bn to help poorer countries buy covid-19 vaccines.

Disney lay off 28,000 staff across its parks.

30 September

Projections by Air Transport Action Group suggest that 46 million jobs could be lost globally due to the reduction in global travel.

1 October

Covid cases have continued to double in areas of the UK under local lockdowns.

SNP MP Margaret Ferrier suspended after she took a train from London to Scotland despite testing positive for coronavirus.

2 October

US President Donald Trump and the first lady test positive for the coronavirus.

3 October

Donald Trump releases video message saying he is "doing well" after being taken to hospital with Covid-19.

France reports 16,972 new cases, another daily record for the country.

4 October

Global cases pass 35 million.

Donald Trump briefly leaves the hospital to make a drive-by appearance waving at supporters from his car.

5 October

President Trump leaves hospital.

UK contact tracing error means that 50,000 contacts may not have been traced.

8 October

World Health Organisation reports record one-day rise in global coronavirus case numbers. Cases in Europe continue to rise. Brazil now has 5 million cases and close to 150,000 deaths.

9 October

Europe records 100,000 cases in 24 hours for the first time.

Spain declares a state of emergency to allow it to keep Madrid in partial lockdown.

12 October

UK government announces a new three-tier system for Covid restrictions in England, with Liverpool immediately entering the highest tier of restrictions.

13 October

President Trump holds a large outdoor rally in Florida after recovering from Covid.

Labour Party leader, Keir Starmer, calls for the UK Government to impose a 'circuit breaker' lockdown on the UK.

18 October

Europe passes 250,000 coronavirus deaths.

19 October

Ireland imposes tough coronavirus restrictions, including banning people from travelling more than 5km from their home.

Wales announces two week 'firebreak' lockdown.

20 October

Government forces tighter restrictions on Greater Manchester after failing to reach an agreement with Mayor Andy Burnham.

21 October

Spain passes one million coronavirus cases.

Scotland announces a five-tier coronavirus system compared with England's three tiers.

24 October

France, Italy, Greece, Luxembourg and Austria all hit record daily increases in coronavirus cases.

More anti-lockdown protestors march in London.

25 October

In Italy, people strongly advised not to leave their homes unless it is for work, health or education purposes.

Spain declares a nationwide state of emergency.

26 October

Protests against new coronavirus restrictions and looting in Italy are met with teargas by police.

President Trump says claims that US cases are rising is a 'fake news conspiracy' and is due to extensive testing in the US.

28 October

France and Germany both impose month long national lockdowns.

White House lists 'Ending the Covid-19 pandemic' as one of President Trump's accomplishments, as half a million Americans test positive for coronavirus in a week.

29 October

West Yorkshire moves into Tier 3 restrictions.

30 October

World Health Organisation declares "Europe is at the epicentre of this pandemic once again".

31 October

Boris Johnson announces a 4 week national lockdown in England with non-essential retail closed, and pubs and restaurants closed except for takeaways. Schools, universities and courts will remain open.

UK passes 1 million confirmed coronavirus cases.

Number of coronavirus related hospitalisations hit new highs in 14 European countries.

1 November

Spain sees weekend of protests and looting after it announced a six month state of emergency.

4 November

France records over 40,000 new cases in 24 hours.

5 November

Chancellor Rishi Sunak extends furlough scheme until the end of March.

6 November

European coronavirus-related deaths pass 300,000.

7 November

France passes 40,000 coronavirus related deaths.

Hospitals in Greater Manchester suspend non-urgent care..

The Queen wears a mask in public for the first time.

8 November

Global coronavirus infections pass 50 million.

Hundreds of protestors gather in Manchester to protest against the national lockdown.

9 November

Pfizer announces that its vaccine is 90 per cent effective as UK COVID-19 deaths reach highest level since May.

11 November

Italy passes 1 million coronavirus cases.

13 November

The number of coronavirus cases reaches 50 million worldwide.

14 November

Anti-lockdown protests in Bristol.

15 November

Boris Johnson forced to self-isolate for a second time after being contacted by NHS test and trace app after coming in contact with someone with the virus.

16 November

Moderna claims research shows its vaccine is 94.5 per cent effective.

18 November

New data shows the Pfizer vaccine to be 95 per cent effective.

19 November

Northern Ireland announces it will go into a tougher two week lockdown with non-essential shops shutting from the 27 November.

20 November

Health Minister, Matt Hancock, states that Pfizer vaccine could be rolled out next month.

22 November

G20 leaders pledge to "spare no effort" in ensuing equitable distribution of vaccines globally but make no concrete commitments on how to achieve this.

Ministers across the UK endorse a shared objective of "some limited additional household bubbling for a small number of days" over Christmas.

Laboratory confirmed coronavirus cases pass 1.5 million in the UK.

23 November

Government says it hopes to inoculate all those most at risk from Covid-19 by Easter.

Boris Johnson details his "Covid Winter Plan" to the UK which includes a tightened three-tier system in England post-lockdown.

24 November

UK announces plans that families can bubble in three-household groups from the 23rd-27th December for Christmas.

France announces a three-stage easing of restrictions beginning with the opening of non-essential businesses.

25 November

Coronavirus cases pass 60 million globally while the Americas report 1.5 million in seven days, the highest weekly number since the start of the pandemic.

Analysis suggests the UK trace-and-trace system reached 58 per cent of close contacts of people in the worst affected areas for Covid-19 since September.

The National Audit Office report on how the government bought extra supplies of PPE during the first virus wave concludes that "the government paid a very high price during unusual market conditions." The report explains that many large orders were fast tracked without the due diligence that would normally occur after companies able to act as a broker in arranging PPE supplies were recommended to the government.

26 November

British stocks fall after Matt Hancock announces that over a third of the population will remain under tough Covid-19 restrictions at the end of the national lockdown.

US President Donald Trump announces that deliveries of a coronavirus vaccine will begin in the US next week.

27 November

Hospitals in England told to prepare for a rollout of the COVID vaccine in 10 days.

28 November

Boris Johnson appoints Nadhim Zahawi as the minister in charge of the rollout of the Covid-19 vaccine.

UK secures another 2 million doses of the Moderna vaccine while more than 150 people are arrested in London at an anti-lockdown protest.

30 November

Final results show the Moderna vaccine to be 94 per cent effective and nobody who was given the vaccine in test trials developed severe disease.

Pubs, bars and restaurants in Wales are banned from serving alcohol and must shut at 6pm.

Sir Philip Green's Arcadia Group including Top Shop, Dorothy Perkins and Burtons goes into administration putting 13,000 jobs at risk.

1 December

MPs approved the UK government's plan for a four tiered system of restrictions to replace the second lockdown in place during November.

Pfizer/Biontech and Moderna file for EU approval of Covid-19 vaccine.

Debenhams goes into administration putting 12,000 jobs at risk.

2 December

Pfizer/Biontech vaccine approved by UK regulator MHRA.

3 December

Global coronavirus deaths pass 1.5 million and UK death toll passes 60,000.

US President-elect Biden states that in his inauguration speech he will ask Americans to wear face masks for his first 100 days in office.

6 December

Italy's death toll passes 60,000.

US hits record daily increase in coronavirus cases for the third day running.

8 December

UK administers its first does of the Pfizer/Biontech vaccine

9 December

A study suggests that Covid-19 was circulating in Italy in November 2019.

10 December

US records more than 3000 deaths in 24 hours for the first time.

London hits 191.8 cases per 100,000 people, the highest rate for any area in England.

16 December

Despite rising COVID cases Boris Johnson says it would be "inhuman to ban Christmas."

17 December

French President, Emmanuel Macron, tests positive for Covid-19 forcing a number of European leaders into self-isolation.

Northern Ireland announces a 6 week lockdown from Boxing Day.

18 December

Italy announces a new national lockdown, 24-27 December, and 31 December-3 January.

France's coronavirus death toll passes 60,000.

19 December

A new strain of coronavirus is identified in South East England; data suggests the "Kent variant", as it is known, could be 70% more transmissible.

Concerned about the rising cases from the Kent variant the UK government announces a new Tier 4 with a "Stay at home" requirement which will include Kent, London, most of Surrey, Berkshire, Buckinghamshire, parts of East England and certain other areas with high rising levels of infection. The previously proposed relaxation of rules over five days of Christmas is cut to just Christmas day.

The total number of coronavirus cases globally passes 75 million.

Scotland announces travel ban with the rest of the UK.

21 December

The number of people in the UK who have received the first dose of the Covid-19 vaccine reaches 500,000.

UK supermarkets warn that there may be food shortages if border issues with France are not resolved quickly.

The EU approves the Pfizer/Biontech vaccine.

22 December

AstraZeneca states that it believes its vaccine, developed with Oxford University, should be effective against the new strain of coronavirus.

23 December

The government announces that more areas of the UK will be moved into Tier 4 on Boxing Day.

24 December

Study suggests that England could face more Covid-19 deaths in the next six months than in the whole of 2020 unless restrictions are increased.

London confirmed as the UK's coronavirus hotspot with more than 2 per cent of Londoners having the virus. Infection rates increase in every region of England.

Italy passes 2 million coronavirus cases.

25 December

The Queen praises the British people for 'rising magnificently to the challenges of the year' in her Christmas Day message

Another 570 COVID-19 deaths are recorded on Christmas Day taking the overall UK death toll over 70,000.

Pope Francis uses his Christmas day message to urge countries to share vaccines.

26 December

1 in 1000 Americans have now died from Covid-19 in less than a year.

Global coronavirus cases pass 80 million.

27 December

The EU starts its vaccination programme.

28 December

UK reports over 40,000 cases in 24 hours for the first time since the start of the pandemic.

29 December

UK records over 50,000 infections in 24 hours for the first time since the start of the pandemic.

30 December

Oxford-AstraZeneca vaccine approved for use in the UK by regulator MHRA.

UK announces plans to delay second-stage vaccinations and prioritise giving more people their first vaccine in order to curb the spread of the virus more quickly.

31 December

A hologram of Captain Sir Tom Moore lights the London night sky on New Years Eve.

1 January 2021

US passes 20 million coronavirus cases.

3 January

UK death toll passes 75,000.

Brazil approves import of 2 million doses of the Oxford-AstraZeneca vaccine although the vaccine is not yet approved for use in the country.

India approves use of the Oxford-AstraZeneca vaccine and a locally developed vaccine.

4 January

England enters a third national lockdown with schools closed and people allowed to leave their homes only once a day for exercise for the next six weeks at least.

UK becomes the first country to administer the Oxford-AstraZeneca vaccine.

5 January

GCSEs and A-Level examinations cancelled in the UK for 2020/21

The UK's Chief Medical Officer, Chris Whitty, says that 1 in 50 people in the UK has coronavirus. The UK has over 60,000 cases in 24 hours for the first time during the pandemic.

Germany extends its national lockdown until the end of January.

6 January

Europe passes 25 million coronavirus cases.

UK records 1,162 coronavirus deaths, the highest figure since April.

8 January

NHS England announces that NHS health and social care staff will be given immediate priority on receiving the vaccine, with the majority vaccinated before February.

The Moderna vaccine becomes the third to be approved in the UK.

'Major incident' declared in London as cases soar.

9 January

The Queen and the Duke of Edinburgh receive the COVID-19 vaccine.

US reports over two million new coronavirus cases in the first 9 days of 2021.

UK passes three million coronavirus cases as deaths pass 80,000.

10 January

Modelling suggests that 1 in 5 people in England may have had the coronavirus.

11 January

Coronavirus rate in Spain highest since the start of the pandemic.

World Health Organisation warns that herd immunity will not be achieved in 2021, despite vaccine rollout.

13 January

The UK passes 100,000 coronavirus deaths. PM Boris Johnson acknowledges that "there are many things we wish we had done differently" based on COVID knowledge now available.

14 January

The UK bans flights from a number of South American countries, including Argentina, Brazil and Chile.

15 January

Coronavirus death passes 2 million globally.

US President-elect, Joe Biden's chief of staff warns that US will hit 500,000 coronavirus death by the end of the month.

Brazil's President, Jair Bolsonaro, says there is little he can do about the pandemic, stating that he "should be at the beach".

16 January

Data from John Hopkins University shows the most recent 500,000 coronavirus deaths occurred in the space of six weeks; at the start of the pandemic it took six months to reach the first 500,000 deaths.

France implements 6pm curfew as its death toll hits 70,000.

17 January

UK announces it will begin vaccinating over 70s and the clinically vulnerable people this week.

South Africa delays reopening schools as the new variant of Coronavirus first found in South Africa continues to spread throughout the country.

Israel announces it will begin vaccinating Palestinians, amidst pressure from human rights groups and Palestinian officials.

18 January

UK had the highest death toll in the world in the week ending 17 January, with 16.3 deaths per million people.

South African variant of coronavirus found to be more infectious.

19 January

UK records 1,610 deaths in 24 hours, the highest since the pandemic began.

Germany extends national lockdown until 14 February.

20 January

US President Joe Biden signs executive orders on his inauguration day, including mandating mask wearing and social distancing in federal buildings and land.

India's vaccination programme hampered by low turnout as misinformation deters people from taking the vaccine.

21 January

Pfizer cuts vaccine deliveries to some European countries by up to a half in some countries due to production changes.

22 January

AstraZeneca warns that a glitch in production means there will be delays to initial vaccine deliveries to the EU.

23 January

Today marks one year since Wuhan entered lockdown, confining its 11 million citizens to their homes.

25 January

Moderna confirms that its vaccine works against mutated versions of the virus first found in the UK and South Africa.

Riots continue in Amsterdam for the third night over the introduction of a night time curfew.

26 January

AstraZeneca says it will prioritise its delivery of vaccines to the UK, over delivering vaccines to the EU, as it signed its contract with the UK first. EU expresses concern.

27 January

Pan American Health Organisation announces that 1 million people have died from Covid-19 across North and South America.

UK announces compulsory hotel quarantine for those arriving from 'high-risk' countries. Those seeking to leave the UK will need to make a written declaration of their need to travel.

28 January

Europe faces vaccine shortages as France announces that supplies of the Moderna vaccine expected in February will be reduced by 25 per cent.

UN announces that the Covid-19 pandemic has cost the tourism industry $1.3trillion.

29 January

EU triggers, and then retracts, a Brexit clause which would have blocked vaccine exports to Northern Ireland.

EU authorises the Oxford/AstraZeneca vaccine for use on over 18s.

Germany bans travellers from the UK, Ireland and Portugal.

30 January

EU and UK agree to a reset in relations following vaccine supply dispute.

Data reveals the UK's daily death toll averaged over 1000 in January, the worst month of the pandemic in the UK so far.

World Health Organisation urges Britain to pause Covid vaccinations after it finishes vaccinating the most vulnerable, to allow those in poorer countries to receive vaccine.

US records half of its 26 million coronavirus cases in the last two months.

1 February

EU tightens travel restrictions on those outside of the block, with only travellers from countries with very low case numbers, and very few cases of the new Covid-19 variants, allowed to enter the EU.

2 February

Study suggests the Oxford/Astra Zeneca vaccine provides sustained protection against Covid-19 for at least three months and cuts transmission of the virus by two-thirds.

6 February

AstraZeneca warns that the Oxford/AstraZeneca vaccine has significantly reduced efficacy against the South African variant of coronavirus. South Africa suspends use of this vaccine.

8 February

UK records 333 deaths, the lowest figure for six weeks as the lockdown and vaccination programme have a positive effect.

9 February

World Health Organisation says that its investigation into the origin of the virus had uncovered new information but not changed its understanding of the outbreak.

10 February

Germany extends lockdown until 7 March.

12 February

The government achieves its ambition of offering, by mid-February, a COVID-19 vaccine to the 15 million Britons in the four most vulnerable categories which includes NHS frontline staff, care home residents and staff, those aged over 70 and others with medical conditions making them extremely vulnerable to COVID-19.

The economy shrunk by just under 10 per cent in 2020, more than following the 2008 banking crisis and the 1929 Great Depression. The largest contraction since the 1709 Great Frost.

The UK virus reproduction R-value drops below 1 for the first time since July.

16 February

Scotland announces plans for phased schools reopening.

18 February

Globally, coronavirus infections fall to their lowest level since mid-October

19 February

Court rules that the UK Government broke the law by failing to publish details of PPE spending within the legally required 30 days of contracts being awarded.

20 February

200 million coronavirus vaccines delivered globally.

UK announces that all UK adults will be offered a first dose of the coronavirus vaccine by the end of July 2021.

21 February

One in three adults in the UK have now received the first dose of a Covid-19 vaccine.

22 February

Boris Johnson announces a staged plan to lift England out of lockdown with schools reopening and outdoor socialising with one other person allowed from 8 March; six people or two households meeting outside and organised sport allowed from 29 March; on 12 April non-essential shops, gyms and hairdressers will reopen and pubs and restaurants can serve people outside; indoor hospitality will be allowed from 17 May together with larger gatherings; and an aim to end all restrictions on social contact and gatherings on 21 June.

US passes 500,000 coronavirus deaths.

23 February

Scotland to ease lockdown from 5 April.

Ireland announces plans to start reopening schools next week.

25 February

The Queen urges those hesitant about getting the vaccine to "think about other people rather than themselves".

Brazil's death toll reaches 250,000.

28 February

UK has given 20 million first dose vaccinations.

The first UK case of the coronavirus variant first identified in Brazil.

2 March

Italy closes schools and increases restrictions on businesses in regions worst hit by the Covid-19 variant first found in the UK.

3 March

Chancellor Rishi Sunak delivers a "spend now, tax later" Budget. The cost of the government's response to the coronavirus pandemic is now £407 billion.

6 March

US passes President Biden's $1.9 trillion Covid relief plan.

The Dalai Lama receives a Covid-19 vaccination.

7 March

England invites those aged 55-59 for vaccinations.

Rangers football fans gather in Glasgow to celebrate winning the Scottish Premiership, despite lockdown restrictions.

8 March

England schools reopen in line with Boris Johnson's roadmap for exiting lockdown.

Italy passes 100,000 coronavirus deaths.

9 March

UK Foreign Secretary, Dominic Raab, writes to the European Council denying claims that the UK has issued an "outright ban" on vaccine exports.

Scotland announces relaxation of outdoor household mixing.

10 March

Brazil has over 2000 Covid-19 deaths in 24 hours for the first time since the pandemic began.

11 March

European Medicines Agency recommends conditionally approving the Johnson and Johnson's Covid-19 vaccine.

12 March

Boost in vaccine supply in the UK further assists the government's vaccination roll-out which is at a much more advanced stage than in European countries.

14 March

Netherlands suspends use of the AstraZeneca vaccine and Irish health regulators recommend deferring the use of the AstraZeneca vaccine in Ireland amid concerns about possible side effects in small numbers of cases.

Head of the Office for National Statistics says that there is "no doubt" that there will be a new wave of Covid-19 cases in the autumn.

France announces plans to evacuate 100 Covid-19 patients from intensive care units around Paris to ease pressure on services.

15 March

Italy, France, Portugal, Slovenia and Cyprus suspend use of the AstraZeneca vaccine pending an assessment by the EU's medicine regulator.

Brazil strikes deal with Pfizer for 100 million doses of the Covid-19 vaccine.

16 March

European Medicines Agency announces it is investigating 30 cases of unusual blood clotting disorders among 5 million recipients of the Oxford/AstraZeneca vaccine.

Sweden adds to countries pausing or restricting use of Oxford/AstraZeneca vaccine.

17 March

Despite last week's positive news on vaccine supplies NHS Trusts now warned that supply issues may lead to a significant cut in the number of vaccines available from the end of March.

18 March

European Medicines Agency declares the Oxford/AstraZeneca vaccine safe to use, declaring that the benefits outweigh the risks.

As a result, a number of European countries including Germany, Italy and France resume use of the Oxford/AstraZeneca vaccine.

19 March

Covid-19 related deaths in Europe pass one million.

PM Boris Johnson, receives his first dose of the Oxford/AstraZeneca vaccine.

Parisians criticised for fleeing Paris on packed trains to avoid new lockdown.

20 March

European Commission President Von der Leyen issues warning to AstraZeneca over reduced vaccine supply.

India reports the biggest surge in new infections in four months.

British MPs urge Home Secretary to allow protests in England, despite lockdown.

21 March

UK sets new record of over 870,000 daily vaccinations.

Germany extends lockdown measures.

23 March

UK lights candles in remembrance of the lives lost during a day of reflection on the anniversary of the first lockdown.

Brazil, where the latest surge of COVID-19 is deemed out of control, has a record number of 3,251 daily Covid-19 deaths as it approaches 300,000 COVID-19 deaths.

Printed in Great Britain
by Amazon

73010876R00175